UNDERSTANDING
BAKING

UNDERSTANDING
BAKING

SECOND EDITION

JOSEPH AMENDOLA

DONALD LUNDBERG

JOHN WILEY & SONS, INC.

New York   Chichester   Weinheim   Brisbane   Singapore   Toronto

This book is printed on acid-free paper. ⊖

Copyright © 1992 by John Wiley & Sons, Inc. All rights reserved.
Published simultaneously in Canada.

This publication is designed to provide accurate and authoritative information in regard to the
subject matter covered. It is sold with the understanding that the publisher is not engaged in
rendering professional services. If professional advice or other expert assistance is required, the
services of a competent professional person should be sought.

Library of Congress Cataloging-in-Publication Data:

Amendola, Joseph.
    Understanding baking / Joseph Amendola, Donald E. Lundberg.—2nd ed.
        p.   cm.
    Includes index.
    ISBN 0-471-28457-2
    1. Baking.   I. Lundberg, Donald E.   II. Title.
TX683.A44   1992
641.7'1—dc20

92-21875
CIP

Printed in the United States of America

CONTENTS

FOREWORD

Bread is the most widely eaten food in the Western world today and has been a staple food over the centuries. A painting on one of the walls of an Egyptian pyramid shows men kneading dough by trampling it with their feet while maintaining their balance with the aid of sticks. Ancient Greece understood the art of puff pastry. Public bakeshops appeared in ancient Rome even before the time of Christ.

During the Middle Ages, dining, like so many of the arts of fine living, became quite simple. At that time food was served on a trencher, a piece of thick bread placed on the plate. Other foods were piled upon it and the trencher soaked up the fats and juices from the various meats, poultries, and game placed on the trencher. The trencher was eaten last.

With the Renaissance, the Italians in the northern city-states again developed a keen interest in food. In the 16th century, Catherine de Médicis was married to the crown prince of France, the Dauphin (later Henry II), and brought with her to Paris a brigade of chefs and bakers. Catherine is credited with stimulating the French to take an interest in finer food preparation. Her bakers brought with them the recipes and skills for baking such items as cream custards, éclairs, tarts, macaroons, and cream puffs.

A school of baking was opened in Paris in 1780. About the same time, pastry baking became a specialized art, and the pastry bakers set themselves up in business apart from the bread bakers.

In this country, wheat flour was at a premium during the Colonial period because wheat did not grow well in New England or along the eastern seaboard. Corn was the staple food of the colonial settlers. By the time of the American Revolution, bread again was an important part of the diet, and Christopher Ludwig, as superintendent of the bakeries for the Continental Army, did much for the morale of the troops. George Washington grew wheat at Mt. Vernon, found milling an honorable profession, and produced flour that was famous for its high quality.

As settlers moved into the Midwest and wheat was grown over large areas, white flour became available to nearly everyone. The leavening agent for the bread made at the time came from several sources: the simplest was the fermentation of bacteria and wild yeast that could be made to grow in dough. A cowboy cook made his starter by mixing flour and potato water in a keg and leaving it in the sun to ferment. He often took it to bed with him to keep it warm through the long, cold nights.

Another starter involved cornmeal, water, and sugar, which was allowed to ferment overnight. It was blended with flour, salt, and other ingredients to yield salt rising or sourdough bread. Commercial yeast, a by-product of the brewing industry, became available in 1868.

Another leavening agent much used in the 19th century was baking soda. It combined quickly with the lactic acid in sour milk or buttermilk to release carbon dioxide, which helped expand and raise the product. If a recipe called for sweet milk, cream of tartar could be added to get the chemical reaction going. Baking powder, a combination of baking soda and an acid, came along in 1856 and served the same purpose. All that was needed to start the reaction was water, salt, and heat. Baking powder and commercially available yeast were great steps forward in the history of baking.

Much of history can be traced in the movement of a baked item from country to country. The croissant or crescent roll dates from the year 1686, when it was created in Budapest. The Ottoman Turks were besieging the city and had tunneled under the city walls into the heart of the city. Bakers who worked during the night heard the sounds of the Turks digging and gave the alarm. To reward the bakers who had saved the city, the privilege of making a crescent roll was granted to them in that the crescent was the emblem on the Turkish flag. The croissant is widely popular as a breakfast item in France today.

Strudel, the marvelous paper-thin dough product, had a similar history. Thin-layered dough was apparently first used in the Near East to make baklava. Baklava is made up of paper-thin sheets of dough piled in layers and filled with honey and nuts. This dessert moved westward with the Turks as they came into Hungary. Later it was carried from Hungary into Germany and Austria when Hungary became a part of the Austro-Hungarian Empire.

The move to convenience in the bakeshop came about the turn of the century. Self-rising flour that contained baking powder was available prior to 1900. Pancake flour was developed during World War I. By the early 1930s a biscuit mix became available to homemakers, and bakers began using doughnut mixes. The first cake mix, that for gingerbread, was sold in the mid-1930s. Soon after, pie crust mixes and corn muffin mixes appeared.

Cake mixes were marketed before World War II but first became popular during that war, when there was a shortage of sugar and shortening. Cake mixes that included these items did not require ration points. Today few home-baked cakes are made from scratch. Only eggs and water are added to most cake mixes now bought in the store.

The first cakes in this country were pound cakes, so called because they contained one pound of butter, one pound of flour, one pound of eggs, and one pound of sugar. Sponge cakes could also be made without baking soda or baking powder. Cakes as we know them today were not possible until the invention of baking powder, when a cake could be leavened and built up in layers. The angel food cake is an exception because it is leavened completely by the hot air and steam initially made available by whipping and folding in egg whites.

A big step forward in cake making came in the 1930s, when emulsifiers were added to shortening. These new shortenings, called *high-ratio shortenings,* made it possible for the batter to carry greater proportions of shortening, sugar, milk, and eggs to flour. Once the high-ratio shortenings were available, flours were introduced to accommodate them. These flours were ground more finely and permitted greater absorption and a finer crumb in the cake. Today pre-mixes are widely used in institutional and commercial foodservice kitchens. Professional bakers, too, are turning to them. It is likely that bakeshops will be using pre-mixes almost exclusively in the near future.

Mechanized equipment in the bakeshop has changed baking from a job demanding long hours and hard work to something approaching an industrial process. Much of the job of baking has been de-skilled. The job is broken down into its separate parts, with most of the work done by machinery and each baker doing only one small part of the total process. The small bakeshop manned by two or three persons is doomed to disappear unless pre-mixes are adopted. Large industrial plants produce most of the bread. In such plants only a few persons direct and control the whole establishment. Most of the employees are machine operators; only a few employees perform the few specialized tasks.

This change to mechanization has given the professional baker a new importance and demanded new knowledge and technical skills. The baker becomes a technician as well as a craftsman, who, in addition to being able to roll and shape doughs, must understand something about the ingredients used and at least a little about the physics and chemistry of baking. The purpose of this book is to provide that simple and elementary understanding.

PREFACE

This book is written for baking and culinary students as well as for the general public who wish to know what baking is all about, the ingredients used, and how they are used to produce attractive, flavorful, and nutritional baked goods. Culinary schools are adding baking courses because they have correctly identified that every good cook should also be a good baker and that most full-service restaurants include fresh baked items produced on the premises on the menu. In this book recipes and references to specific manual skills bakers require are covered only inasmuch as they contribute to a better understanding of what takes place in the baking process.

This current edition further develops the material of the first edition published in 1970. Much of what has been learned about human nutrition since then has been incorporated into this revised edition. New baking ingredients and additives have become available, as have modified starches, fat substitutes, and new sweeteners. A variety of gums and alginates are being used as thickening agents and as substitutes for foods high in calories. Information about the uses of these products has been added.

For the baking research results referred to in this edition, we have drawn heavily upon E. J. Pyler's *Baking Science and Technology*, Third Edition (Sosland Publishing Company, Merriam, Kansas, 1988). This two-volume book incorporates much of baking science research over the past 40 years into its analysis and commentaries.

Baking and cooking have much in common. In fact, most cookbooks include dough and butter products, pies, and pastries. Bakers and cooks are concerned with the control of time and temperature in the transfer of heat to the food material. Enzymatic action, the control of acidity, and the texture, mouth feel, flavor, and sweetness are considerations held in common by both bakers and cooks.

When bakers fry doughnuts, they face the same problem with the smoking point of the fat medium, the fat flash points, fat breakdown, and rancidity control as do fry cooks. The thickening of starches is of interest to both sauce cook and pie maker.

There are differences. The baker works with precise formulas, whereas the cook uses recipes. The baker *scales* ingredients in terms of weight, which is measured in comparison to the weight of the flour. Once the ingredients for bread or rolls are in the oven, no adjustments can be made; the cook making a stew or sauce can add salt or water or make other adjustments that are not possible in a bake oven. In other words, much of baking must be more precisely done than is necessary in cooking.

CHAPTER 1

INTRODUCTION

I. TYPES OF BAKERIES

II. PRE-PROOFED FROZEN BAKED GOODS

III. THE STALING PROBLEM

   A. Retardation of Staling

   B. Replacement of Air in the Product Package

I. TYPES OF BAKERIES

In the past, bakeries produced the bulk of their products from raw materials: flour, water, yeast, sugar, eggs, shortening, and a few other ingredients. Many still do today. Smaller bakeries today can be called *scratch-mix* operations. Most of their products are produced from raw ingredients, but prepared mixes and bases are also used.

A third type of bakery is the fresh-baked, in-store bakery that uses frozen dough and bake-off in the supermarket. Hundreds of supermarkets include this type of bakery, where the basic preparation and freezing are done at a central location and the product is "baked off" in the store. Many other in-store bakeries operate as combination bake-off and scratch-mix bakeries.

1. Supermarkets sell the largest percentage of baked goods. Some companies have hundreds of in-store bakery operations. The Winn-Dixie Stores, for example, in 1991 had more than 1,222 stores, 91.4% of which included bake-off bakeries.

It means that the small bakery must fit into a market niche not already served by the supermarket or produce a product different from or superior to that of the supermarket. The independent baker can also offer more personal service and perhaps a location preferred by a number of people (a market).

What does this mean for the independent, small, from-scratch bakery?

II. PRE-PROOFED FROZEN BAKED GOODS*

A recent development in baking is the ability to pre-proof, freeze, and bake off a bakery item, in contrast with the widely used method of producing a product that is not proofed before freezing. With the pre-proofed product, the yeast is fully activated prior to freezing.

Using the typical frozen-dough process, the time from mixing until baking is at least 2 hours, and in some cases 7 or 8 hours, most of it for fermentation. The pre-proof and freeze method permits bake-off times of 6 to 18 minutes, depending on the size of the product. The key to the new process, which eliminates the long time needed to proof after the dough has been thawed, is the removal of "free" water and the flattening of air bubbles in the dough before freezing.

No chemicals are involved, only physical pressure in pressing the water into the dough system so that the water is bound to the other dough ingredients. When frozen, free water expands and forms crystals, which rupture the dough structure, as seen in Figure 1-1.

In the new system, any water present in the dough is evenly distributed and combined with the starch and gluten so that no ice capsules are formed during freezing. The micrograph in Figure 1-2 (enlarged 500 times) shows no tearing or scoring.

By pre-proofing the dough, 2 to 4 hours can be saved. The pre-proofed product preserves its elasticity for more than a year and can be presented freshly baked at any time during that period.

To force the free water to bind with the molecular gluten structure, the

---

* This section is based on Makato Nakagowa's presentation, Pre-Proofed Baked Goods, at the 67th Annual Meeting of the American Society of Bakery Engineers.

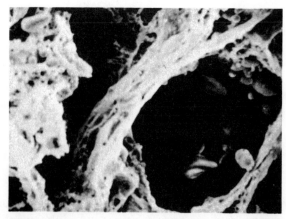

Figure 1-1

dough is stretched and pressed into sheets, which are then rolled into the shapes required for bread, rolls, croissants, baguettes, and other products.

Bread dough ordinarily expands about six times to form bread, four times during fermentation. The pre-proofed frozen dough method obtains the same expansion as occurs when freezing is not involved.

2. To review, until recently frozen dough products were shipped as an unproofed dough. The new process gently presses the water present in the dough to combine it with the gluten so that when the dough is frozen the water present does not crystallize and rupture the gluten starch structure.

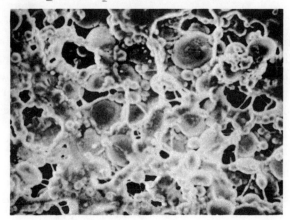

Figure 1-2

Air present in the dough is also pressed into many small bubbles. The strips of dough are then formed into the desired product shape.

The new system eliminates the need to thaw and proof frozen dough before it is baked off.

How can water crystallization be avoided in a dough?

By stretching and pressing the dough to bind the water to the gluten and starch.

III. THE STALING PROBLEM

A principal problem for bakers is *staling,* the falloff in quality of baked products beginning soon after the product comes out of the oven. About 5% of all bread is returned because of staling, which is seen by the consumer as a loss in pleasing appearance, texture, and flavor. Loss of aroma is a big part of flavor loss.

In technical terms, the bread, cookie, roll, or other baked product has lost moisture in the crumb, and the crumb has firmed and become less elastic because of changes in the starch, called *retrogradation* (reverting to a former, inferior state). Cereal starches have two kinds of starch molecules, amylose and amylopectin. It is the amylopectin that retrogrades, reverting back to its original firm state as rigid crystalline granules.

3. The obvious thing that takes place in staling is the loss of moisture. A chemical change also takes place, the hardening of the amylopectin molecules called _____.

Retrogradation.

The amylopectin starch molecules are made up of long, branched chains, as compared with the amylose molecules, which are straight-chain molecules.

Another cause of staling can be mold growth. Fungi, which may be present in the air of the bakery, may get into the dough. Mold growth can be controlled by mold inhibitors such as propionates, sorbates, and benzoates used at a 0.2% level (relative to flour proportional content).

A. Retardation of Staling

Several things can be done to retard staling, among them cryogenic freezing and the addition of bread softeners and antifirming agents to doughs. Bread made from high-protein flour does not stale as rapidly and its crumb is not as firm as bread made from low-protein flours.

4. Knowing this, would the addition of vital gluten to a formula retard staling?

> Yes. It is added to increase the protein content of the bread.

Soy flour or soy isolates (soy proteins) added to a bread formula also slow staling. Fats, too, extend shelf life and result in a softer crumb.

Adding 2% to 4% of sweeteners such as sucrose, dextrose, and fructose act to reduce staling slightly.

> Raisin paste contains 30% dextrose and 36% fructose. Raisin juice concentrate is 85% to 90% sugars. Both extend shelf life not only because they help to retain crumb moisture but also because they contain propionic acid, a natural mold inhibitor.

5. Would you guess that adding raisins (high sugar) would help the staling problem?

Special enzymes that can be added to the dough are also effective against staling. They split the long dextrose starch chains and prevent the formation of the rigid, cross-linking starch structure associated with staling.

B. Replacement of Air in the Product Package

6. One way to increase the shelf life of the baked good—by as much as 200%—is to replace the air in the package that wraps the products with either carbon dioxide or nitrogen. Nitrogen is best for bread products; carbon dioxide is best for high-fat products. Because of the high cost, this technique is used almost exclusively for premium baked goods.

   Do you think this procedure, known as *flushing*, would reduce mold growth?

> Yes. Molds need oxygen to grow. Replacing the oxygen in the package deprives the mold of the oxygen necessary to grow and live.

CHAPTER 2

FLOURS AND MEALS

Wheat flour, the basic ingredient bakers use, was present as long ago as 7000 B.C.; it was probably first found growing wild as grass mixed with rye grass. In its endosperm, the heart of the grain, were the right proteins, that, when mixed with water and then kneaded, formed the elastic gluten needed for formation of a dough. Yeasts in the vicinity, when mixed with the flour, leavened the dough. When baked, the dough became bread. Pieces of the dough could be used to "start" new batches of dough.

Bread, beer, and onions were the ancient Egyptians' staple foods. Later in Europe, rye grain, originally viewed as a weed in the wheatfields of northern Europe, was harvested along with wheat and used to make rye bread.*

The two key components of wheat flour are protein and starch. Let's first consider wheat protein. Like all proteins, it is made up of amino acids, which in turn are composed of 50% to 55% carbon, 20% to 23% oxygen, and 12% to 19% nitrogen. Protein molecules consist of different amino acids linked together into long chains. Of the 150 known amino acids, only 18 occur in wheat protein and only 4 account for approximately two-thirds of the wheat protein important to bakers.

1. The baker is most concerned with what two components of flour? | Protein and starch.

2. What are the building blocks of protein? | Amino acids.

Flour is the finely ground meal of wheat and one of the most important ingredients used in bakery products. Therefore, flour quality has a major influence on the quality of finished baked products.

I. REASONS FOR IMPORTANCE OF FLOUR

- It is the backbone and structure of baked goods.
- It acts as a binding agent and an absorbing agent.
- It affects the keeping quality of products.
- It is important to the flavor of products.
- It adds nutritional value to the baked product.

*Reay Tannahill, *Food in History.* New York: Stern and Day, 1973.

II. WHEAT

Wheat, from which flour is made, is the most essential grain used in bread-making because it is the only cereal that contains the proper combination of glutenin and gliadin. When combined with water, these properties form gluten, which is essential for retaining the gas produced by yeast. No other grain can replace wheat in breadmaking.

The primary types of wheat flour used in baking are hard wheat and soft wheat.

A. Hard Wheat

There are several kinds of hard wheat:

1. One hundred percent straight flour is a strong type of flour. It is preferred in the production of high-quality hard rolls and hearth breads.
2. Patent flour is generally used when a formula calls for bread flour. It is used in making bread, rolls, and the usual products made with bread flour.
3. First clear flour and second clear flour are used in making rye breads because of their darker color and higher gluten content.
4. Bran is used mainly in the production of muffins.
5. Whole-wheat flour (including graham) is used primarily in making whole-wheat bread and muffins.

B. Soft Wheat

There are three kinds of soft wheat: Cake flour is used to produce high-quality cakes. Pastry flour and cookie flour are used for pie crust, cookies, and pastry.

Soft wheat flour made from soft wheat, when squeezed in the hand, remains together; hard wheat flour crumbles. Hard wheat flour is rough when rubbed between the fingers.

Generally, high-quality bread depends on a high protein level, but a high-quality wheat produces good bread over a range of protein levels. Protein quantity is mainly influenced by growing conditions, whereas protein quality is genetically determined.

3. True or false: the baker cannot rely completely on protein level to assure a good-quality bread.   **True.**

Figure 2–1 shows the general separation of the various grades of flour, but does not show the exact system of the separation of flour streams.

III. RYE FLOUR

Rye flour is secured from the milling of the rye berry or grain. Although the composition of rye is quite similar to that of wheat insofar as the actual amounts of moisture, protein, carbohydrate, fat, and ash are concerned, the nature or kind of protein in wheat and rye is different.

Some of the gluten components are present in rye, but when rye flour is made into a dough by the addition of water, it does not form gluten such as is formed when wheat flour is treated in the same manner.

In making rye bread, some wheat flour is necessarily used as a source of gluten so that a porous, well-risen loaf may result. If rye flour were used alone, the loaf would be heavy and somewhat soggy, with a consequent impairment of its palatability and digestibility.

Rye is milled into flours of different grades, such as rye patent flour, rye straight flour, various dark rye flours, and pumpernickel.

A. Grades

There are four grades of rye flour:

1. Light—practically as white in color as wheat flour, it is intended for use in rye products where a white color is desirable. It does not have the strong rye flavor of the darker grades.
2. Medium—darker in color because it contains a larger percentage of the rye grain, which also accounts for its pronounced rye flavor and, therefore, its popularity.
3. Dark—containing some of the outer part of the grain, it is used principally by bakers in making very dark rye bread.
4. Straight—consisting of about 70% light flour and about 30% dark flour, it is often used interchangeably with the medium grade.

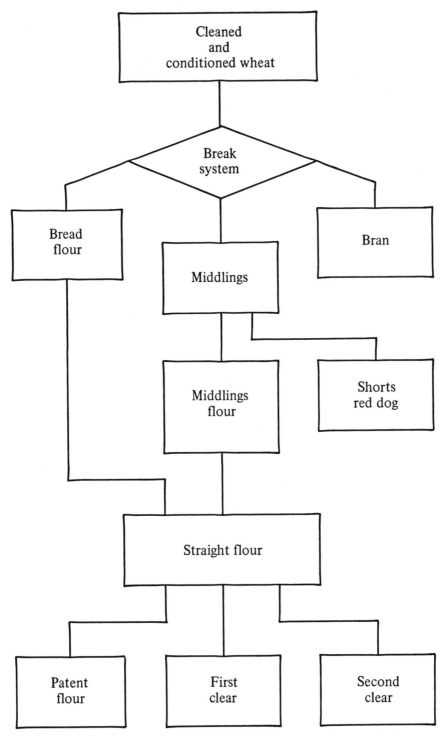

Figure 2–1 *The milling of wheat into flour. Reprinted from* A Treatise on Cake Making, *by permission of Standard Brands, Inc., copyright owner.*

RYE BREAD AND RYE FLOUR

I. POINTS OF INTEREST CONCERNING THE PRODUCTION OF RYE BREAD

A. There are many different kinds of rye bread made and sold in this country, ranging from dark, sour rye to a very light rye loaf.

B. The flavor of rye bread depends on the process of fermentation employed and on the quantity and quality of the flour used for the blend.

C. Rye flour is more apt to ferment than white wheat flour. The fermentation period of rye doughs, especially those in which sour is used, must be carefully watched and regulated.

D. Care should be taken to avoid excessive steam in the oven during the baking of rye bread.

B. Pumpernickel Flour

This is a coarsely ground, whole-rye flour. It is quite dark and is used chiefly in making pumpernickel bread. This flour is known in some sections as *rye meal* and *rye graham*. A 100% coarsely chopped rye is also known as *rye meal.*

C. Rye Blend Flour or Rye Flour, Bohemian

Rye flour is blended with hard wheat flour (a high gluten and a clear flour) to give it the necessary rising power.

IV. SELF-RISING FLOUR

This is ordinary flour to which calcium acid phosphate, baking soda, and salt have been added. As calcium acid phosphate and baking soda are the ingredients of phosphate baking powder, self-rising flour is the same mixture obtained by mixing flour with baking powder and salt. However, the baking powder ingredients and the salt used in preparing the self-rising flour are mixed with the flour much more thoroughly and uniformly at the mill than they can possibly be mixed in the home; they cost the consumer less than flour, baking powder, and salt bought separately; and the use of self-rising flour does away with the work of mixing the ingredients in the kitchen.

V. POTATO FLOUR

This is used in the making of potato bread by mixing it with either wheat or rye flour. It is also used in making bread. For all practical purposes, today potato flour is purchased. However, prior to this convenience, cooked potato water was used.

VI. CORN FLOUR

This flour is produced by pulverizing white corn grits.

VII. CORNMEAL

This is the coarsely ground kernel of the corn, either yellow or white. Yellow cornmeal is a very good source of vitamin A; white cornmeal lacks this vitamin. The term *old process* is used in connection with cornmeal; it is manufactured by grinding the entire kernel, with the exception of just the outer bran coat. In manufacturing *new process* cornmeal, the germ, which contains the corn oil, and all of the bran is removed. New process cornmeal keeps better because of the lack of oil, but the old process article, because of the oil in the germ, is decidedly superior, both in food value and in flavor.

VIII. RICE FLOUR

Rice flour is produced by grinding uncoated rice. It is used like pastry flour and is also used in many diets in which other flours are objectionable.

IX. ALL-PURPOSE OR FAMILY FLOUR

This flour, also known as *blend flour* or *general-purpose flour,* is a flour so prepared that it may be used quite satisfactorily for all baking and cooking purposes in the home. It may be a blend of hard wheat flours, a blend of soft wheat flours, or a blend of both hard and soft wheat flours. As a rule, family flour prepared from hard wheat flours is superior for making yeast breads, and that prepared from soft wheat flours is superior for making quick breads.

X. GLUTEN FLOUR

Gluten flour is made from hard wheat flour from which a large part of the starch has been removed. It is used for making bread for diabetics and others who must abstain from starchy foods.

XI. GRAHAM FLOUR

There is no difference between graham flour, whole-wheat flour, and entire-wheat flour. The terms are used interchangeably for the product made by grinding the entire wheat grain, including the bran—a 100% wheat flour.

XII. BLEACHED FLOUR

Flour requires proper aging in order to produce best results in baking. Storing newly milled flour for 2 or 3 months not only gives the flour the necessary aging but also gives it a much whiter color—a whiteness consumers generally expect in flour of high quality. In order to eliminate the expense of storing the flour and in order to place the newly milled flour on the market immediately after it is milled, flour now is commonly bleached by chemicals approved by food officials, which in no way affects the palatability or nutritive properties of the flour. The bleaching process also gives the new flour the proper aging so that it is ready for use as it leaves the mill. All flour thus artificially bleached and aged is known as *bleached* flour.

XIII. IDENTIFYING HARD AND SOFT WHEAT FLOURS

When hard wheat flour is rubbed between the fingers, it feels dry and somewhat granular. If a tablespoonful or so of the flour is pressed tightly in the hand and then shaken, it falls to powder readily, showing practically no imprint of the fingers. When soft wheat flour is rubbed between the fingers, it feels smooth and soft. If a tablespoonful or so of the flour is pressed tightly in the hand and then shaken, it remains more or less in lumps, showing the imprint of the fingers.

XIV. STRONG AND WEAK FLOURS

Whether a flour is strong or weak depends upon the gluten that can be developed in it. When liquid is added to the flour, two of the flour proteins combine to form gluten, an elastic substance that gives the doughs and batters their ability to stretch. Good-quality gluten is very elastic; it can easily double in bulk without breaking. Flour that contains this high-quality gluten is called *strong* flour. It is made from hard wheat and is the baker's first choice for making yeast bread. A strong flour absorbs more liquids than a weak one and thus makes more loaves of bread than could be made from the same quantity of a weak flour. In weak flours, the gluten is less in quantity and weaker in quality than it is in strong flours—just right for making cakes and pastry. Weak flours are made from soft wheat.

XV. ENRICHED FLOUR

This is a white flour containing certain minimum amounts of at least two important vitamins and one added mineral. These added food values (vitamin B_1, nicotinic acid, and iron) help to replace those lost from the wheat grain in the process of milling refined flour. Enriched flour may also contain certain amounts of riboflavin, vitamin D, calcium, and phosphorus; these additions, however, are optional. (It is deficient in one of the essential amino acids—lipine.)

The added vitamins and minerals do not change the flavor of the flour or its color, appearance, and baking and keeping qualities. The minimum requirements for added food values in enriched flour per pound are: 1.66 milligrams of vitamin B_1 (thiamin), 6.15 milligrams of nicotinic acid, and 6.15 milligrams of iron. (Nicotinic acid is a vitamin found naturally in wheat and other foods. It is a pellagra-preventative factor and has none of the qualities of nicotine found in tobacco.)

Creamy-colored enriched flour is made by a special milling process that retains in the flour the amounts of vitamins and minerals that are lost in the ordinary method of milling refined wheat flour. Actually, such flour has not been enriched; it comes from the mill rich in the vitamins and minerals required for "enriched" flours. Although it is labeled "enriched," nothing has been added to it either during or after the milling process. It has its own nature-given vitamins and minerals, instead of having synthetic food values added to it.

Enriched flour has synthetic vitamins added, which serve the same purpose in the diet as the natural vitamins.

XVI. BREAD FLOUR

This is a hard wheat flour, usually a blend of hard winter and hard spring wheat flours, sold both bleached and unbleached, and used largely by the bakery trade for making bread. It is slightly granular to the touch and yields gluten that is quite strong and elastic.

Flour should be stored in a cool, dry place. A temperature of 65 to 70°F is satisfactory. The storage room should be well ventilated and free from any odors whatsoever. Flour readily absorbs odors that often prove ruinous to the finished baked product.

A. Soy Flour

Soy flour has the advantage of containing up to 50% protein. The soybean is nature's most nutritious bean and can be grown in many parts of the world. A disadvantage of soy flour is that it completely lacks elasticity when blended with water.

4. True or false: Wheat flour is highly nutritious but is somewhat deficit in lysine, one of the essential amino acids.

True.

Wheat protein is unique among the cereals in that it alone, when water is added (hydrated), can form a dough that can be fermented and expanded. When heat is applied, it sets to form an aerated bread. This is made possible by the gluten proteins in wheat, particularly, those called gliadin and glutenin. When fully hydrated, glutenin becomes tough and rubbery and gliadin becomes a viscous, fluid mass. When hydrated together, they become cohesive, elastic, and viscous.

5. The unusual quality of wheat protein is that it contains two proteins—glutenin and gliadin—that are extensible and when made into a dough and fermented expand and form a cellular mass. With heat the proteins become firm, and the result is _____.

Bread and other baked dough products.

B. Rye and Oats

Other cereals such as rye and oats and tricale (a cross between wheat and rye) contain about the same amount of protein as wheat and are about the same nutritionally. Rye flour also contains gliadin. The glutenin of rye flour, however, differs from that of wheat and is responsible for its inability to form the gluten structure provided by wheat protein.

6. Why is it impossible to make rye bread with only rye flour?

Rye protein alone cannot form the elastic, gluten matrix that when fermented and expanded gives a loaf its volume.

Vital wheat gluten is the dried gluten protein of wheat flour from which most starch has been removed. It can be added to dough to increase its protein content. It is usually added at the sponge stage with other dry ingredients before water is added.

The gluten adds strength to the flour and makes it better able to withstand continuous mixing and high-speed dough development. Only a small percentage of vital gluten (based on the flour) is added; 2% to 3% can be added to doughs for hard rolls and French and Italian breads. Raisin and related heavy breads get the same percentage. Sweet rolls and yeast-raised doughnuts get 0.5% to 1.5% of the vital wheat gluten.

7. Gluten is composed of almost all ____.

Protein.

2. Rye is milled into flours of different grades, such as rye patent flour, rye straight flour, and various dark rye flours.

B. Rye blend flour is usually made by mixing from 25% to 40% of rye flour with baker's clear. The exact amount of rye flour used depends on local conditions and the character of the bread desired.
C. Pumpernickel flour is a coarsely ground, whole-rye flour. It is quite dark and is used chiefly in making pumpernickel bread.

III. TYPES OF RYE BREAD

A. Most popular types of rye bread are made with either a straight or sponge dough, and either plain or with caraway seeds.

1. Plain rye bread
2. Light rye bread
3. Dark rye bread
4. Bohemian rye
5. Jewish rye
6. Swedish rye
7. Pumpernickel rye

B. These breads may be made with or without sour—sour fermented dough used for leavening.

IV. PREPARATION OF SOUR

4 lb sour*
  To this add:
2 qt water
5 lb dark rye flour   (1st sour)
  Let stand 3 hours and add:
4 qt water
10 lb dark rye flour   (2d sour)
  Let stand 3 hours and add:
12 qt water
30 lb dark rye flour   (3d and final sour)

When sour starter is used, remove the onion and proceed as described.

These sours should be made 3 hours apart. See that these sours are not made too stiff. Temperature of water for these sours should be 60°F in summer and 80°F in winter.

If more than one batch is required, take 30 lb from the final sour and add 12 qt water and 30 lb dark rye flour to make again 84 lb sour. In this manner, continuous batches can be made as required.

Always leave enough sour for use the following day. Use ½ lb sour for every 10 lb final sour required.

* If it is impossible to secure this sour as a starter, it may be started as follows:
  Mix together: 2 lb rye flour
                       1½ lb water
                       1 large onion (split into four parts)
                       6 oz ground caraway seed
                       2 oz Fleischmann's Yeast
Let stand 24 hours.

REVIEW

1. What is flour?

2. What are some reasons for the importance of flour?

3. Why is wheat the most essential grain used in breadmaking?

4. What are the two primary types of wheat flour used in baking?

5. Why is rye flour alone not recommended for making bread?

6. What is all-purpose or family flour?

7. Why is flour bleached?

8. What is "strong" flour, what is it made from, and what is it used for?

9. What is "weak" flour, what is it made from, and what is it used for?

10. What is enriched flour?

11. How should flour be stored?

CHAPTER 3

THE MAGIC OF GLUTEN*

> ***This chapter is to be used as a Question and Answer section for Chapter 2 *Flours and Meals*.**

1. Mix flour and water together and knead. Lo and behold, the combination begins to become stretchy and elastic. The proteins in the flour take up the water (hydrate). *Gluten* is being developed. The proteins and water form a molecular network that can be stretched. When heated to about 165°F it becomes firm and provides the structural framework of the baked dough product.

   What ingredient permits doughs to enlarge and take on a new shape when baked?

   Gluten.

2. Mixing flour and water to form a dough is something like mixing sand, cement, and water to form concrete. Protein in the flour resembles the cement; starch in a flour is like sand.

   Mixing water with the flour develops the gluten to give strength to the dough, just as mixing water and sand with cement sets off a chemical reaction that gives strength to the sand and cement.

The water must be mixed with the flour so that the gluten strands can develop. Try forming a pie dough using only fat and flour. When baked, the crust would have no strength and would crumble.

To form an elastic dough with strength, the flour must be mixed with _____.

Water.

3. As wheat flour and water are kneaded, gluten is _____.

Developed.

4. Not all of the protein in flour will form gluten, but that which does is the part that enables the dough or batter to stretch and rise. Proteins in flour vary in the amount and quality of gluten that are developed. Flour is said to be strong or weak according to the amount and toughness or elasticity of the gluten formed.

What ingredient in flour largely determines the strength of the flour?

Protein.

5. A dough's elasticity or stretch is related to the _____ of the flour used.

Strength.

6. Strength of the flour depends primarily, but not entirely, on the amount and type of protein present in the flour.

Gluten strength depends mostly on the wheat variety, the kind of wheat, but also upon the growing conditions and the storage conditions. For bread and rolls we need a *strong* flour, but strength is not necessarily an asset. Cakes, for example, should be made with *weak* flour, and pastries with a flour of intermediate strength.

Strength of the flour is most closely related to what constituent in the flour?

Protein.

7. The amount of gluten present in flour is related to the amount of protein in the flour. Wheat flour ranges in protein content from about 6.5% to 15%.

If a baked item is to rise and assume a new, enlarged form, some gluten must be present so that the dough will stretch and harden in the expanded form.

The amount of gluten needed for a product varies considerably. Bread, éclairs, and pound cake may contain large amounts of gluten to give the desired structure; cakes, cookies, and some pastries require much less because fewer structure-building properties are desired. In a product such as pie dough, low gluten is wanted so that the crust has a "sharp break" (breaks easily).

Do cakes and cookies need comparatively large or small amounts of gluten development?

Small.

8. Much of baking knowledge is concerned with the amount, nature, and control of the gluten that is developed in a particular flour.

Breads baked on the hearth (on stones and not in pans) require high-protein flour that when baked is strong enough not to flatten under the weight of the dough and to withstand the strong leavening action of the large amount of carbon dioxide gas developed by the yeast.

Cake flour, by contrast, must be made from soft wheat (low protein content). If bread flour were used, the cake would be tough. You can make a cake with bread flour if you increase the fat, but the product is never as good as when cake flour is used.

Flours in a middle range are necessary for pastries and hot breads such as rolls, biscuits, and muffins.

Are the protein content and gluten development of flour that are best for pastries and hot breads more or less than those contained in bread flours?

Less.

9. Muffins are characteristically light and fluffy, and the problem in making them is to avoid developing the gluten in the flour. Mix the batter as little as possible. Even during the process of putting the

batter into a pan, too much manipulation causes a tough muffin. In a baking powder biscuit dough, we want a stronger structure, and so we work the dough more than a muffin batter. However, too much kneading or working destroys quality in the biscuit.

If we mix biscuit dough too much, what will we get? | A heavy, tough biscuit.

10. For Danish and sweet rolls, bread flour can be used, but some formulas call for the addition of some pastry flour. Why? | So that less gluten development takes place.

11. Only wheat flour can be kneaded to develop gluten to any extent. Rye flour contains enough protein to do so, but other substances present do not permit gluten development.

To develop gluten, we need what kind of flour? | Wheat.

12. The variety of wheat, the growing conditions, and the soil produce wheats of different hardness and softness. Hard wheat produces strong flours. From strong flours, gluten can be developed that stretches farther before tearing. Taking a guess, what kind of flour, strong or weak, would you use for bread? | Strong, because the dough must stretch a great deal to form a large loaf.

13. Again thinking about strength, what kind of flour would be used for a cake? | Weak. The thing we prize about cakes is their tenderness. Weak flours make tender cakes.

14. Soft wheat produces weak flours. Hard wheat results in flours that are *strong*. Although we speak of the *strength* of a flour, the wheat it is made from is spoken of as being *hard* or *soft*. Soft wheat produces a _____ flour. | Weak.

15. Hard wheat results in a _____ flour. | Strong.

16. Factors other than the amount of protein affect the quality of the flour. These are not well un-

derstood. The principal factor in wheat and flour that determines the baking characteristic is the amount of _____ in the wheat.

Protein.

17. As flour is worked (kneaded) by hand or by mixing machine, the dough becomes elastic. The amount of kneading or mixing determines how much gluten is developed.

    In some products, like bread, we want maximum gluten development. For tender biscuits, would you want maximum gluten development?

No. If all the gluten is developed, the biscuit would be chewy like bread. Most of us like tender biscuits.

18. Gluten is not like rubber or gum that springs back after many stretchings. Stretch dough too much, and the gluten strands break.

    Can we overmix a dough?

Quite easily. The gluten is broken down, and the dough loses its ability to expand.

19. Much of the skill of baking centers around the control of gluten development. The more protein present and the more gluten developed, the chewier the product. Hearth-baked breads, those that are not panned (baked in a pan), require maximum gluten to support the loaf. Cake that is supposed to be light and tender requires minimum gluten. Flaky crust pastry calls for some gluten development.

    The substance that provides a frame and is the principal support for baked goods is _____.

Gluten.

20. Suppose we use whole-wheat flour—that containing the bran and the germ as the endosperm. Would we get more or less gluten development than with white flour?

Less. The bran apparently cuts the gluten strands and has a diluting effect on the protein. The loaf will be smaller.

21. Gluten is strengthened by the presence of most minerals. Water contains minerals, and the so-called dough improvers contain minerals that act to strengthen gluten.

    Does the presence of minerals strengthen or weaken gluten?

Strengthen.

22. The amount of water absorbed by a dough largely depends on the amount of protein or gluten present. The more protein, the greater the amount of water required to make up the dough. Starch absorbs comparatively little water.

    Which dough would take more water: bread dough or pastry dough?

    Bread dough, because of its higher protein content.

23. The amount of water absorbed by the dough is a guide to the amount of protein present. Which dough would take up more water: cookie dough or pastry dough?

    Pastry dough, because it is likely to contain more protein.

24. Knowing that fat (shortening) surrounds gluten strands, do you think that adding shortening to a dough would help or hinder the development of gluten?

    It hinders the development because it makes the gluten strands less continuous. Fat is a tenderizer, as is sugar.

25. Separated out from wheat flour, vital wheat gluten is often added to a variety of dough products for what purpose?

    To give the dough added strength, which means that the baked product will have better structure. It also adds nutritionally valuable protein.

Two other high-protein flours are available: cottonseed and peanut flour. Neither is used but could be added at levels of 5% based on wheat flour. One reason they are not used is that they alter the appearance and flavor of the product unfavorably.

Potato flour is added to some products. Potato flakes added at the 3% level based on wheat flour increase water absorption and improve texture and softness in white and raisin breads. Potato flour contains 8% protein and is high in thiamin, riboflavin, and niacin.

26. Flours such as soy, oat, potato, and rye are high in protein, and their protein is of high quality. However, they cannot by themselves be made into a raised dough product because their protein lacks the amino acids necessary to form what substances?

    Gliadin and glutenin.

27. Composite flours are wheat flours with percentages of other flours, such as millet, soybean, corn, banana, and rice, added to make specialty yeast-raised products.

Will adding small percentages of these flours weaken the wheat dough?

Yes. None of the flours, other than wheat, contains the gluten-forming proteins needed for aeration.

The protein content of wheat range from 6% to 18%, depending upon its variety, where it is grown, and the growing conditions. Generally speaking, wheat grown in low-rainfall areas has higher-than-average protein content. The high-protein wheats are called *hard* because they have hard kernels. Hard wheats are generally high in protein. *Soft* wheats have softer kernels and are lower in protein.

The four major categories of wheat are: hard red spring, hard red winter, soft red winter, and spring white wheats. Winter wheats are grown where the winter weather is relatively mild and dry. They begin to grow before the cold weather sets in and are harvested in early summer. Spring wheats are planted in the spring and harvested in late summer.

The hard wheats yield flour with strong glutens and are best for hearth and pan breads. Cake and pastry flours come from soft wheats. Pasta flour is made from durum wheat. Durum wheat is not used for breads because of its yellowish color, even though it is high in protein.

28. Winter wheats are planted when?

In late fall or early winter.

29. Spring wheats are harvested when?

In the late summer.

30. Which wheats—the hard or soft wheats—contain the most protein?

The hard wheats.

31. As gluten is developed in a dough, it takes up water and becomes stretchable.

To roll into pie dough, strudel dough, and Danish pastry dough, the gluten stretches into longer and longer strands. After gluten is stretched it tends to shorten up and partially regain its original length. A dough that is rolled out handles much better than if it is allowed to relax.

True or False: When gluten is stretched as a dough is rolled out, the gluten strands then tend to shorten.

True.

32. To allow the gluten to adjust to its new length after being stretched, a dough is *relaxed*. With pie dough the dough must be relaxed overnight. With Danish pastry the dough is usually relaxed for 30 minutes or more between each rolling. During the period of relaxation, the starch takes up some of the water, and the gluten strands are given time to adjust to their new, longer length.

   We relax dough primarily so that it will roll out more easily and take on a new and flatter form. What part of the dough are we most concerned with in the relaxing period?

   The gluten strands.

   Yes. By overmixing the dough, some of the gluten strands are broken. The dough begins to resemble that made with pastry flour. This practice is not recommended because bread flour is usually costlier. Overmixing is also costly in time and power.

33. Ordinarily pie dough is made from pastry flour. Pastry flour contains less protein than bread flour and more than cake flour. Is it possible to use bread flour for pie crusts?

34. Gluten is strengthened by the presence of _____ and weakened by the presence of _____ or by _____.

   Minerals, fat, overmixing.

35. To stretch a dough, it is rolled out. Usually, to allow the gluten to adjust to the new length of the strands, it is _____ for a period of time.

   Relaxed.

36. The amount of gluten developed in a dough depends primarily on the kind of _____ used.

   Wheat flour.

37. In some products we want maximum gluten development; in others, minimum gluten development. How about angel food cakes?

   Minimum gluten development.

REVIEW

1. The kind and amount of protein in the flour relates to the type of gluten that can be developed from it. Is flour that produces a large amount of elastic gluten a strong or weak flour?

2. For cakes, is a strong or weak flour wanted?

3. For bread, is a strong or weak flour wanted?

4. In some products we want to develop the maximum gluten possible. If dough is overmixed, what happens to the gluten?

5. For tender biscuits, is maximum or minimum gluten developed?

6. What effect do minerals have on gluten?

7. Which dough absorbs more water: that with high protein or that with low protein?

8. To "relax" a dough, we allow it to stand and the gluten to _____.

9. Is a relaxed dough easier or more difficult to handle than a dough that is not relaxed?

10. Which contains more protein: cake flour or pastry flour?

CHAPTER 4

SELECTING THE RIGHT FLOUR

I. WHEAT KERNEL TO FLOUR

II. FLOUR ADDITIVES AND MATURING
   AGENTS

   A. Additives

   B. Oxidants in Flour

I. WHEAT KERNEL TO FLOUR

The wheat kernel is made up of three parts: the wheat germ, which is the seed; the endosperm, comprised mainly of starch and protein; and the bran. There is also a small percentage of ash. The bran covers the wheat germ, and the endosperm provides the reservoir of food on which the germ feeds as it grows into a wheat plant. (See Figure 4–1.)

The problem of the miller is to separate the three parts with the intent of retaining (extracting) the endosperm and making it into a powder as flour. About 92% by weight of the kernel is endosperm, which contains starch granules embedded in a matrix of gluten-forming protein. The separation process is called *extraction*.

1. Around the outside of the kernel is the _____. | Bran.

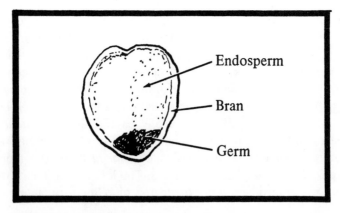

Figure 4–1 *A kernel of wheat.*

2. From the baker's viewpoint which part of the wheat kernel is most important? Why?

> The endosperm. Because it contains the starch and gluten-forming proteins necessary to make leavened (raised) dough products.

The miller wants to obtain the maximum extraction (separation) of the endosperm and to do so without excessively breaking up the starch granules.

3. Would it be possible to make bread by simply grinding up the whole wheat kernels?

> Before milling became a science and had the use of modern equipment, the flour produced included the germ and the bran.

The germ contains about 9% to 11% lipids (fats and fatlike substances), which affect flavor and readily turn rancid when exposed to air. Bran imparts a coarse texture to baked products not appreciated by many consumers. If bran is wanted in a dough product, it is added separately, not as part of the flour.

Before sending the wheat kernels through a series of rollers that flatten and break them up, the wheat is first cleaned and tempered, the moisture context adjusted so that the bran and germ can be efficiently separated, and the endosperm made more friable (easily crumpled and pulverized).

The wheat (which may be a blend of several wheats) is then sent through a series of five or six rollers, each set to grind finer than the one before. The crushed wheat, now called *stock*, is sifted into three sizes: the coarsest size; the medium size, called *middling;* and the finest, called *break* flour. The coarsest grind is then sent through successive "breaks" until, after the fifth or sixth passage (or break), nearly all of the endosperm has been removed. The germ is removed by flattening it so that it cannot pass through sieves.

The endosperm that has been separated out is further purified by passing through flat rollers and sifting. As many as 150 different *streams* (flours subjected to different grinding operations) are produced. When all of the streams are combined, the result is called *straight* flour. The more refined flours are sold separately as *patent* flours. The less refined flours are labeled *clear* and are graded according to degree of refinement: fancy clear and second clear.

4. Grind the entire kernel into flour, and we have whole-wheat flour. It is very difficult to keep "fresh" because it contains the germ, which is about 9% to 11% fat. This fat turns rancid when exposed to oxygen because of the action of some enzymes naturally present in the wheat.

   Whole-wheat flour contains the endosperm, the bran, and the _____.   **Germ.**

5. White flour is made using only the endosperm. The kernel is broken up into a meal and then bolted (sifted). The bran is lifted off by air. The germ is separated off.

   White flour is made up of what part of the wheat kernel?   **Endosperm.**

6. About 72% of the wheat kernel comes out as flour. What's left is used for animal feed.

   The finest flour is known as *fancy patent* or *extra short.*

   Then come *short, medium,* and *patent* flours. Straight flour is a combination of the others.

   The finest ground flour, most free of bran and germ, might be labeled _____.   **Fancy patent or extra short flour.**

Wheat on the average contains about 85% endosperm, and 100 lb of cleaned wheat yields 72 lb of flour and 28 lb of animal feed.

The baker cannot be sure which flour will produce the desired product and may blend different flours in-house. Milling produces several grades of flour quality, and the baker buys the grade wanted for a particular product or blends flavors to achieve the desired product.

7. What is the primary purpose of milling?

To separate the endosperm from the bran and germ.

8. Why not leave the germ, which is highly nutritious and contains fat, in the flour?

The fats oxidize, turn rancid, and impair flavor. They also add an unwanted color to the flour.

9. What is a straight flour?

One that contains all of the flours of various degrees of refinement.

The patent contains the best of the endosperm and therefore is more expensive.
   Patent flours come from the wheat kernel first in the milling process. Middlings come next, and clears last. A straight flour is a mixture of the entire kernel minus the bran.

10. Which flour costs more: patent or clear?

11. Would it be wise to use only the patent flours for baking?

No. The baker selects the flour best suited for a particular product.

The miller selects the wheat or blends of wheat to extract out the endosperm, and produces several degrees of refined flours. Even so, the baker cannot be sure of the baking quality, which depends on its genetics and growing conditions.

The ultimate test of flour quality is the product produced. The baker may blend flours, include various additives, vital wheat gluten, or starch to arrive at the flour he wants.

12. True or false: The same kind and grade of flour may vary from one milling to another.

True.

13. Next, let's look at the composition of wheat flour:

Protein: 6.5% to 18%

Starch: 68% to 76%

Lipids (fatlike compounds): 1.5%

Ash (minerals): 0.3% to 1%

Fiber: 0.4% to 0.5%

Moisture: 11% to 13%

Although the largest constituent of wheat flour is starch, it is the _____ that primarily affects its baking quality.

Protein.

14. Rub some of the white flours found in the usual bakeshop between your fingers. Some are found to be gritty or hard. Others are extremely powdery or soft.

The hardness or softness is related to the proportion of protein to starch in the flour. Starch grinds into a fine powder. Protein is broken into larger particles that can be felt when rubbed.

Rub a white flour between the fingers. If gritty, is it likely to be high or low in protein?

High.

15. Besides wheat flour, we have available rye, graham, soy, potato, corn, and farina flour.

Although rye flour contains sufficient protein to develop gluten, gummy substances in the flour prevent gluten from developing and its glutenin is different. It is usually available in three grades of color: white, medium, and dark. Because rye flour does not form gluten, it is mixed with strong wheat flour in varying proportions, depending on the type of rye bread wanted, such as American rye, sour rye, pumpernickel, and sweet or pan rye.

What do you think would happen to the bread if no wheat flour were added to the rye flour?

The bread would rise very little and would be extremely heavy and dense.

16. Soy flour is more nutritious than any other flour. Although soy flour is highly nutritious, its flavor is not well accepted by North Americans. Up to 8% soy flour can be added to wheat flour if additional oxidizing agents such as potassium bromate are added. Rolls containing soy flour and oxidizing agents can be made superior to bread baked from wheat flour alone, as measured by volume and fineness of grain.

Can you make bread from soy flour alone?

It would not rise properly because soy flour does not develop gluten. Americans would not eat it because of its flavor.

17. Soft wheat flour (low protein) is called for in making cookies, crackers, and pretzels. Soft wheat is also used in cakes, doughnuts, and other cake-like products.

True or false: Soft wheat flour is used for items that do not need strong gluten.

True.

18. Graham flour is flour to which bran has been added but which is very finely ground. It was named after a miller of whole wheat who advocated its use.

Is graham flour similar to whole-wheat flour?

Yes. Both contain bran, but in the graham flour the bran is finely ground.

19. Suppose you have nothing but bread flour and would like to use it for making pastry or even some types of cake. Would it be possible to soften the flour by adding starch?

Yes. This is done at times.

20. A flour made from durum wheat is especially high in protein and has its own yellow-amber color and nutty flavor. It is used mostly for pasta products such as macaroni, spaghetti, and noodles.

Would durum flour be desirable for French or Italian types of breads, which require high protein content?

Yes. It is so used, especially in France and Italy.

II. FLOUR ADDITIVES AND MATURING AGENTS

A. Additives

Potassium bromate has routinely been added to wheat flour by the miller or the baker since about 1916 and has proved to be an inexpensive oxidant that may increase bread loaf volume by 10% to 15%. Only a few parts per million of potassium bromate are needed. Just why this chemical is so effective is not clear. It is clear that its use allows for shorter fermentation and mixing times and faster processing times, which together reduce production costs. In 1991, California declared that any product sold in the state that contains potassium bromate must carry a warning label that the chemical is in the product and that it may be a cause of cancer.

Even though tests have shown that bread containing a few parts per million of potassium bromate retains only a few parts per billion of the chemical after baking, bakers are searching for replacements for potassium bromate that are inexpensive and have the same effects.

Some of the replacements are ascorbic acid, azodicarbonamide (DADA), and ethoxylated monoglyceride. Small amounts of fungal amylose have been tried. Longer fermentation makes the bromate less necessary. Adding vital wheat gluten or increasing the amount of yeast helps. Surfactants (agents that reduce surface tension) also can perform some of the functions of potassium bromate.

Potassium bromate has been an effective, inexpensive oxidant in bread-making. It also strengthens the dough. Substitutes—either one or a combination—will need to be found.

21. Why is a replacement for potassium bromate being sought?

It has been declared to be unsafe and a carcinogen (cancer-causing agent).

22. After reading about the several chemicals that may partially replace potassium bromate, we can see why cereal chemistry and bakery engineering are separate specialized disciplines. On what basic science do they depend?

Chemistry.

The federal government requires that all bread flour be nutritionally enriched by the addition of iron and the B complex vitamins, thiamin, riboflavin, and niacin. The reason for the *enrichment* requirement is that substantial amounts of these and other vitamins are lost in the milling process, when most of the bran and germ are removed. Bran and germ contain much of the vitamins and iron. Most bread flour is fortified by the miller, but bakers may also enrich their products with premeasured tablets or preweighted soluble-film packets.

B. Oxidants in Flour

Oxidants are chemicals that cause oxidation, a change involving the loss of electrons. Oxidation is important to the baker because flour that has not had oxygen added by exposure to air during storage needs to be oxidized by the addition of an oxidizing agent. This is usually done by the miller but can be done by the baker.

The Food and Drug Administration approves the following oxidants for use in flour: potassium bromate ($KBrO_3$), ascorbic acid (vitamin C), and azodicarbonamide ($NH_2CO.N$:)2. A very small amount of oxidant is sufficient: 75 parts per million (ppm) of potassium bromate, for example.

For optimal baking performance, each flour requires a certain level of oxidation. Those flours not oxidized produce doughs that are excessively soft, exhibit insufficient elasticity, and produce small loaves. The loaves have a coarse texture and poor crumb color.

23. Using a freshly milled flour that has not been oxidized is not a good idea. Why?

> The baked product will be smaller than desirable, with a coarse texture and poor crumb color.

Because wheats and their growing conditions vary, the resulting flours may not be exactly what is wanted. Flour is bleached to whiten them.

Enzymes may be added to the flour so that fermentation can take place properly, and the gluten in the flour can be strengthened by adding oxygen to it. Bakers may want to increase the vitamins and iron content. For these and other reasons, some flours are bleached and certain additives are put into them.

Such additives improve the flour in various ways. An *additive* is something added to a food for a particular purpose. Flour additives aid the baker and the consumer.

24. True or false: An additive can be a "dirty" word.

> True, for some people who do not understand their purpose. But flour additives as allowed by law are good for the purposes intended.

Bleached flour has had one of several bleaching agents added to it by the miller. These agents whiten the flour by removing the yellow color (the carotenoids) present.

Some bleaching agents also mature or "age" the flour, which means that oxygen is added to the flour and the gluten becomes stronger or more elastic.

White cakes are made with bleached flour because of the white color desired. Cookies, pies, and crackers are usually made with unbleached flour.

25. Some bleaching agents, besides whitening the flour, also _____. | Mature it by adding oxygen to it.

Flour can be *matured* by letting it sit in storage. Gradually, the surrounding air combines with some of the flour. This is a slow and costly process, and the oxygen does not reach the flour uniformly; therefore, the miller is likely to add a maturing agent to the flour, which accomplishes the same purpose in a shorter time.

The most widely used additive for this purpose is potassium bromate. It is one of several gluten-oxidizing agents that have the effect of making the gluten more elastic and stretchable.

26. Would bromated flour most likely be used for bread or cake? | Bread; we need strong gluten for bread.

Potassium bromate is added to flour by the miller, not the baker. Only a few parts per million are added. This amount is so small that it is no health hazard; it is less than what normally occurs in many seafoods.

Potassium bromate has no bleaching effect on the flour. It is inert until water is added. Because it makes the gluten more elastic and stretchable, the dough is easier to handle. The fermented dough will stretch and hold gas better. The baked product is bigger.

27. Would you use bromated flour for cakes? | Probably not, because the bromated flour is not bleached.

Not all flour is bromated; some flour does not need it. Other flours need a combination of maturing agents. Chlorine dioxide and bromate are sometimes added together.

28. Is addition of maturing agents to flour best done by the baker or the miller? | The miller. The process is much too complicated to do in the bakeshop.

29. The most widely used maturing agent added to flour is _____. | Potassium bromate.

30. What does potassium bromate do to the gluten? | Makes it more stretchable and elastic.

Other additives are put in flour to accomplish particular purposes. Malted wheat or barley flour (from germinated grain) is added to flour that contains too few of the natural enzymes needed to convert starch into sugars. The word *enzyme* comes from the Greek "to leaven."

If there are too few of these enzymes, dough fails to rise properly. With too many, the dough is sticky and tends to run. The baked product may contain gummy spots.

Dough that is leavened by yeast must have enough enzymes present to provide sugars on which the yeast can act.

31. The reason malted wheat may be added to flour is to provide more of the right kind of _____. | Enzymes.

Another flour additive is *calcium phosphate*. This substance provides acid in the flour for persons who want to make sour milk or buttermilk biscuits. The added acid (between 0.25% and 0.75%) bolsters the leavening action of baking powder used for making these products.

32. Phosphated flour is used primarily for making _____. | Sour milk or buttermilk biscuits.

Mold inhibitors are added to bread dough ingredients to discourage the growth of various molds and bacteria. Some bacteria form spores (bacteria with thick walls) that are not killed by baking. Under the right conditions of warmth and moisture, these spores grow and turn pieces of bread into sticky, yellowish patches that can be pulled into rope-like threads. These *rope spores* can be held down by vinegar or other acids. Various molds also grow in bread products under the right conditions.

Propionates (salts of propionic acid) are added to baking formulas to combat the growth of molds and rope-forming bacteria.

33. Mold inhibitors are additives used for the purpose of reducing the growth of _____.

Spores and molds.

34. Rope spores in bread is a condition caused by certain _____.

Bacteria.

35. Does an acid condition favor or inhibit the growth of rope-forming spores?

Inhibits.

Self-rising flour is used widely in the Southeast. It is flour that contains a leavening agent and salt.

36. Self-rising flour is like any other flour except that the _____ has already been added.

Leavening agent.

A special *gluten flour* or high-gluten flour is made by adding extra protein to the flour so that it will have more than 40% protein. Such flour can be added to ordinary flour to improve its baking quality or to produce high-protein bread and rye breads.

37. Suppose you had a soft wheat flour, low in protein, which you wanted to use for making bread. Would it make sense to add some gluten flour to the weaker flour?

Yes, this is done on occasion.

REVIEW

1. From which part of the wheat kernel does most of the flour come?

2. Which part of the wheat kernel is removed from most flour?

3. Why is whole-wheat flour less stable than white flour?

4. The largest component of wheat flour is _____.

5. Protein content of flour varies from about _____ to _____.

6. Which of these flours feels grittier to the finger: the high protein or the low protein?

7. Rye flour has about the same protein as wheat flour, but little gluten can be developed in it. Why?

8. Soy flour is highly nutritious. Why is it used so little?

9. In what other products besides cakes is soft wheat flour likely to be used?

10. To soften bread flour, what would you add to it?

11. Which of these breads would use the "strongest" flour: French or American?

12. What is the advantage of bleached flour over unbleached?

13. When oxygen combines with the flour, it matures it and also strengthens the gluten that will be developed. Potassium bromate added to the flour does the same thing. Does the baker add potassium bromate to flour?

14. Potassium bromate is added to flour because it makes the gluten more _____.

15. Some flours lack sufficient enzymes to provide sugars on which the yeast can act. Name an additive that provides these enzymes.

16. Propionates are added to baking formulas for what purpose?

CHAPTER 5

LEAVENING AGENTS

I. DEFINITION

Webster's definition for the word *leaven:* "1. to raise (a) a substance (as yeast) used to produce fermentation in dough or liquid, esp. sour dough; (b) a material (as baking powder) used to produce a gas that lightens dough or batter. 2. Something that modifies or lightens a mass or aggregate."

The two types of leavening most commonly used in baking today are organic (yeast) and chemical (baking powder, baking soda, cream of tartar, and ammonium carbonate).

II. PURPOSES OF LEAVENING AGENTS

Many factors determine the quality of any baked product, but none is more important than the manner in which the batter or dough is raised or leavened and the control of this leavening action.

If a cake batter or dough possessed no leavening power or, in other words, did not rise during baking, the resulting product would be dense, heavy, and unpalatable. It would have little volume and would in no way resemble the light, porous, and appetizing product we know as cake or bread. Proper leavening makes cake more digestible.

III. CLASSIFICATION

There are several reasons why a cake batter or dough rises or becomes light during baking. The different types of cakes or breads have been roughly classified into three groups, each characterized by the principal reason causing its leavening or rising. However, in a great number of cakes or breads, the leavening is the result of a combination of the actions explained in the following paragraphs.

A. Chemical Leaveners

1. BAKING POWDER

In many of the cakes made today, such as loaf and layer cakes, wine cakes, various packaged cakes and cupcakes, as well as different kinds of cookies and biscuits, the principal leavening agent is baking powder. If it were not for baking powder, the many different varieties of delicious cakes produced today would not be possible. Therefore, the tremendous opportunity for the growth and development of the cake business today is in a measure due to the fact that baking powder in its present standardized form is available to the baker.

It must be remembered, however, that when converting a small, hand-made, household recipe to a large-quantity batch for bakeshop use, proportionate reductions should be made in the baking powder content to take care of the extra leavening brought about by creaming through mechanical means, which is much more thorough than the hand method of creaming employed in the home.

a. Baking Powder, the "Soul of the Cake"

Although the other ingredients used can be considered the "body of the cake," the action of the baking powder is mainly responsible for the conversion of the heavy mass of batter into a light, well-risen, appetizing cake. As a matter of fact, the action of the baking powder influences many of the characteristics of the cake, such as symmetry, crust characteristics, volume, cell structure—which directly affect grain and texture—and to a very marked degree the eating and keeping quality of the cake.

b. Baking Powder Defined

Baking powder is a leavening agent made up of a mixture of an acid, an acid-reacting salt, or a combination of acid-reacting salts with bicarbonate of soda. These substances are intimately mixed in balanced proportions, usually with a certain amount of specially dried starch, which aids in keeping the powder dry and acts as a separator of the constituents of the powder until it is used.

c. Action of Baking Powder Explained

In the presence of both heat and moisture, the acid-reacting salts act upon the bicarbonate of soda, releasing carbon dioxide gas. Part of this gas is absorbed by the liquid of the batter. The rest of this gas gradually pushes its way into the air cells (formed in creaming), helping them to expand and produce greater volume until the batter is finally "set" by the baking process. In this way the finished cake secures its light, porous cell-like structure. (See Figure 5-1.)

Baking powder distributed throughout the cake batter in the mixing process gradually loses its identity as the reaction producing the carbon dioxide gas proceeds. When this action is completed in the oven, the baking powder will have been used up, or destroyed, and in its place are left residual substances, possibly together with traces of the original ingredients, which form a part of the cake itself. The character of this residue depends on the original composition of the powder used and may affect the flavor and color of the finished cake interior.

2. CREAM OF TARTAR

Cream of tartar is refined crude tartar, which precipitates from grape wine during and after the process of fermentation. The pinkish crystallized sediments called *lees*, found at the bottom of the wine cask, and the pinkish crystalline substance called *argol*, which collects on the sides of the cask, are nothing but crude tartar.

The refining consists of a process of alternate decrystallizing of the crude tartar by cooking in boiling water and then allowing the resulting liquid to crystallize. The liquid is finally bleached to pure white and allowed to crystallize once more. As the liquid cools, a thin layer of white crystals forms on the surface. It is from this layer of white crystals that cream of tartar takes its name.

Cream of tartar is sold in powdered form. It has an acid taste and is used chiefly in the preparation of cream of tartar baking powder. For leavening purposes, two parts of cream of tartar are mixed with one part of baking soda.

3. BAKING SODA

Baking soda (bicarbonate of sodium) is a side product in the manufacture of the common washing soda, also known as *sal soda*.

Sodium bicarbonate contains carbon and oxygen, which form carbon dioxide gas. Hence, the reaction is similar whether a baking powder is used containing both the acid component and the sodium bicarbonate, or whether the sodium bicarbonate is added to a batter that has sufficient acidity in other ingredients to release the gas from the sodium bicarbonate.

An example is the addition of sodium bicarbonate to spice cakes containing molasses. The molasses is acid and is able to release the carbon dioxide gas from the added sodium bicarbonate.

4. AMMONIUM CARBONATE TYPE

This type is a little different in its action. Like sodium bicarbonate, it also contains the constituents of carbon dioxide gas. Unlike the acid type, however, it does not require an acid or other substance to cause a reaction.

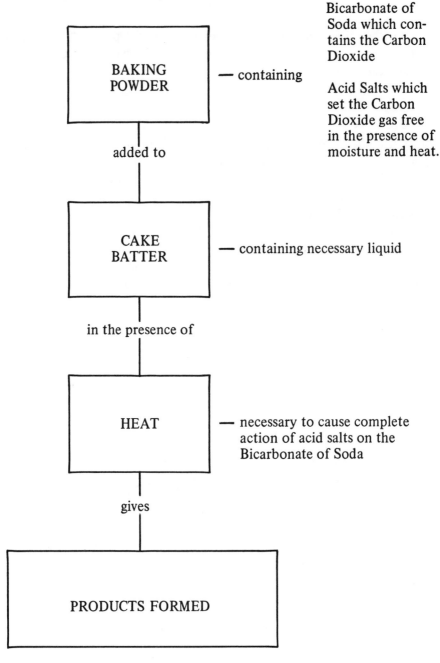

Figure 5–1 *The action of baking powder.*

Carbon dioxide gas is liberated from the ammonium carbonate by decomposition from heat and moisture in the baking process. As it decomposes rapidly, it is used for the most part in cream puffs and cookies, where a sudden expansion is desirable.

B. Yeast

1. COMPRESSED YEAST

Yeast is a microscopic, one-celled plant belonging to the group known botanically as fungi, which ordinarily multiplies by a process known as *budding*, and which under suitable conditions causes fermentation.

Each individual yeast plant is round or oval in shape and measures about $1/3,600$ inch in diameter. Each yeast cell is surrounded by a thin membrane of cellulose, and the interior of each cell is made up of finely granular protoplasm.

2. DERIVATION OF THE WORD *YEAST*

Our word *yeast* comes from the Sanskrit *yas*, "to seethe or boil," descriptive of its action in suitable sugary solutions from which it produces alcohol and carbon dioxide gas.

3. THE FUNCTION OF YEAST IN BREADMAKING

Yeast raises and conditions the dough batch or, in other words, converts the inert, heavy mass of dough into a light, porous, elastic product that, when baked, is appetizing, easily digestible, and nutritious. Yeast itself also adds food value to the loaf.

Without yeast, bread and other yeast-raised products as we know them today would not be possible.

Panary fermentation, brought about by the action of the yeast, represents the life process of the dough, and upon this the creation of bread depends. Because of its fundamental and indispensable function in the production of leavened bread, yeast has been rightly termed the soul of the bread.

4. CHARACTERISTICS OF A GOOD COMPRESSED YEAST

Purchased from a reliable manufacturer
Purity and uniformity are important
Hardness

Consistency, feel, and fracture are firm and springy
Taste and odor should be fresh and pleasant
Appearance is light cream with a hue of yellowish or gray

5. USE OF ACTIVE DRY YEAST

1. Determine amount of active dry yeast required. If the formula is set up for compressed yeast, replace the compressed yeast with 40% as much active dry yeast. On a weight basis, this will actually amount to 6.4 oz (use 6½ oz) of active dry yeast to replace 1 lb of compressed yeast, or 1 lb of active dry yeast for each 2½ lb of compressed yeast.

2. Weigh out the exact amount of active dry yeast required. Active dry yeast is convenient to use. Simply weigh out in the same manner as sugar, salt, or any other dry ingredient. Use a dry scoop because moisture affects the keeping quality of active dry yeast.

3. Dissolve active dry yeast in at least four times its weight of warm (not hot) water. Use part of the formula water for this purpose. In commercial practice, the temperature of the dissolving water may be from 90 to 115°F. However, for best results the temperature of the water in which this yeast is dissolved should be from 108 to 112°F.

Temperatures lower than 90°F should not be used. As the water temperature is decreased, there is a tendency toward longer dissolving time, longer fermentation time, smaller loaf volume, and poorer internal bread characteristics. Particularly when small amounts of active dry yeast and water are used in cold weather or in cold utensils, the temperature of the water may fall below 90°F before the active dry yeast is dissolved in it.

If at all possible, use a thermometer to determine dissolving water temperature. If active dry yeast is dissolved in water below 90°F, it will take longer to dissolve. At 140°F active dry yeast, like compressed yeast, is "killed." Using the same water temperature to dissolve the yeast for each dough will ensure uniform fermentation activity.

If a thermometer is not available, the correct dissolving water temperature can be estimated fairly well with practice. The water should feel slightly warmer than body temperature.

4. Dissolving procedure: If 1 lb of compressed yeast is replaced by 6½ oz of active dry yeast,

a. Weigh 6½ oz of active dry yeast
b. Run 1 quart (about 2 lb) of the formula water into pail or mixer. Water temperature should not be lower than 90°F (108 to 112°F for best results).

c. **Add yeast to water** IN A SLOW STREAM **while stirring water so as to wet each yeast particle. (Yeast must be added** SLOWLY. **Add yeast to water. Do not add water to yeast.**

d. **Allow to soak 3 to 4 minutes while scaling other ingredients.**

e. **Stir until yeast is dissolved.**

f. **Use like compressed yeast. Be sure to** SUBTRACT **the dissolving water (in this example, 2 pounds) from your formula water.**

5. Doughs made with active dry yeast rather than compressed yeast will generally require from about 1¾ to 2 lb more water for each 1 lb of active dry yeast used. The exact amount of added water can be determined by observing the doughs made with active dry yeast. This additional water, most of which compensates for the difference in moisture content between active dry yeast and compressed yeast, should be added to the sponge, or to the dough in the case of straight doughs.

6. If dough temperature is increased, dough time may be reduced slightly. The exact dough time can be determined by experience.

7. Dough mixing time may be decreased. The exact amount of reduction in time will vary according to shop conditions and can be determined by observing the first few doughs made with active dry yeast.

Storage: Active dry yeast, like compressed yeast, is a form of plant life. Even though it is a dry product, it is actually alive and should be stored in a cool, dry place.

For best results, active dry yeast for bakers should be kept under refrigeration (below 45°F) *in a closed container.*

If refrigeration is not available, active dry yeast should be stored in a cool dry place *in a closed container.* Cover container *tightly* after each use.

C. Leavening Achieved Mechanically

1. LEAVENING BY CREAMING

When shortening and sugar are creamed together, we know that as the creaming process goes on, the mixture becomes lighter and occupies more volume. This is due to the fact that air is gradually being whipped into the mixture. Naturally, when this creamed mass is incorporated with the other ingredients in the cake mix, this air is locked up in the batter. When heated in the oven, these air cells, because of vaporization of moisture in the batter, expand and cause the cake to rise. The proper incorporation of air in the creaming process to a large extent controls the volume and structure of the finished cake. Old-fashioned pound cake is an example of a cake in which this type of aeration, or leavening, is most prominent.

2. LEAVENING BY BEATEN EGGS

When eggs are beaten, the result is a fluffy, foamlike mass, full of air. When this whipped mixture is incorporated into cake batter, the air it contains is carried and held in the batter. The expansion of these air cells during baking causes the cake to rise and to become light and porous.

Angel food cake, containing the beaten whites of eggs, and sponge cake, containing whole eggs previously whipped, are examples of cakes in which most of the leavening is secured in this way.

IV. STORAGE OF YEAST

A. Proper Temperature

Upon arrival at the bakery, the yeast should be placed in the refrigerator immediately. The temperature of the refrigerator for ideal yeast storage should be kept at about 45°F.

In handling yeast, never forget that it is a living plant; like all plants, it breathes in oxygen from the air and exhales carbon dioxide. This vital process of respiration is going on all of the time, proceeding very slowly indeed at low temperature, such as should be maintained in a refrigerator, and very rapidly at high temperature, such as is often met with in the bakeshop in summer weather. As this vital process continues in the absence of food for the yeast, it gradually weakens. When the yeast is in a dough at 80°F, the case is different, for there is plenty of food in an ordinary dough for the requirements of the yeast. It is very important, therefore, that yeast should be kept cool to retard the respiration as much as possible until it is used.

In order to prevent any deterioration of yeast, extreme care is observed during manufacture and shipment, and the same precaution should be exercised by the baker so as to ensure the greatest activity of the yeast in the dough batch.

B. Storage of Baking Powder

Practically all baking powders deteriorate with age. If bought in quantity and kept in storage for any length of time, they lose their strength, for they absorb some moisture and slowly give off gas. Furthermore, after storage for any considerable period of time, baking powder may become "caked" or lumpy, thus rendering it difficult to mix in uniformly with the flour.

In using a baking powder that has lost part of its original strength or uniformity through age, a baker is taking a dangerous and unnecessary gamble. It is certain that with such a baking powder the quality of the finished cake will suffer noticeably and will not justify the expenditure made for the other ingredients it contains. Therefore, the freshness of any baking powder can be considered as one of its foremost quality characteristics. Store baking powder in a cool dry place.

REVIEW

1. Name the two types of leavening agents most commonly used and give an example of each.

2. What is the importance of leavening in baking?

3. What is the principal leavening agent in cakes today?

4. What gas is liberated in the presence of moisture and heat?

5. What are the characteristics of a good compressed yeast?

6. What is the recommended procedure for storage of active dry yeast?

7. Name two ways to achieve leavening mechanically.

8. Why do baking powders deteriorate with age?

9. Why is yeast called the soul of bread?

10. What should the temperature of the dissolving water for active dry yeast be to yield the best results?

11. What is the effect of a lower dissolving water temperature than 90°F?

12. If the dissolving water temperature reaches 140°F, what is the effect on the yeast?

CHAPTER 6

SUGARS AND SYRUPS

I. GENERAL INFORMATION

Webster's New International Dictionary, second edition unabridged, gives this definition of *sugar:* "A sweet crystallizable substance, colorless or white when pure, occurring in many plant juices and forming an important article of food. . . . The chief sources of sugar are the sugar cane and the sugar beet, the completely refined products of which are identical."

By definition, therefore, and by long-established common usage, sugar means sucrose (beet or cane sugar) and nothing else. The word *sugars,* however, can refer in the chemical sense to the family of carbohydrates known as the *saccharides,* any member of which is correctly called a *sugar*—but not simply *sugar.* Chemists recognize dozens of sugars of varying sweetness, such as *milk* sugar (lactose), *corn* sugar (dextrose), and *malt* sugar (maltose). Maple sugar is largely sucrose, but is distinguished by its flavor.

A. Refined Sugar

The refined, granulated sugar of commerce is derived from sugar cane and sugar beets. It is 99.94% pure and is thus the purest of all organic substances produced in such volume. Sugar is distinguished by (a) its lack of flavor other than sweetness, (b) its ability to blend other flavors and accentuate aromas, (c) its ready solubility in water, and (d) its high caloric value. It is pleasant to the taste, clean, uniform in quality, and easily assimilated, contains no waste, and keeps indefinitely.

II. PURPOSES SERVED BY SUGARS

Sugar as a whole serves the following important purposes in baking:

1. Adds sweetness.
2. Aids in the creaming process.
3. Creates a softening or spreading action of batter.
4. Imparts crust color.
5. Retains moisture in loaf, prolonging freshness.
6. Forms body of icings and fillings.
7. Adds food value.
8. Aids in the fermentation of yeast.

III. CLASSIFICATION OF SUGARY AGENTS

The principal groups of sugars used in baking are disaccharides and mono-saccharides. Each contains several different types of sugars commonly used in the bakery. In addition to these two groups of sugars, a third group of sugary agents includes sugary syrups.

A. Disaccharides

1. CANE AND BEET SUGAR

Without further qualification, the single word *sugar*, as ordinarily employed and as used in this book, refers to that form of sugar secured principally from the sugar cane and beet. This sugar is known technically as *sucrose*. Frequently refined sucrose, regardless of its source, is spoken of as *cane sugar* or *common sugar*. As purchased today in its white form, this sugar is nearly 100% pure.

Sugar of the same high purity may be obtained in different degrees of fineness or size of granule. This difference has a marked effect on the value of the sugar when used for various purposes in cakemaking.

Types and Uses

GRANULATED SUGAR

Ultrafine: Especially suited for cake work in the bakery, in dry mixes, such as dessert powders and cake mixes, and for coating confectionery pan goods.

Very fine: Ideal for dry mixing with other finely divided materials in the production of cake mixes, pudding preparations, gelatine dessert powders, and the like.

Fine or extrafine: This is "regular" granulated sugar used for all-purpose general food and beverage manufacture. It is the type of sugar usually served at the table.

Medium coarse: Generally employed in the production of crystallizing syrups in confectionery and in making fondant, where an unusually white product is required. It is well adapted to the manufacture of cordials. Medium coarse is a "strong" sugar that resists color changes and inversion in high-temperature cooking.

Coarse: Sometimes preferred for the purposes to which a medium-coarse grain sugar is put.

Special sugars: These have been carefully tested to meet the critical requirements of commercial canners and soft drink manufacturers.

POWDERED SUGARS

Ultrafine (confectioners' 10X type): Recommended for smoothest-textured frostings and icings and uncooked fondants.

Very fine (confectioners' 6X type): Recommended for cream fillings in biscuit work and for sprinkling on buns, pies, and pastries. It is also suitable for uncooked fondants, frostings, and icings. It mixes well with melted fats to make certain confectioners' coatings.

Fine (confectioners' 4X type): Used in the manufacture of lozenges and chewing gum and in packing such confections as marshmallows and Turkish paste. Extensively employed in chocolate manufacture, it is also used for a finish coating for pan goods where a smooth surface is needed.

Medium coarse: Generally applicable to dusting mixtures for which other powdered sugars are too fine, and the product is prone to accumulate surface moisture. It is used for dusting doughnuts and crullers.

Confectioners' sugars are usually packed with small amounts of cornstarch to prevent caking.

2. BROWN SUGAR

Brown sugar is cane or beet sugar in which the refining process has not been completed. It is sometimes spoken of as *soft sugar* because of its characteristic soft feel. Such sugar naturally has a tendency to cake in storage. Various grades of brown sugar (available in light and dark) are produced, containing from about 85% to 92% of sucrose, together with a small amount of invert sugar. Turbinado sugars, although not so white as highly refined granulated sugars, also are economically advantageous in a wide variety of products.

The characteristic flavor and color of brown sugar are due to the caramel and other substances present in the natural sugar syrup before refining. The lower grades of brown sugar possess a more pronounced molasseslike taste than the higher grades. Brown sugar can be used advantageously in certain dark cake mixes and icings, especially where its characteristic flavor is desired.

3. MALT SUGAR

Malt sugar or maltose, as the name implies, is the chief constituent of malt syrup. When malt syrup is used in bakery products, some malt sugar is thereby introduced into the dough. The use of malt syrup in cakes is explained later under "Syrups."

4. LACTOSE OR MILK SUGAR

Lactose is the natural sugar of milk. It is often termed *milk sugar*. While obtainable, it is not used as such in bakery products but is carried into the batter by the milk used. Although of relatively low sweetening value, lactose is a good food value and contributes to crust color.

B. Monosaccharides

Sugars in this classification are often termed *simple sugars*. Although the different sugars in this group have the same chemical composition, they vary considerably in their degree of sweetness and other physical characteristics.

1. CORN SUGAR (DEXTROSE)

Dextrose is a form of sugar found in the bakery in the form of corn syrup. Dextrose is not as sweet as cane sugar. The corn sugar of commerce is manufactured from cornstarch. Various grades of corn sugar can be produced, having a dextrose content of from about 80% to over 99% on a dry basis. In cakemaking, corn sugar is sometimes used in combination with cane or beet sugar and is often employed where excessive sweetness is not required.

2. LEVULOSE

Levulose is a form of sugar often known as *fruit sugar* or *fructose*. It is of the same chemical composition as dextrose but is much sweeter, even sweeter than cane sugar. Levulose is present in molasses. It is the principal sugar in honey and contributes 50% of invert sugar. High fructose syrups are available commercially and are widely used.

C. Sugary Syrups and Moisture-retaining Agents

1. MOLASSES

The best grade of molasses used by the baker is a viscous, sugary liquor obtained by concentrating the juice of sugar cane that has been previously treated in order to contain sufficient invert sugar to prevent crystallization. The brown color and characteristic flavor of molasses are due to the caramel and other substances derived from the original cane juice in the process of abstracting the sugar.

There are various grades or types of molasses, varying in composition and depending on the degree of refinement. In general, molasses contains approximately 35% to 50% sucrose, about 15% to 30% invert sugar, about 20% to 25% water, and from 2% to 5% mineral matter, together with a small amount of protein and other constituents.

Low grades of molasses are usually lower in sucrose content, higher in invert sugar content and mineral matter, and harsher in flavor than the higher grades of molasses. The invert sugar contained in molasses assists in prolonging freshness in cakes.

Molasses is used mainly in certain dark cakes and cookies where its peculiar flavor is considered desirable. In selecting molasses for use in cake-making, its flavor should be of foremost consideration.

2. MALT SYRUP

Malt syrup is a specially prepared concentrated syrup made by evaporating a water extract of malt under carefully controlled conditions. It is used primarily in yeast-made products.

3. INVERT SUGAR (STANDARDIZED)

a. Definition

Invert sugar is equal parts of the two simple sugars, dextrose and levulose. Although sweeter than cane sugar, invert sugar is otherwise neutral in flavor. It is used commercially in cake- and candymaking, often in the form of a syrup that contains about 50% invert sugar, 30% sucrose, and 20% water. It is also obtainable in either plastic or paste form. Invert sugar occurs naturally in honey and molasses. In bread doughs, invert sugar is formed from the cane or beet sugar present by the action of an enzyme known as *invertase,* which is present in the yeast.

b. Commercial Preparation

Invert sugar is produced in the form of a syrup by heating a solution of cane or beet sugar to which has been added a small amount of acid, such as tartaric acid, or of invertase, an enzyme contained in yeast. Under these conditions the acid or invertase acts on the cane or beet sugar and converts it into the new form of sugar known as *invert.*

Although invert sugar may be a new idea to many bakers, it has been used for a number of years in candy and biscuit plants. Some bakers have been in the habit of making their own invert syrup, as described previously, through the use of acids. However, in the average bakery, it is quite difficult to prepare a uniform invert sugar. The acid that is carried along in the invert syrup as it is made must be neutralized either prior to its incorporation in the cake mix or afterwards by the addition of the proper amount of soda. It is exceedingly difficult for the average baker to know just the correct amount of soda required, and quite often this means either an excess of soda or an excess of residual acid remaining in the dough. Furthermore, in preparing invert sugar in a bakery by the use of acid, there is some danger that the acid used may attack the metal of the container with decidedly detrimental results. Either of these conditions is undesirable and may be eliminated by the use of an invert sugar that has been commercially prepared under carefully controlled conditions and in which the acidity has been properly and correctly neutralized.

c. Functions in Cakemaking

i. Prolongs Freshness

Invert sugar has the remarkable ability to hold or retain moisture. Thus the use of invert syrup aids in delaying the staling of the cake. It is especially valuable in sweet mixtures that have a tendency to dry out too rapidly.

ii. Promotes Smoothness in Icings

The presence of some invert sugar prevents the crystallization or graining of cane or beet sugar. In this way, invert syrup promotes that smoothness desirable in many icings.

iii. Sweetness

Invert syrup is very sweet and naturally imparts this characteristic to the finished cake.

iv. Crust Color

Invert sugar aids in the promotion of a rich, brown crust color.

d. Amount and Manner of Use

In cakes of the pound cake class, which are very slowly baked, the amount of invert sugar to be used without incurring a slight discoloration of the crumb is quite limited. In cakes that are baked faster, larger amounts may be employed with no such discoloration. For light fruitcake, use from 10% to 20%; as high as 30% may be used for dark fruitcake. The amount employed in cupcakes and plain layer cakes can range from 5% to 20%. In sponge cake, from 4% to 6% of the sugar may be replaced with invert sugar. The use of too much invert syrup, especially in light cakes, may adversely affect the volume, cell structure, and crumb color.

The invert syrup may be creamed together with the remainder of the sugars used and the shortening, or it may be added to the creamed sugar–shortening mass at the completion of the creaming process. It may also be mixed with the milk or milk solution.

4. HONEY

One of the first sugary agents known to man is a natural invert syrup produced from the nectar of flowers through the agency of the honeybee.

Honey varies in composition, depending on its source, but an average sample would contain about 75% invert sugar, about 15% to 20% water, and a small amount of other substances, some of which give honey its natural delicious flavor. This characteristic honey flavor, which is not present in commercial invert syrup, is the principal reason for the use of honey in special types of cakes and cookies.

5. GLUCOSE SYRUP (CORN SYRUP)

Glucose syrup, perhaps better known as *commercial glucose* or *corn syrup*, is produced commercially from cornstarch. It varies somewhat in composition, depending on the manner of manufacture, but an average glucose syrup contains about 40% corn sugar, or dextrose, and a considerable amount of dextrin. It possesses some moisture-retaining properties, probably because of its relatively high content of dextrin, and is used to some extent in both cakes and icings. It aids in the promotion of a glossy surface in certain types of icings.

IV. STORAGE

Storage of sugar should be in a cool, dry place.

V. SUGAR COOKING

To cook sugar, approximately three parts sugar to one part water are placed in a copper or stainless-steel pot and stirred until the mass comes to a boil. The sides of the pot are brushed with water to clear them of any sugar crystals. The formation of crystals will start a chain reaction of crystallization that makes the mixture grainy.

Another way of clearing the sides of the pot is to cover the pot while it boils, letting the steam from the syrup wash down the sides of the pot. This is a very important step in the early stages. Continue to cook the syrup until it reaches the proper proportion of water to sugar.

Expert confectioners usually judge the degree of the syrup by dipping the index finger into cold water and then immediately dipping the same finger into the boiling syrup. This method is definitely not recommended for a novice because of the danger involved. A candy thermometer should be used. While the thermometer is not in actual use, place it in a jar of warm water close to where the cooking takes place. This practice eliminates the breakup that occurs if a cold thermometer is placed in hot syrup.

A. Boiling Stages

The chart below indicates the temperature reading for each stage of sugar that reflects the amount of water in the sugar. The less water present, the higher the temperature of the boiling sugar. The less water, the more solid or harder is the sugar mixture when cooled. Temperatures may vary because of humidity and altitude conditions. Because it only takes a few degrees to bring syrup to another stage, temperature control is extremely important.

STAGES OF SUGAR BOILING	
Stages	Temperature Range
Thread	230–235°F
Soft ball	240–245°F
Ball	250–255°F
Hard ball	260–265°F
Small crack	270–275°F
Crack	275–280°F
Hard crack	285–315°F
Caramel	325–350°F

The next chart shows how the concentration of sugar is reflected in the temperature of boiling. As the concentration of sugar increases, so too does the temperature at which the mixture boils. Knowing the boiling temperature also tells the concentration of sugar.

BOILING POINTS OF VARIOUS CONCENTRATIONS OF SUGAR AND WATER		
Boiling Degree Water and Sugar	Sugar Present (%)	Water Present (%)
212.7°F	10	90
213.8°F	30	70
215.6°F	50	50
223.7°F	70	30
225.2°F	75	25
238.8°F	85	15
243.8°F	87	13
249.5°F	89	11
252.7°F	90	10

REVIEW

1. What are the two chief sources of sugar?

2. Which of the following statements may be applied to the use of sugar?
   a. Aids in the creaming process.
   b. Imparts crust color.
   c. Retains moisture, thereby prolonging freshness.
   d. Aids in the fermentation of yeast.

3. What are the two main groups of sugars in bakery products?

4. What is brown sugar?

5. What is lactose?

6. Give two examples of monosaccharides.

7. What is invert sugar composed of?

8. In what form is invert sugar generally used commercially?

9. How does the use of invert sugar delay the staling of cake?

10. How does the presence of invert sugar promote smoothness in icings?

11. Name a natural invert sugar.

12. From what is glucose syrup produced commercially?

CHAPTER 7

EGGS AND EGG PRODUCTS

I. GENERAL INFORMATION

Eggs and egg products are important ingredients used by bakers principally in the production of cakes and sweet goods. In these products eggs and egg products comprise approximately one-half the cost of the ingredients. In some cakes, such as sponge cake, the cost of eggs may amount to as much as 70% of the total ingredient cost.

Eggs are commercially available to the baker in four forms: shell eggs, liquid eggs, frozen eggs, and dried eggs. The separated whites and yolks may also be procured in liquid, frozen, or dried form. Certain modified egg products, such as sugar yolks and glycerin yolks, are also produced for use by the baking industry. Because of cost and good quality, frozen eggs are much more widely used in the bakery than fresh eggs. Dried eggs, despite advantages of exceptional keeping quality and convenient form, have failed to attain popularity with commercial bakers chiefly because of the adverse changes that occur in the egg material upon drying. Dried eggs are an important ingredient in most prepared cake mixes, however.

II. FUNCTION OF EGGS IN CAKEMAKING

Eggs are most widely used in cakes. Generally speaking, without eggs there would be no cake. They are the major factor in giving cake the dominant characteristics that differentiate cake from other baked products.

A. Binding or Texturizing Action

The most essential factor in the making of a cake is the formation or development (in the mixing and the maintaining or retention in the baking) of cell structure. Eggs (wholes, whites, or yolks) hold together as an emulsion the other ingredients of a cake batter: the flour, the fat, the sugar, and the moisture. Eggs are also of prime importance in the production of the smooth-flowing batter that is necessary for proper handling of cake mixes in scaling or depositing machines.

B. Leavening Action

Beaten eggs form a fluffy, foamlike mass that is much lighter and occupies a much larger volume than the unbeaten egg. When this foamlike mass is added to other cake ingredients to make a cake batter, the foam structure makes up to a certain extent the cell structure of the cake. When the individual cells are subjected to the heat of the oven, the expansion of air, together with the vaporization of moisture in these bubbles or cells, tends to expand the cells and raise or leaven the cake.

This same final action or leavening in a cake can be obtained from eggs that are simply creamed into a sugar–shortening creamed mass. Here the eggs tend to stabilize the air cells developed by creaming by rendering the cells elastic so that they can expand on heating without rupturing. This expansion raises the cake. Here, as before, the leavening is due to the expansion of air and the vaporization of moisture into the cells from the cell walls.

C. Shortening Action

Approximately one-third of the egg yolk is fat, which adds shortening value.

D. Flavor or Eating Quality

Eggs have a characteristic flavor that cannot be duplicated. Fresh eggs impart a delicious flavor to a cake. Also, the eating quality of the cake is definitely enhanced by their texturizing effect.

E. Color

Where whole egg, yolk, or egg product containing egg yolk is used in cake mixes, color is of primary importance. Eggs produce in the cake that golden color associated with richness of cake quality.

F. Food Value

The nutritive value of eggs needs little explanation. Rich in fat, protein, and essential mineral substances necessary to growth and health, eggs are rightly considered one of humankind's basic foods. Naturally, their food value is imparted to the products in which they are used. Egg yolks are high in cholesterol; egg whites have none, an important distinction for people with heart disease.

III. IMPORTANT CHARACTERISTICS OF EGGS

In purchasing eggs for the purpose of cakemaking, the following points should be kept in mind.

A. Body of Whites

A strong, firm-bodied white is desirable for cakebaking, inasmuch as it whips up better and gives strength to the framework of the cake. A thin, watery white produces soft, soggy cake devoid of lightness and fluffiness. Spring-laid eggs have the best type of whites. During and for some months after the molting season, which begins in July, the whites are usually weak. Spring-laid eggs are available throughout the entire year in the form of frozen eggs. In other words, eggs that are laid in the spring are promptly collected, candled, broken, inspected, and frozen.

B. Richness and Color of Yolks

Spring-laid eggs excel on both these points: the yolks contain a higher percentage of fat, and the color is much better than in eggs laid during the summer, fall, and winter months. During the spring, hens have more opportunity to get fresh green fodder, which produces the preferred type of yolk. Egg yolk contributes richness, flavor, appetizing color, softness, and nutritive value to a cake.

C. Uniformity as to Wholesomeness

A good baker sometimes runs into a lack of uniformity and wholesomeness, particularly in shell eggs, and instead finds musty eggs, "hay" eggs, and other types of inferior eggs. If shell eggs are bought, it is the better part of wisdom to buy them from a reliable house and pay a fair price to secure a high grade. A saving of 2 cents in the price of a dozen eggs is not always sound economy, for one bad egg in a dozen may give a bad flavor to a batch of cake costing perhaps $2 or $3.

D. Uniformity as to Other Properties

It is essential that the eggs be uniform in other properties, such as the body of the whites and the color of the yolks. Shell eggs are likely to vary in quality from month to month.

E. Size and Yield

Buy shell eggs according to yield. It may be found that a case of shell eggs, selling at 20 or 30 cents a dozen more than another grade, produces more egg meat at a lower cost per pound than the cheaper eggs. This is because eggs vary so widely in size. Occasionally, exceedingly large eggs may be secured that will give a yield of 37 and 38 lb of egg meat but with small eggs the yield may not be over 28 or 30 lb per case.

F. Inferior Grades

Deterioration in eggs is caused chiefly by bacterial action. "Cracks" may be a snare and delusion, because in the use of "cracks" there is a tremendous loss from leakage that may far more than offset the difference in the price per dozen.

IV. CLASSIFICATION OF EGGS

Eggs, from the standpoint of the baker, may be classified as shell eggs, dried eggs, and frozen eggs.

A. Shell Eggs

Shell eggs are ordinary hens' eggs as they are usually marketed to the baker in crates or cases of 30 dozen each. The quality of such shell eggs is determined by candling or "lighting" the egg. Candling is done by holding the egg before a lighted opening, usually in a dark room, in such a manner that light rays pass through the shell and illumine the interior of the egg.

Various localities or cities may designate the same grade of shell eggs by different names, letters, or numerals, and it is, accordingly, practically impossible to list classifications that would be applicable in all cases.

B. Dried Eggs

At one time dried eggs were used to a considerable extent in certain types of bakery products. Today, however, dried eggs constitute only a small fraction of the total amount of eggs used in baking in the United States and Canada.

Dried eggs are produced by removing the bulk of the moisture from liquid eggs. This is done by either a spray-drying or a tray- or pan-drying process. Dried eggs are usually available as dried whole egg, dried white (albumen), and dried yolk.

Type	Liquid Weight Desired (lb)	Solids Needed (oz)	Water Required (oz)
Egg whites	1	2	14
Whole eggs	1	4¾	11¼
Fortified eggs	1	5½	10½
Sugar yolk	1	8	8

CONVERSION TABLE FOR DRIED EGGS

C. Frozen Eggs

Frozen eggs are produced from shell eggs by removing the edible liquid and freezing it. After the packing and freezing process, the eggs are held in freezer storage at 0°F or below until withdrawn for delivery.

Definite standards for purchasing frozen eggs have not been adopted because of the difficulty that would be experienced in grading the product either in its frozen state or by sampling. Although shell eggs may be individually candled or lighted to determine their quality, the baker buying frozen eggs must depend principally on the reputation of the packer. It has therefore become advisable for the baker who desires top-quality frozen eggs to purchase from a firm not only in a position to guarantee the quality of its products but is also experienced in the handling and delivery of refrigerated products to bakers.

It is the combination of these two factors that has brought about the continued and steady increase in frozen egg consumption since 1928 has been accompanied by improvements in frozen egg processing and delivery.

The best-quality frozen eggs present to the baker the most economical means of securing eggs for year-round use. They make it possible to have spring-laid eggs every season of the year.

V. TYPES OF FROZEN EGGS AND FROZEN EGG PRODUCTS

Frozen eggs are generally available in convenient 10- and 30-lb cans in any of the following types:

A. Frozen Whole Egg

Frozen whole egg is the product as separated from the shell, packed, and frozen. The suggested government "solids" specification is minimum 24% and maximum 28%.

B. Frozen Egg White

Frozen egg white is that part of the edible egg that encloses and protects the egg yolk in the shell. It is almost pure albumen and, according to suggested government standards, should run from 11% to 13% egg white solids.

C. Frozen Egg Yolk

Frozen egg yolk is the separated yolk of the egg, which, in commercial separation, carries with it a small amount of egg white. Government specifications suggest minimum solids of 42.5% and maximum solids of 45%.

D. Fortified Eggs

Fortified eggs are whole eggs to which extra yolks are added to give greater egg solids content.

VI. ADVANTAGES OF HIGH-QUALITY, SPRING-LAID FROZEN EGGS

A. Strictly Fresh Eggs Assured

High-quality, frozen, spring-laid eggs come from certain sections of the grain belt that produce the finest eggs in the country. These eggs are selected for their adaptability to the production of high-quality cake and sweet goods. This means that strictly fresh eggs are collected, brought to the plants, inspected, broken and inspected again, and then frozen. In their frozen state, all their fine qualities are conserved intact.

B. Quality of Cake

For high-quality cake and sweet goods, the baker needs high-quality eggs. It is mistaken economy to use inferior eggs that will offset the advantages of other costly cake ingredients. High-quality, frozen, spring-laid eggs possess whites that are firm and have excellent whipping qualities and yolks that are uniform and enhance the eating qualities and golden color of the cake.

C. Uniformity Ensured

When high-quality, frozen, spring-laid eggs are used, the baker is assured of uniformity in the various important functions performed by eggs in cake-making. The use of shell eggs purchased throughout different seasons of the year represents a gamble insofar as uniformity is concerned because eggs vary in composition with the changing seasons and character of feed. The use of high-quality, frozen, spring-laid eggs eliminates all worry on this score.

D. Time Saved in the Bakery

The edible portion of the egg is made up of about 36% egg yolk and 64% egg white, and the baker purchasing shell eggs must accept them on this basis. Then the baker must break and remove the shells in order to obtain the whole egg and, if either egg white or egg yolk is desired separately, separate the white from the yolk, which frequently results in an oversupply of one type.

The resultant labor cost, time lost, unsanitary procedure, and oversupply of white or yolk have been eliminated by the use of frozen eggs. These may be purchased as needed, when needed, and in accordance with the baker's requirements.

E. Economy through the Elimination of Waste

When shell eggs are employed, there is likely to be a loss through shrinkage, spoilage, and breakage, as well as in the process of breaking and separating the eggs at the bench. Furthermore, there is danger of one bad egg occasionally slipping in and spoiling a measure full. When high-quality frozen eggs are used, the baker is insured against such a mishap.

F. Frozen Eggs Mean Greater Profits to the Baker

When a crate of shell eggs is purchased by the baker, the proportion of yolks and whites is predetermined. In ordinary bakeshop separation of shell eggs, the yield is about 19 lb of whites and 16 lb of yolks. When high-quality frozen eggs are employed, they can be purchased or withdrawn from the warehouse in amounts and kinds to meet production needs. Day in and day out, this means an economy that should not be overlooked.

VII. HANDLING FROZEN EGGS IN THE BAKERY

Frozen eggs, when they are delivered to the baker, are in a solid, frozen mass at a temperature of about $-15°F$. Before they can be used, they must be thawed out and mixed to secure uniform consistency. There are two ways in which frozen eggs may be thawed prior to using, namely, to set out the eggs required for the day's baking in a temperate part of the shop, where they may thaw slowly, or to set them in running cool water.

The latter method is decidedly preferable. Frozen eggs thaw out much more rapidly when the container of eggs is placed in running water than when merely exposed to air of the same or even somewhat higher temperature than that of running water.

At room temperature a can of frozen eggs may require from 18 to 24 hours for proper thawing, whereas it probably would be completely defrosted in 5 to 6 hours if placed in a tank of cool, running water.

In bakeries where large quantities of frozen eggs are regularly used, the installation of a defrosting or thawing tank is a wise investment. Several such tanks are on the market, but one may be built very simply and of a size conforming to the amount of eggs used. Care should be taken in constructing such a tank to be sure that the drain is installed at the proper height so that the water will be carried off at a level below the top of the cans of eggs to prevent water from getting into the cans.

After the eggs have been thawed, it is good practice to stir them thoroughly before incorporating them in the cake batter.

Frozen eggs should never be thawed by placing them in hot water or over the oven. Egg albumen begins to coagulate at 120°F. Coagulation means the whites will not whip up lightly and that the yolks will show up in the form of yellow specks throughout the cake.

Formulas calling for a given number of shell eggs or a given number of whites or yolks are essentially inaccurate because eggs vary so much in size. However, for general work in the bakery, use the following basis for conversion:

1 lb whole egg = 9–11 shell eggs
1 lb egg white = 15–17 whites
1 lb sugar-yolk = 22–24 yolks

REVIEW

1. In what four forms are eggs commercially available?

2. What form of eggs is an important ingredient in most prepared cake mixes?

3. Name the most important function of eggs in cakemaking.

4. Why is a strong, firm-bodied white desirable for cakebaking?

5. What does the egg yolk contribute to a cake?

6. What is the important consideration in buying shell eggs?

7. What is candling, and for what purpose is it done?

8. Why should bakers buy their frozen eggs from a packer with a good reputation?

9. What are the four forms in which frozen eggs are generally available?

10. What are fortified eggs?

11. What are the advantages of high-quality, spring-laid, frozen eggs?

12. What are the two ways in which frozen eggs may be thawed prior to using?

13. Why should frozen eggs never be thawed by placing them in hot water or in the oven?

CHAPTER 8

SHORTENING:
FATS AND OILS

I. FATS AND OILS

The triglycerides, made up of glycerol and fatty acids, which are called *fats,*
oils, and *shortenings,* have been used by bakers for centuries to assist in the
leavening action, provide the feeling of moisture in the mouth without wet-
ness, and to lengthen the shelf life of baked goods. The flakiness of pies,
pastries, and related items would not be possible without fats, and until
recently it was felt that only fats could provide the tenderness that charac-
terizes cakes. Above all, the human animal enjoys, in fact often craves, fat,
perhaps because of evolutionary demands that recall the necessity of stored

fat for the storehouse of energy within the body tissues when food was not always available.

Nutritionally, fats provide 9 calories per gram for daily use by the body as energy or to be stored for later use. Two of the fatty acids, linoleic and linolenic, are needed by the body for a number of physiological processes.

1. Is it safe to say that most baked goods contain some fat, without which they would taste quite different? | **Yes.**

Fats and oils are similar chemically; both are esters of glycerine and fatty acids. By definition, a *glyceride* (glycerine and fatty acid) is a fat if solid at 68°F and an oil if liquid at this same temperature. In this book the term *fat* includes oils.

On average, fats contain a high percentage of saturated fatty acids attached to the glycerine, whereas oils contain more unsaturated acids.

2. Fats are different from oils in that at the usual room temperature fats are solid and oils are liquid. Most fats have more _____ fatty acids than oils. | **Saturated.**

Fats are composed of glycerine and fatty acids, the fatty acids constituting about 95% of the weight. Most of the fats we eat are called *triglycerides* because they contain one glycerol molecule to which three long-chain fatty acids (made of 16 or 18 carbon atoms) are attached.

3. A triglyceride is a fat made up of one glycerol molecule and three molecules of _____. | **Fatty acids.**

Fats that are solid at room temperature are usually white and tasteless; when formulated especially as a bakery ingredient, they are called *shortenings*. Like all fats, the shortenings "shorten" gluten strands and in doing so tenderize the product. Shortenings surround the gluten and other bakery ingredients and lubricate them so they cannot stick together.

Fat or oil used in baking is selected to perform a particular function. Shortenings are fats that are used to shorten the gluten strands, surround them, and make them more easily broken. In the language of baking, the product is made more *tender*. Shortenings also add flavor and color and help to leaven the product when it is creamed. *Creaming* is working the fat until it is soft and creamy; air is added to the fat during this process, which helps in the leavening.

4. Shortening is called by that name because it shortens what?

> The gluten strands,
> making them less
> continuous and the
> product more tender.

Knowing something about the chemical and molecular makeup of fat helps
in understanding how it functions in baking and in nutrition. More than 95%
of the weight of most fat foods are triglycerides, called that because their
molecules are composed of one glycerol and three fatty acids. One hundred
grams of fat yields about 95 grams of fatty acids.

5. Triglycerides are made up of glycerol and _____.

> Three fatty acids.

Fats commonly used by bakers include soybean, cottonseed, coconut, palm
kernel, lard, and tallow. Oils growing in popularity among people concerned
about their diet are canola and olive, high in monounsaturated fatty acids.

In the past, the price of the various fats has determined, to a large extent,
which fat was to be used in baking. Nutritionally, fats are classified as saturated, polyunsaturated, and monounsaturated. These terms obviously need
explanation.

Fatty acids have molecules made up of chains of carbon atoms that are
bonded together electrically. When fatty acids contain one or more carbon-
to-carbon double bonds, they are termed *saturated.* Tropical oils, which contain a high proportion of short-chain fatty acids, are clear liquids at room
temperature. Lard, which contains about 37% saturates, most with long carbon chains, is semisolid at about 80°F.

6. Most saturated fats, such as animal fats, are what
form at room temperature?

> Seemingly solid.

7. Tropical fats, such as coconut and palm kernel,
are highly saturated. What is their form at room
temperature?

> Liquid.

8. Why?

> Because they are
> short-chain fats.

9. Fats contain varying amounts of fatty acids that
are saturated, monosaturated, and polyunsaturated. Canola oil is a fat that contains fatty acids
high in _____.

> Monounsaturates.

The length of the molecule chain (the number of carbon atoms) influences whether a fat is solid or liquid. Fatty acids have from 4 to 22 carbon atoms. The longer ones, those with 14 to 22 carbon atoms, are more likely to be solid at room temperature.

Short-chain (4 to 12) fatty acids are likely to be liquid. This accounts for the peculiar quality of tropical oils—coconut, palm kernel, and palm nut—which are liquid but highly saturated. Coconut and palm kernel oils have the advantage of being exceptionally stable with respect to oxidation rancidity. However, they are subject to hydrolysis.

10. Whether a fat is seemingly solid at room temperature depends both upon the degree of saturation of its fatty acids and upon what else?	**The length of the carbon chain.**

Fatty acids whose molecules all contain single carbon-to-carbon bonds are termed *saturated.* Fatty acids that contain only one double bond are called *monounsaturated.* The saturated and unsaturated linkages are illustrated here:

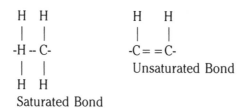

Saturated fats are more stable and less likely to react chemically with other atoms than fatty acids high in unsaturated bonds. Animal fats, such as lard and tallow, are saturated and therefore more stable than unsaturated fats. Vegetable fats found in corn, rapeseed (canola oil), safflower, and olives contain a higher percentage of unsaturated fat and monounsaturates. A number of fatty acids with double bonds means they are more chemically reactive and will combine with such atoms as hydrogen and oxygen. Short saturated fats are plastic at room temperature.

What does all this mean for baking? Baked goods containing fats high in unsaturates turn rancid more quickly because they combine with hydrogen and oxygen. Unsaturated fats used in frying break down more quickly and develop off flavors.

11. Would a vegetable fat such as corn oil be good for use in making puff pastry?

No. It is not plastic enough and will turn rancid more quickly.

II. FAT HYDROGENATION

Hydrogenation of fat was a milestone for baking in that fats could be produced with a desired level of plasticity and increased resistance to rancidity.

In the period 1911 to 1925, the chemist Hilditch found a way to add hydrogen atoms to monounsaturated or polyunsaturated fats that changed their unsaturated oil molecules into saturated ones. Saturated fats are less susceptible to oxidation and therefore to rancidity. Baked goods with saturated fats have longer shelf lives. Hydrogenation also raises the smoke point, important for fats used in frying foods.

To visualize what takes place in hydrogenation, look at two-hydrogen carbon molecules, one unsaturated and the other saturated. If the molecule has two fewer hydrogen atoms than when saturated, it is called monounsaturated. In the diagram, the locations of the carbon atoms connected by a double bond lack hydrogen atoms.

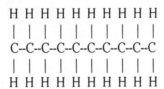

When all of the carbon atoms are bonded to hydrogen atoms, the molecule is saturated, as seen in the next diagram.

```
H H H H H H H H H H
| | | | | | | | | |
C--C--C--C--C--C--C--C--C--C
| | | | | | | | | |
H H H H H H H H H H
```

The fact that the double bond is the location of reactivity seems misleading. The double bond does not mean double strength. Actually double bonds are weaker and are the location where an oxygen atom can join the hydrogen atom.

12. Hydrogenation is a process in which a hydrogen atom is added at the double bond, making the bond saturated. An oil can be made into a solid fat by hydrogenating it. Adding a hydrogen atom at a double bond is called _____.

Hydrogenation.

A basic cause of rancidity in fat is the addition of oxygen to the fat (oxidation). The more unsaturated a fat, the less stable it is.

13. Which fat is more likely to turn rancid: soybean oil that has been hydrogenated or soybean oil that has not been hydrogenated?

The unhydrogenated one. Hydrogenation makes the oil more saturated and more stable.

III. VISIBLE AND INVISIBLE FATS

For the consumer, fats are divided into those they can see before eating, the visible fats, and those that are not seen, the invisible ones. Most pastries contain a large amount of invisible fat, but the consumer is increasingly aware of the invisible fats, and bakers are reacting by producing lower-fat items and specialty items that are marketed as having reduced calories and cholesterol. Fat substitutes in baked products are also being marketed. Note that only animal foods contain cholesterol. Fat itself contains no cholesterol, but adding any fat to your food will raise the cholesterol level in your blood.

A. Butter

Fresh butter is still widely used because of its special flavor, and because it melts in the mouth, which shortenings do not. Butter is used in some cake formulas and by some bakers for pie dough. It is avoided by others because of cost and because its tendency to soften and melt at fairly low temperatures makes it difficult to work with.

Because butter is about 16% water, it cannot be substituted ounce for ounce for other shortenings that contain almost all fat. To substitute regular shortening for butter, multiply by 0.8. To substitute butter for regular shortening, multiply by 1.25.

Although considerably more expensive and more difficult to work with, butter is often used in puff pastry.

B. Margarines

Bakers' margarine is quite soft and has superior creaming quality. Roll-in margarine is firmer and somewhat waxy. Puff pastry margarine is still firmer and waxier. Both roll-in and puff pastry margarine are plastic over a range of temperatures and have high melting points. Roll-in margarine melts at a temperature of 116°F; puff pastry melts at 130°F.

14. Margarines used by bakers are produced specifically for one product. Why would bakers want high melting points for roll-in and puff pastry margarines?

When fats are worked into the dough, the dough temperature rises. The high melting point keeps the fats plastic and workable.

15. Bakers' margarine is made quite soft for what reason?

To provide it with superior creaming quality, which means a greater amount of air can be incorporated. A temperature of between 65 and 70°F (18 to 21°C) is necessary for butter to remain workable. At 50°F it is too hard to work, and at 80°F it is too soft.

Margarines consist of a variety of ingredients. By federal regulation it, like butter, must contain at least 80% fat unless the label clearly states otherwise. Margarine fat is either vegetable or animal in origin and may have a single hydrogenated fat or two or more different fats. Lecithin or another emulsifier is usually added.

C. Fats and Nutrition

When eaten in excess, fats pose a health problem, and bakers are cutting back on fat and using fat substitutes. The U.S. Department of Agriculture found that about 38% of the calories consumed in the United States come from fat, whereas nutritionists and the American Heart Association recommend that not more than 30% of calories consumed come from fat sources.

For overweight people and those at risk for heart problems, a number of cardiologists recommend reducing fat intake to 10% of total caloric consumption.

16. Will high-fat baked products become more or less popular in the future? | Less popular.

Substitutes for fat in baked goods include a modified high-amylose food starch that can provide up to 100% replacement of fats. Some bakers use egg whites instead of whole eggs and nonfat milk in place of whole milk to reduce fat content. Some of the low-fat or nonfat products, however, contain added sugar. Fat-free cakes are made by including emulsifiers, maltodextrins, and gums in the formula. One such formula for 98% fat-free devil's food cake includes egg whites (instead of whole eggs), monoglycerides and diglycerides as emulsifiers, and xanthan and guar gums. Maltodextrin used in pie crust formula permits up to a 20% reduction in shortening while still producing a flaky pie crust.

17. What are some of the substitutes for fat being used in baking formulas? | Gums, egg whites, emulsifiers, maltodextrins, and high-amylose starch.

Knowing something about the molecular makeup of fats and oils helps in understanding their performance during baking and their effects on the taste and texture of the finished product. Also important is how fats behave nutritionally in the body. Excessive fat consumption is associated with heart disease, high blood pressure, and strokes. Although bakers cannot predict what their customers will eat, it is well known that consumers are growing more aware of the dangers of eating too much fat, particularly saturated fat, the kind that has all of the valence bonds between the carbon atoms in the fat molecules filled. Saturated fats resist turning rancid and developing off odors.

Fat and oil play a large role in baking and contribute flavor and mouth feel to a variety of baked goods. Bakers have selected fats for use in their products largely because of customer preference, availability, and price. New knowledge about fat, its molecular structure, and the energy that holds the carbon atoms together has provided a better understanding of how fats affect the baking process and the finished product. Nutritional information about what happens to fatty acids in the body has become a part of general knowledge. A large number of consumers have become aware of the nutritional effects of fat in the diet, good and bad, and look for products low in fat, particularly those low in polyunsaturated fats (those containing many fatty acids in which the carbon atoms are connected by single bonds).

18. Large numbers of consumers of baked goods prefer products low in fat and avoid fats that are
_____. | Saturated.

Most of the fats used by bakers today come from vegetable sources—soybean, cottonseed, and corn—but these are unsaturated. Fat processors add hydrogen gas molecules to many of the double-bonded carbon linkages to make them more saturated. The process called *hydrogenation* makes the vegetable fats less subject to turning rancid.

19. Does partial hydrogenation of vegetable fats make
them more or less saturated? | More saturated.

Now we have a dilemma: saturated fats are easier for the baker to work with, they do not break down readily in frying, and they do not turn rancid easily. Nutritionally, saturated fatty acids in the bloodstream combine with cholesterol to form plaque in the arteries, which can lead to high blood pressure, strokes, and heart disease. What is the baker to do?

The baker can offer both kinds of baked goods—those with saturated fats and those with unsaturated fats—and make the consumer aware of the difference.

The temperature at which a fat melts is also a factor in making baked goods and depends in part on the number of carbons in the molecule's carbon chain. For a given carbon chain length, saturated fats have a higher melting point than unsaturated fatty acids.

Fat serves to lubricate batters and doughs and allows them to "slip" and move easily. The fat must be of the right degree of plasticity for a particular purpose. For example, soft poultry fats shorten gluten well but blend too easily with flour to produce a flaky crust for pies. Too much fat mixed with flour gives a greasy crumb of an oily quality.

20. Because fat shortens a baked product, what
would happen to a cake with excessive fat in the
batter? | The cake will fall
while baking because
it is too tender.

Fats and oils that contain a high percentage of unsaturated fats have more shortening power than saturated fats. Shortening power is also increased as free fatty acids increase. Thus animal fats such as butter, lard, and chicken fat make tender baked products because they contain large quantities of free fatty acids. Vegetable fats contain fewer free fatty acids and therefore do not make a tender product. However, a fat can have too much shortening power, which is why we prefer vegetable fats for some baking uses. Butter and margarine contain water (butter and margarine are only 80% fat).

21. Can we substitute one fat for another to achieve a particular shortening effect?

Not pound for pound, because of the difference in saturation, free fatty acids, and water content in various fats and oils.

Until the 1930s, when *emulsifiers* were added to fats used for baking, butter, lard, and margarine were the commonly used shortenings. Lard is still popular as a shortening for pie crusts. Modification of food fats came in the development of margarine as a substitute for butter by the French during the Franco-Prussian War. Today's margarine is likely to be hydrogenated soybean, cottonseed, corn, or safflower oil.

IV. FRYING FATS AND FAT BREAKDOWN

The fat used for frying partly determines the quality of the fried foods. Special frying fats are used for frying doughnuts because they do not smoke at temperatures required for frying and also resist breaking down chemically in the presence of heat and moisture. Such fats are treated so that their original smoke point is 450°F or higher.

22. What would be wrong with filling a deep-fry kettle with butter?

The butter burns at the required frying temperatures and would soon break down chemically. It is also expensive.

Saturated fats have several advantages for frying over the unsaturated fats. The saturated fats have a higher smoke point, are more stable, and are less likely to foam.

23. Does the carbon chain of saturated fats contain double bonds?

It contains no double bonds.

Most fats for frying have only 0.05% of free fatty acids in them and have a smoke point greater than 440°F. If the free fatty acids are increased to 0.1%, the smoke point is lowered to 400°F. At 0.5%, the smoke point is 350°F.

24. As the free fatty acids increase in fats, does the smoke point increase or decrease?   Decreases.

V. THE TREND TOWARD PRODUCING MORE HEALTHFUL BAKED GOODS

A "healthy" revolution in baked goods took place in the late 1980s based on the results of medical research showing that fat calories should be less than 30% of total caloric intake and that animal fats and tropical oils such as palm and coconut should be limited or avoided in the diet. Consumption of sugar and salt in the American diet were shown to be excessive and could be associated with high blood pressure, heart disease, and stroke.

Excessive fat consumption is associated with heart disease and with stroke due to arteriosclerosis (thickening and hardening of the arteries). Bakers do not mandate consumer tastes and will continue to produce high-calorie desserts, but they should be aware that Americans are becoming more concerned with the amount and kind of fat they eat.

Saturated fats are known to increase a blood component, low-density lipoprotein (LDL), which is associated with the formation of plaque in the arteries. Bakers can expect to produce more products low in saturated fats, the kind present in animal fats, and will probably be using more fat substitutes in the future.

A. Low-fat, Low-cholesterol Products

In many baked goods fat functions to provide flavor, good mouth feel, and texture. It tenderizes and extends shelf life and in some products is important because of the aeration when it is creamed. To replace fat to meet market demand for reduced or no-fat products has been a challenge to food scientists and bakers, a challenge summarized by James P. Zallie.*

Fat is a significant ingredient of several baked goods.

---

*"Fat Free Products," a presentation at the 67th meeting of the American Society of Bakery Engineers, Chicago, 1991.

Product	Fat (%)
Bread and rolls	2–5
Cakes, shortening type	20–60
Sweet goods	10–30
Pie crusts, fried	20–30
Pie crusts, baked	25–60
Cookies	20–70
Crackers	7–10
Doughnuts, cake	5–9
Doughnuts, yeast raised	6–14

Cookies contain up to 70% (based on flour) of fat and in some cakes as much as 60% of the weight of flour is fat. Baked pie crusts may also have as much as 60% of the weight of the flour in fat.

Replacing the fat can make dough less extensible and sticky and make the product drier and with poor crumb texture. Without fat, some products have smaller volume and their shelf life is shorter. In cakes the absence of fat results in large air cells that make the cake coarse in texture and restrict its volume.

To be called *fat-free* the Food and Drug Administration permits up to 0.5 grams of fat per serving. A *reduced-fat* label indicates that the product contains at least one-third less fat than is contained in the standard product.

25. Ordinarily fat serves one or more functions in particular baked products. It extends shelf life, tenderizes, adds flavor, and contributes to texture. Fat used in cake batter has what functions other than providing tenderness and flavor and extending shelf life?

Fats for cakes are creamed (beaten), and tiny air cells are created that when heated help in the leavening process.

B. Fat Replacement

The search is on for ingredients that can replace some or all of the fat in doughs and batters and result in a product that has the flavor and texture of fat. Skim milk and egg whites, along with starches and gums, are used to replace fat and reduce calorie content.

Gums and starches do not replace fat completely but can serve to retain moisture. In icings and fillings, maltodextrin and dextrin are carbohydrates that provide a smooth texture and excellent mouth feel. Polydextrose is a reduced-calorie polymer made up of dextrose (corn syrup, glucose) molecules, plus about 10% sorbitol and 1% citric acid. A carbohydrate, it can be a partial replacement for sugar, starch, and fats. Sorbitol is a close relative of sugar and is about 60% as sweet as sugar. Polyglycerol esters are used as an emulsifier and look and taste like fats but are lower in calories.

REVIEW

Fats and oils, both animal and plant, are important bakery ingredients and partly responsible for the texture, taste, mouth feel, and nutrition for many baked items. Since about 1970, nutritional concerns about fats have caused bakers to think in terms of calorie, cholesterol, and saturated fat reduction in formulas. Only animal fats contain cholesterol. Fats are termed saturated, polyunsaturated, or monounsaturated depending upon the number of carbon linkages in a molecule that are connected by double bonds. Saturated fats are generally easier to work with and less likely to turn rancid or break down chemically in frying than less saturated. Adding hydrogen to oils can give them a desired level of saturation and plasticity but also makes them more likely to clog the eater's arteries. Fats that are seemingly solid at room temperatures are usually more "saturated" than oils. Tropical oils such as coconut and palm nut are highly saturated even though they are oils at room temperature. This is because they are made up of short-chain fatty acids.

Several fat substitutes are available for use by bakers which produce products that are similar in taste and mouth feel to products containing fats.

CHAPTER 9

SALT

I. SCIENTIFIC DEFINITION

From a strictly scientific standpoint, salt represents a certain class of sub-stances or chemical compounds produced by the action of an alkali on an acid. In other words, if an acid and an alkali are mixed together they react with each other and form a new substance known as a *salt*.

Although hundreds of different kinds of salts are well known to the chem-ist, the word *salt* in ordinary language refers to one particular salt, namely, sodium chloride, which is the common salt universally used by everyone as a mineral food.

This is the salt that is used in bakery products, salted butter, salted meats, and a multitude of other foods, as well as for seasoning or flavoring in connection with practically every meal.

Salt is naturally present in many everyday foods and has been recognized since very early times as an indispensable article of diet, necessary to sustain life and health.

II. SOURCE OF SALT

Nature has supplied us with salt in great abundance. It is found deposited in the earth in the form of salt beds and also dissolved in the water of the oceans, salt seas, and lakes.

III. METHODS OF OBTAINING SALT FROM NATURAL SOURCES

A. The Mining of Rock Salt

In some sections of the United States and other countries, salt is "mined" from deposits of salt located below the surface of the earth, often at a depth of several hundred feet. Salt is secured from these mines in rather large irregular pieces known as *rock salt*, which is crushed, graded, and used as such, largely for the curing of hides, as food for cattle, and for many general industrial purposes.

Occasionally rock salt is obtained in a very pure state, but usually it contains small amounts of clay and other impurities. To render this salt edible, it is first put through a careful process of purification in order to remove any objectionable substances that would impart an undesirable color or flavor to the salt.

B. Salt Obtained from Salt Brines

A very large part of the salt used in this country is removed from the natural salt beds by first dissolving the salt in water to form a very strong salt solution known as *brine*. This is done by drilling down a 6- or 8-in. hole until the salt deposit is reached. A pipe large enough to fit this hole is driven into the salt bed, and inside of this another pipe about half as wide is driven down still further into the deposit of salt. Fresh water is forced into the outer pipe and soaks down through the salt bed, dissolving considerable amounts of the salt together with some impurities. The salt water thus produced is known as "artificial" brine and is pumped up through the inner pipe. In this way salt is removed from the underground deposit without the necessity of constructing a mine. In certain localities, however, "natural" brine is obtained by merely boring into natural salt wells, which furnish a convenient source of salt.

In addition to common salt, both artificial and natural brines contain a small amount of other mineral substances, some of which impart an objectionable bitter or biting taste. The brine is evaporated in such a manner that these impurities may be separated out. Eventually, practically all of the water of the brine is driven off by evaporation, leaving the salt in crystallized form. This is then dried, sifted, and graded.

In general, the size of the salt crystals secured can be more or less controlled by the method of evaporation employed. The salt sold for edible and baking purposes today is highly refined and free from objectionable substances. It is exceedingly pure and snow white in color.

C. Salt Secured from Oceans, Seas, and Lakes

In certain areas, usually where the climate is dry and hot as in California and Utah, salt is recovered from the water of oceans, salt seas, and lakes. The salt water is first collected in large, shallow open ponds or vats so that it will cover a large surface. The water is slowly evaporated by the heat of the sun until finally the salt crystallizes and separates out. Because of the use of the sun's rays for this purpose, salt thus produced is often called *solar salt*. At various stages of the evaporation or concentration process, impurities separate out from the brine and are removed by passing the strong salt solution from one pond or vat to another. Finally, salt begins to crystallize out of the highly concentrated brine and continues to do so until practically all of the water has disappeared by evaporation. This salt is then collected, further purified, dried, crushed, sifted, and graded.

IV. FUNCTION OF SALT IN BAKERY PRODUCTS

A. Palatability Improved by Salt

One of the most important functions of salt is its ability to improve the taste and flavor of all the foods in which it is used. Without salt in a dough batch,

the resulting bread would be flat, insipid, and lacking in flavor. The notice-
able improvement in palatability brought about by the presence of salt is
only partly due to the actual flavor of the salt itself. Improved palatability
promotes the digestibility of food; because of this, salt enhances the nutritive
value of bakery products. From the standpoint of palatability, the most pronounced effect of salt is its peculiar ability to intensify the flavor created in
bread as a result of yeast action on the other dough batch ingredients that
are blended together in the loaf. This results in bringing out that characteristic taste and flavor of good bread that is so eagerly sought by the discrim-
inating customer. The best-flavored bread is obtained by the maintenance of
cool dough temperatures, the liberal use of salt, and the use of sufficient
yeast to bring about the necessary softening of the dough and the production
of a light loaf in a reasonably short fermentation time.

B. Effect of Salt on Dough Fermentation

Although the action of yeast is responsible for the fermentation of the dough,
it is the salt present that helps to govern or control this activity.

Although the amount of salt used in bread dough tends to lessen the rate
of yeast activity, its ability to prevent the development of any objectionable
bacterial action or wild types of fermentation is much more pronounced. In
this way, salt, when used in proper amounts, aids in checking the development of any undesirable or excessive acidity in the dough batch.

Thus, salt performs a very valuable function in breadmaking. It governs
the important changes involved in the conditioning of the dough, affords
protection against any undesirable action in the dough, and in general assists
in the promotion of a normal, healthy panary fermentation process, which
is necessary in order to secure a finished product of high quality.

C. Effect of Salt on Gluten: Texture and Grain of Product

Salt has a binding or strengthening effect on gluten and thereby adds strength
to any flour. The additional firmness imparted to the gluten by the salt enables it to hold water and carbon dioxide more efficiently and to expand
nicely without tearing. This results in a finer-grained loaf of superior texture.
Although salt has no direct bleaching effect on bread, the fine grain and thin
cell walls produced give the crumb of the loaf a whiter appearance.

D. Effect of Salt on Crust Color

By lessening the destruction of sugar in the dough, salt indirectly assists in the promotion of a deeper crust color.

V. USE OF SALT IN BREAD DOUGH

Because of the very important action of salt in breadmaking, it is essential that liberal quantities of refined high-grade salt are used. The average amount is about 1¾ to 2¼ lb to every 100 lb of flour. Some authorities recommend that the amount of salt used should be based on the actual quantity of water employed in making up the dough batch, namely, about ½ oz to every pound of water.

The upper limit of the quantity of salt that can be successfully used is usually governed by the taste of the resulting loaf. During the hot summer months, many bakers find it advantageous to use slightly more salt than in the winter as a safeguard against the development of any undesirable changes in character of the dough fermentation.

In bread made by the sponge-and-dough method, it is advantageous to use a small portion of the salt in the sponge part, where it is valuable in strengthening the gluten.

Salt is usually first dissolved in the bulk of the water together with the sugar and malt syrup before mixing into the dough. It is very important to see that the salt is not dissolved in that portion of the water in which the yeast is dissolved before incorporation into the dough batch.

VI. STORAGE OF SALT

Salt is very stable and does not spoil under ordinary conditions. However, it may have a slight tendency to absorb moisture and to get somewhat lumpy or hard. Therefore, it is advisable to store it in a clean, cool, dry place. Inasmuch as salt can absorb odors, the storage room should be free of any odors that might be taken up and carried by the salt.

REVIEW

1. How are salts produced?

2. What is the chemical name of common salt?

3. Name two sources of salt.

4. How does salt improve the palatability of bread?

5. What is the effect of salt on dough fermentation?

6. What is the effect of salt on gluten?

7. Why does salt give a whiter appearance to the crumb of the loaf?

8. How does the use of salt help to promote a deeper crust color?

9. What is the average amount of salt that should be used for every 100 lb of flour?

10. Why should salt be stored in a clean, cool, dry place?

CHAPTER 10

MILK

Inasmuch as milk is called for in many cake recipes because it definitely improves the quality of these cakes, and in view of the fact that several forms of milk are available, this chapter is especially worthy of the attention of every cakebaker.

The word *milk* unqualified is generally understood to refer to liquid whole cow's milk. If the cream is separated from the whole milk, we secure skim milk. If the water is evaporated from whole milk, we have whole milk solids left as a dry substance. If the water is evaporated from skim milk, the dry substance left is skim milk solids.

I. BENEFITS OF MILK IN CAKE

The benefits imparted to cake by milk are derived from two sources, namely, the butter fat in the milk and the skim milk solids. The value of butter fat has been previously covered. The value of skim milk solids, whether contributed by the use of skim milk or contained in the whole milk is apt to be underestimated. The milk solids content—

Aids in prolonging the freshness of the cake
Assists in promoting a desirable appearance and preventing greasiness
Adds to the richness and flavor of the cake
Adds food value

II. DIFFERENT FORMS OF MILK

In order to prolong its keeping qualities and to facilitate handling and shipping, milk is now available not only in its original liquid state but also in various concentrated forms such as evaporated, sweetened condensed, and dried milk, either whole, skim, or partially skim.

A. Liquid Milk

Liquid milk needs no introduction. It is one of our oldest and best-known natural foods. Although liquid milk may vary from time to time in composition, excellent results can be secured with it, provided that it is secured fresh from a neighborhood dairy that is operated under sanitary scientific conditions.

It should be used as promptly as possible and always kept properly refrigerated in clean cans.

A gallon of liquid whole milk weighs about 8½ lb and is about ⅞ water and ⅛ milk solids. Liquid whole milk should be thoroughly stirred directly before use to ensure a uniform distribution of the cream.

B. Evaporated Milk

Evaporated milk, sometimes termed *unsweetened condensed milk,* is milk from which a large portion of the water has been evaporated. The resulting milk is sterilized by heat and then cooled, tested, and canned. Evaporated milk keeps indefinitely if the cans are unopened. Once the cans are opened, however, the evaporated milk is perishable and should be used promptly.

C. Sweetened Condensed Milk

The term *condensed milk* usually refers to sweetened condensed milk. It is prepared from fresh liquid milk that has been sterilized. A considerable quantity of cane sugar is added to the liquid milk, which is then evaporated down until a syrupy milk is obtained, containing about 30% water and about 40% sugar.

The main purpose of incorporating the cane sugar is to preserve the keeping qualities of the condensed milk. The amount of sugar contained must be taken into consideration by the baker when using this form of milk in a product.

If kept too long or in a warm place, this form of milk goes bad in time; stored in a cool place in a tightly covered barrel, it may be safely kept for several weeks. It is advisable to examine and taste this milk from day to day, especially in warm weather, to be sure that it is in good condition prior to using.

D. Dried Milk

Dried milk is milk from which practically all water has been removed, leaving the milk solids. The main reasons for removing the water from liquid milk are

1. To get milk in its most concentrated form
2. To facilitate handling and transportation
3. To eliminate the necessity of refrigeration in storage

Although dried milk in general is quite often referred to as *powdered milk*, some brands of dried milk are produced in the form of tiny flakes.

The development of modern processes of drying makes possible today the production of excellent dried milk that is whole, partially skim, and skim for bakers' use.

In cakemaking, the dried milk may first be mixed thoroughly with the sugar employed in the creaming process, or it can be dissolved thoroughly in water and incorporated as liquid milk. The latter procedure is usually preferable.

Dried milk should be stored in a cool, clean, dry place.

III. COMPOSITION OF MILK

Although the composition of fresh liquid milk may vary depending on the breed of cow, time of year, and other factors, the manufacturers of the more concentrated forms of milk can regulate the percentage of milk solids in these

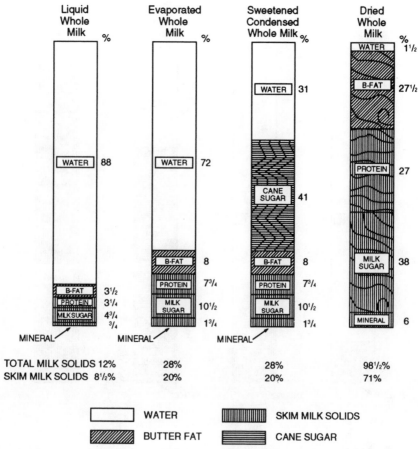

Figure 10–1 *Approximate composition of typical samples of whole milk products.*

forms of milk by controlling the extent to which the liquid milk is evaporated or dried.

Although the U.S. government has fixed certain minimum requirements for butterfat and milk solids in the various concentrated forms of milk, many manufacturers produce these forms of milk with higher milk solids than is necessary to meet the specified U.S. standards. Although the various brands of each form of concentrated milk may differ somewhat in the exact percentage of milk solids, Figures 10–1 and 10–2 show the approximate composition of typical samples of various forms of whole milk and skim milk.

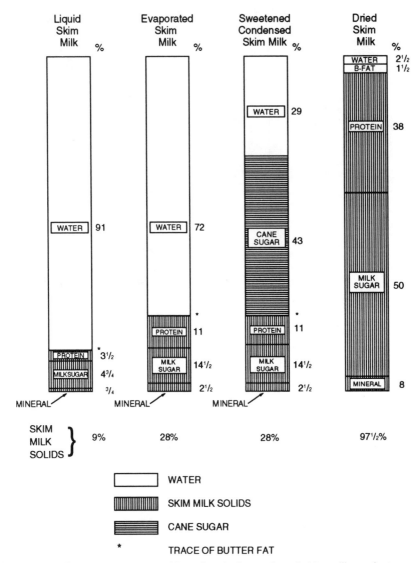

Figure 10–2 *Approximate composition of typical samples of skim milk products.*

IV. MILK EQUIVALENTS

In replacing one form of milk with another form, the new form should contain the same amount of milk solids as was introduced by the type of milk previously used. Obviously, the weight of the two forms of milk in question will be different, but the actual weight of the milk solids contained in each should be the same.

For instance, 1 gallon of liquid milk weighs about 8½ lb and contains about the same amount of milk solids as 1 lb of dried whole milk. Therefore, 8½ lb of liquid whole milk is approximately equivalent to 1 lb of dried milk and 7½ lb of water.

Although these "equivalent" values can be figured out on the basis of relative percentage of milk solids in any given two forms of milk, a conversion table saves time and trouble and prevents errors.

Naturally, any such table can be accurate only for milks of a certain definite composition. However, if based on the average composition of the different forms of milk, such a table can be used for most general purposes in the bakery when changing from one form of milk to another.

V. CONVERSION TABLES

Following are two conversion tables, one for forms of whole milk and the other for forms of skim milk having compositions as indicated in the preceding diagrams. Tables 10–1 and 10–2 show not only the equivalent amount of certain forms of milk necessary to replace 1 lb of other forms but also the adjustment that should be made in the amount of water, sugar, or both used in the formula when these changes are made.

TABLE 10–1
MILK EQUIVALENTS FOR WHOLE MILK PRODUCTS

Form of Milk to be Replaced	Liquid Whole Milk			Evaporated Whole Milk			Sweetened Condensed Whole Milk			Dried Whole Milk		
	Amount (lb)	Water Adjustment	Sugar Adjustment	Amount (lb)	Water Adjustment	Sugar Adjustment	Amount (lb)	Water Adjustment	Sugar Adjustment	Amount (lb)	Water Adjustment	Sugar Adjustment
Liquid whole milk	1	—	—	0.43	+0.57	—	0.43	+0.75	−0.18	0.12	+0.88	—
Evaporated whole milk	2.33	−1.33	—	1	—	—	1	+0.41	−0.41	0.28	+0.72	—
Sweetened condensed whole milk	2.33	−1.74	+0.41	1	−0.41	+0.41	1	—	—	0.28	+0.31	+0.41
Dried whole milk	8.2	−7.2	—	3.5	−2.5	—	3.5	−1.1	−1.4	1	—	—

Table 10–1 holds true only for milks of the composition shown in diagram on page 95). The water adjustment may have to be varied slightly.

Examples

One pound of liquid whole milk can be replaced by 0.43 lb of sweetened condensed milk, provided 0.75 lb additional water is also used and the added sugar in the dough is reduced 0.18 lb.

One pound of sweetened condensed milk can be replaced by 0.28 lb of dried whole milk, provided 0.3 lb extra sugar and 0.41 lb additional water are employed.

The exact quantity of water indicated may have to be altered slightly to produce the desired consistency in the batter. This factor is variable and dependent on local shop conditions.

	Liquid Skim Milk			Evaporated Skim Milk			Sweetened Condensed Skim Milk			Dried Skim Milk		
Form of Milk to Be Replaced	Amount (lb)	Water Adjustment	Sugar Adjustment	Amount (lb)	Water Adjustment	Sugar Adjustment	Amount (lb)	Water Adjustment	Sugar Adjustment	Amount (lb)	Water Adjustment	Sugar Adjustment
Liquid skim milk	1	—	—	0.32	+0.68	—	0.32	+0.82	-0.14	0.09	+0.91	—
Evaporated skim milk	3.1	-2.1	—	1	—	—	1	+0.43	-0.43	0.29	+0.71	—
Sweetened condensed skim milk	3.1	-2.53	+0.43	1	-0.43	+0.43	1	—	—	0.29	+0.28	+0.43
Dried skim milk	10.8	-9.8	—	3.5	-2.5	—	3.5	-1	-1.5	1	—	—

TABLE 10–2
MILK EQUIVALENTS FOR SKIM MILK PRODUCTS

Table 10–2 holds true only for milks of the composition shown in the diagram on page 96.

Similar equivalents can be worked out for partially skim milk products depending on their exact composition.

Examples

One pound of liquid skim milk can be replaced by .09 lb dried skim milk, provided 0.91 lb of extra water is also used.

One pound of sweetened condensed skim milk can be replaced by 0.29 lb dried skim milk, provided 0.28 lb extra water and 0.43 lb extra sugar are also used.

In the event that some form of skim milk is used to replace whole milk, the amount of the skim milk used should be such that it contains the same amount of solids as the content of the "milk solids not fat" in the whole milk. Then sufficient butter must be added to supply the exact amount of butterfat contained in the whole milk previously used.

REVIEW

1. Please list the benefits and uses of milk in cake.

2. List the different forms of milk used in baking products.

3. What proportion of milk is solids compared with liquid?

4. Explain evaporated milk compared to sweetened condensed milk.

5. List advantages for the use of dried milk in bakery products.

6. Dried milk is also referred to as _____ milk.

7. What is the proper way to reconstitute dried or powdered milk?

8. What is the removal of butterfat referred to?

9. What are the milk equivalents to reconstitute from dried to liquid:
   Water _____   Solids _____

10. What is the equivalent of liquid whole milk needed to replace 1 lb of sweetened condensed milk?

CHAPTER 11

WATER IN BAKING

I. PURPOSE
II. ACIDITY AND ALKALINITY
III. HARDNESS

1. Water is the liquid that makes possible the wetting of the protein in flour; this, when mixed, forms gluten. The water may come from the tap or from milk or eggs that are added.

   Without water the development of _____ would not be possible.

   Gluten.

2. Water is the agent that moistens the starch and sugar in bakery products, making it possible to form them into batters, pastes, and dough.

   Water acts as a mixing agent and is needed to moisten the proteins in flour so that _____ can be formed.

   Gluten.

   No. No gluten would form to provide the framework or structure of the cake or bread.

3. Could you bake a cake or bread without water?

4. The mineral content and acidity of the water used in baking may greatly affect the finished baked product. The acidity or alkalinity of the water in part determines the rate of fermentation of the dough or batter. Fermentation slows down when

alkaline or hard waters are used. To overcome (neutralize) the alkalinity, more yeast can be added or an acid, such as vinegar, can be added. Does an alkaline water speed up or slow down fermentation?

Slow down.

5. The degree of hardness is usually expressed as the number of parts per million of calcium carbonate present in the water.

Degree of Hardness	Parts per Million Calcium Carbonate
Soft	10–50
Slightly hard	50–100
Hard	100–200
Very hard	Above 200

Hard water contains at least _____ parts per million of calcium carbonate.

100.

6. Soft water contains less than _____ parts per million of calcium carbonate.

50.

7. Water hardness can be measured in other ways, too. The amount of calcium present is one such measure. The most common way of expressing the degree of water hardness is to talk in terms of the parts per million of _____.

Calcium carbonate.

8. Water containing a small amount of minerals would be called _____ water. That containing a large amount of minerals is _____.

Soft.
Very hard.

9. Closely related to water hardness is the pH of the water, that is, its degree of acidity. The acidity or alkalinity of liquid is measured in terms of an index number and expressed as pH. It is a short way of saying *potential hydrogen* and is a measure of the potential hydrogen concentration. The more hydrogen ions present, the more acid the product. Hard water is likely to be alkaline—but not al-

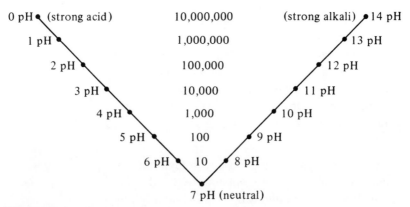

Figure 11–1

ways. Soft water can be slightly acid—but not always.

The pH (degree of acidity) of water is related to the degree of water _____.

Hardness.

10. The pH value of a liquid is expressed as a number between 0 and 14. Pure water has a pH of 7. With a pH below 7, the water is said to be acid. The lower the pH, the more acid the liquid.

When the pH is above 7, the liquid is alkaline. The higher the pH, the higher the alkalinity.

The pH is the measure of the _____ of water and other liquids.

Acidity or alkalinity.

11. The pH of any solution is a measure of its degree of acidity or alkalinity.

Does a low pH number indicate a high or low degree of acidity?

High. The lower the pH, the more acid the solution.

12. Is water with a pH of 8 more acid or alkaline?

Alkaline.

13. Is water with a pH of 6 more acid or alkaline?

Acid.

14. Water that contains no minerals, or is completely "soft," has a pH of 7 and is said to be neutral.

Because the amount of water added to bread dough represents a large proportion of the dough, even small quantities of minerals or other ingredients in the water can have marked effects upon the dough.

In general, water of medium hardness—from about 50 to 100 parts per million—and slightly acid is preferred for baking uses. Water for use in the bakery ideally would be of medium hardness and have a pH below _____.

7.

15. Excessively hard waters, those with high mineral content, may retard fermentation by toughening the gluten. The minerals present apparently prevent the proteins from absorbing water.

What can be done if the water you use is excessively hard?

1. Reduce the pH by adding vinegar or other harmless acid.
2. Use more yeast.
3. Decrease the dough improver (which contains minerals).

Does vinegar added to an alkaline water reduce or increase the pH?

Reduce the pH (make the water less alkaline and more acid).

16. When using very hard water would you increase or decrease the amount of yeast used?

Increase (to overcome the effect of hardness in the water).

17. Dough improvers or conditioners are discussed later. Let's just say that they include minerals and tend to increase the alkalinity of the dough.

If very hard water is used, would we probably not use improver or add more?

Probably not use any dough improver.

18. Water that is too soft can result in sticky doughs. Minerals in hard water tighten the gluten. This condition seldom happens because of the use of dough improvers and yeast foods that add minerals to the water.

What do minerals do to gluten?

Tighten or toughen it.

19. The hardness of water varies widely. In most
parts of Florida, Utah, Arizona, New Mexico,
South Dakota, Nebraska, and Iowa, the water is
quite hard. In Oregon, Washington, and most of
New England, the water is quite soft. However,
within a given area some of the water may be
hard and some soft.

    True or false: In hard water areas you may have
to use water that has been treated to remove
some of the minerals, or you may have to add
acid to the water to make it suitable for use in
baking.

True.

20. True or false: The hardness or softness in water
used in bakeries can be important factors in the
softness or pliability of doughs and can affect the
rate of fermentation of yeast in the doughs.

True.

21. The pH (acidity) and hardness of the water used
in baking affects the development of what important ingredient in dough?

The gluten.

22. In general we would like to have water for use
in baking to be of _____ hardness and with a pH
below _____.

Medium.
7 (slightly acid).

23. Water varies widely in its pH. Water stored in
small reservoirs may accumulate leaves and grass
that ferment and form carbon dioxide. This, in
turn, creates an acid condition in the water. The
pH of water in Amherst, Massachusetts, for example, may go as low as 5. In such cases it may
be necessary to raise the pH by adding an alkali
to the water.

    True or false: Water with a pH of 5 is about
right for baking purposes.

False. It is likely to
be too acid.

REVIEW

1. In order to develop gluten, we must have wheat flour and _____.

2. Does alkaline water slow or speed up the rate of fermentation?

3. The hardness of water is usually expressed as the parts per million of _____ contained in it.

4. Is water with a pH of 7 neutral, acid, or alkaline?

5. Is water with a pH of 7.3 slightly alkaline or slightly acid?

6. If the water available for baking is excessively hard, it could be neutralized by adding vinegar. Is another way of overcoming the effects of hardness to use more or less yeast?

7. Do dough improvers or conditioners increase or decrease the alkalinity of a dough?

8. Why is very soft water not desirable for making a dough?

9. Suppose rainwater (no minerals present) is used for baking. Would you expect the dough to be tough or sticky?

10. The two important factors concerning water that is used for baking are the amount of minerals present and the _____ of the water.

CHAPTER 12

FLAVORINGS: COCOA AND CHOCOLATE

```
I. FLAVORINGS IN BAKING
II. SPICES
III. SPECIAL CHARACTER OF CHOCOLATE
    FAT
```

I. FLAVORINGS IN BAKING

Flavor as experienced by the brain results from the stimulation of nerve receptors in the tongue, mouth, and nose. Taste, one component of flavor, is set off by taste buds, about 9,000 of them located mostly on the tongue, but also on the inside of the cheek and on the epiglottis. Taste buds detect sweetness, saltiness, sourness, and bitterness. The nose is the receptor for odors, of which there are thousands. Odors are the volatile constituents of fruits, spices, some oils, and other foods. Odors are the principal determinants of flavor.

Other receptors in the mouth excite feelings of pressure, pain, heat, and cold. Together the excitation of taste, smell, and feel produce flavor.

The way a food feels in the mouth, called *mouth feel*, depends on the size of the particles and the presence of liquid such as saliva or oil. Pressure receptors tell the brain about a product's coarseness. "Chewiness" in a bread item, for example, depends largely upon the pressure needed by the teeth to shear the food. Seeds add interest to foods because of the variation in texture and the "bite" needed to chew them.

Flavors that are enjoyed are partly the result of experience. All babies like sweet flavors and avoid bitter ones, yet some adults have learned to enjoy bitterness (as in some beers).

Flavor is a large part of what a baker produces and sells. Think of the yeasty aroma of fresh baked bread, the delightful array of flavors in a spice cake, the smooth texture of cake, and the dozens of flavors of other baked products. Flavor is complex. Coffee, for example, is thought to have 600 food flavor volatiles.

Flavor ingredients used by bakers can be divided into spices and herbs, which are the dried parts of various plants, and extracts and essential oils, which are solutions in ethyl alcohol and the oils or odorous parts derived from aromatic plants. Seeds such as anise, caraway, poppy, and sesame are also considered spices.

1. Taste comes as a response to receptors in the mouth for sweetness, sourness, saltiness, and _____. **Bitterness.**

2. The experience of flavor is a response to taste, mouth feel, and _____. **Odors.**

The vanilla bean is an example of a plant that is made into an extract that is used in cakes. The aromatic components of vanilla begin to volatilize at about 280 to 300°F (138 to 149°C), which makes it unsuitable for inclusion in cookies whose temperatures exceed 300°F. (Cake internal temperatures seldom exceed 210°F because of the large amounts of liquids present.)

Liquid flavors such as citrus oils can be bought as powders that have been encapsulated in sugar.

Commonly used bakery spices and their applications are listed in Table 12–1.

TABLE 12-1

Spice	Suggested applications
Allspice	Spice cakes and cookies, fruit icings
Anise	Sweet dough products, cakes, cookies
Caraway seed	Rye bread and toppings, pies, cakes
Cardamon	Breads, rolls, cakes, cookies
Celery seed	Breads, rolls
Cinnamon	Icings, cakes, cookies, fruit and dry toppings, specialty breads, buns
Cloves	Spice cakes and cookies, stewed fruit fillings
Coriander seed	Pastry, cookies, buns, cakes
Fennel seed	Bread, rolls, pastries
Ginger	Spice cakes and cookies, orange coffee cake, fillings
Mace	Spice and butter cakes and cookies, pastry crusts, doughnuts, dry topping for custard pastry
Poppy seed	Toppings for rolls and bread, batters and fillings of cakes and cookies
Saffron	Cakes, cookies, biscuits
Sesame seed	Topping for rolls and bread
Tumeric	Cakes, breads
Vanilla	Cakes, custards

Principal Source: E. J. Pyler, *Baking Science and Technology*. Merriam, Kansas: Sosland Publishing Company, 1988, p. 959.

3. As noted earlier, flavors are detected by the nose. The olfactory patch in the nose reacts to just a few molecules of an odor given off by the volatiles in a food or other material.

What does this say about how spices and flavorings should be stored?

To retain the volatility of the spice or flavoring, it should be stored in an airtight glass or metal container, away from light and high temperatures. Plastic containers are not recommended.

4. Flavor chemists are putting together a variety of flavorings, some that imitate butter flavor, vanilla, lemon, and lime.

Are these synthetic flavors likely to be as good as the natural oil essence or ground spice?

It is very difficult to assemble all of the flavor elements contained in the natural product. Even so, synthetic fruit flavors and vanilla are widely used in the home.

Too much of a spice or flavoring ruins the baked product. If a flavoring or spice comes in a dry form and is particularly strong, it is mixed with sugar, which provides volume and permits more accurate measurement.

Some flavors blend well with others. Cake bakers may use a blend of flavoring extracts such as one part lemon, one part orange, and two parts vanilla. For angel food cake, a blend of 50% uncolored vanilla and 10% each of orange, lemon, cherry, peach, and almond is often used.

In some cakes the amount of a flavoring extract such as lemon or vanilla is so small that it is not discerned, yet it adds to the overall flavor of the cake.

5. Bakers are urged to use only the best spices and flavorings available, even though they may be expensive. Why is this so important?

Spices and flavoring are made up of hundreds of flavor notes, and an inferior spice or flavor detracts rather than adds to the baked product. Very small amounts are used so that the final cost of top-grade flavors and spices is low.

Cocoa and chocolate, although not considered flavorings, have such a characteristic flavor of their own that they are treated both as flavorings and as substantial foods. Powdered cocoa is about 38% carbohydrates and 20% protein. In processing, part of the cocoa has been changed to dextrin, which has a molecular weight between starch and sugar. It absorbs moisture.

6. In a cake mix the added cocoa or chocolate requires that the flour in the formula be reduced. Why?

The dextrin present absorbs moisture and stiffens the batter. Reducing the flour (which also absorbs moisture) reduces the stiffness.

7. Vanilla extract is usually used in chocolate cake mixes, and malt syrup blends well with chocolate. Malt syrup, besides adding sweetness, has another advantage. What is it?

As a syrup it provides moisture and prolongs freshness.

II. SPECIAL CHARACTER OF CHOCOLATE FAT

Chocolate fat, which comes from the cacao bean, makes up 52% to 54% of the bean and is widely used by bakers in cakes, cookies, and icings. The roasted cacao beans have their moisture content reduced and shells removed.

They are then ground, which releases their fat (cocoa butter). Chocolate liquor is about 54% fat; cocoa powder contains 11% to 23% fat. One of the reasons chocolate is so popular is that it contains a small amount of theobromine, a mild stimulant. Cocoa butter, called a *hard butter*, is solid at room temperature (50 to 70°F), but melts rapidly at body temperature (98.6°F), another reason for its popularity and wide use in candy and icings. Unfortunately, from a nutritional viewpoint, chocolate also contains mostly saturated fatty acids, which are associated with vascular diseases.

8. One of the reasons for the popularity of chocolate, besides its delectable taste, is that it is solid at room temperature but melts at _____.

Body temperature. That is, it melts quickly in the mouth.

REVIEW

1. How are flavors experienced by individuals?

2. In what forms do flavor ingredients used by bakers come?

3. What flavors are most prominently used in baking?

4. How should flavor and spices be stored?

5. What proportions of fat are derived from the cocoa bean?

CHAPTER 13

STARCHES AND BAKING

I. STARCH COMPONENTS
II. STARCHES AS THICKENERS
III. MODIFIED STARCHES AND THEIR USE
IV. INSTANT STARCHES

I. STARCH COMPONENTS

Starch is the largest component in baked goods, and bakers are interested in how the various starches function during the baking process and in which starch is best for a particular purpose.

Starch is the reserve carbohydrate of plants and is found abundantly in such common foods as corn, rice, wheat, and potatoes. Rice is about 80% starch, wheat approximately 70%, and potatoes about 19% starch.

Starch provides body for baked goods and is a food in its own right, providing the calories for energy. Wheat starch interacts with proteins and absorbs water to form dough. Part of the water absorbed comes from the gluten, which causes a film to set and is rigid enough to lose its expansion potential and prevent the gluten film from breaking. In baking, the starch absorbs water and gelatinizes (as explained later). The starch firms and provides structure to the loaf. When acted upon by amylose enzymes, some starch becomes maltose (malt sugar) and dextrins, upon which yeast feeds and forms the carbon dioxide that expands the dough.

As seen under a microscope, starch is composed of granules of various sizes, with each granule containing many molecules. The size of the granule is measured in microns, with 1 micron measuring about 1/25,000 of an inch.

Amylose

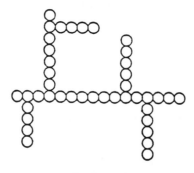

Amylopectin

Figure 13–1 *Amylose* (top) *and amylopectin* (bottom) *molecules.*

The average size of a rice granule is about 5 microns, and that of corn 15 microns. Potato is the largest in size, up to approximately 100 microns.

Even smaller are the molecules that make up starch *granules*. These molecules are long, thin chains composed of more than 2,000 glucose units linked together in chains. Those linked in straight lines are called *amylose;* others in branched chains are *amylopectin*. (See Figure 13–1.)

Each branch consists of 20 to 30 glucose units, and each molecule contains several hundred branches.

Amylopectin starches are called *waxy* because their seed coats appear waxy. These starches have the advantage of not breaking when made into pastes, frozen, and then thawed.

Each starch source has distinctive granules that vary in size and shape. Figure 13–2 illustrates potato granules.

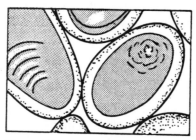

Figure 13–2 *Potato granules.*

II. STARCHES AS THICKENERS

Wheat starch is of particular interest to the breadbaker but is not used in pie fillings because it becomes stringy and develops an unattractive yellowish color. Cornstarch gel is also relatively cloudy. Rice, potato, and arrowroot produce gels that are more translucent and tender.

A starch–water mixture is usually stirred in during the early cooking stage to disperse the starch uniformly in the liquid. Continued vigorous stirring after thickening ruptures the starch cells and causes the mixture to thin out. If it sits up so that it stands without support, it is a starch gel.

The amylose starches set very rapidly and gel firmly upon cooling. In fact, the high-amylose starches set so firmly that they are excellent for use in batters for foods to be deep-fried. The batter adheres so completely to the food that it is almost impossible to remove without pulling off a portion of the food material along with the batter.

The branched-chain starches, the amylopectins, behave differently than the amylose when heated in the presence of water. When the starch granules are heated and imbibe water, they expand in a process called *gelatinization*. In other words, a gel is formed. The amylopectin gels are thinner than gels formed by the straight-chain amylose starches.

In breadbaking, the starch granules undergo partial gelatinization. When the bread cools, the amylose fraction forms an elastic, relatively firm gel. However, the amylopectin retrogrades and becomes rigid. This is the principle cause of staling.

Fillings cooked with starch and water that barely flow (which contain approximately 5% of the regular starches) tend to gel, but most of the waxy starches require as much as 30% in a paste to gel when cooled.

Most recipes for pie fillings call for a range of 4% to 7% starch. The kind of starch, the amount of cooking, stirring, time of cooking, amount of acid, and amount of sugar all affect the viscosity of the paste and the strength of the gel formed.

Cornstarch gives a clear paste that tends to thicken more as it cools. About ³/₄ of a tablespoon of cornstarch has the equivalent thickening value of 1 tablespoon of cake flour. Tapioca also firms more when it cools, and the two starches can be used together to produce a pleasantly clear sauce (or glacé) for fruits that is not rubbery when cooled. A paste made from the two gives a nice sheen to fruit, but waxy maize thickening agents have a superior sheen.

Adding up to 50% sugar to a starch paste increases its viscosity but decreases the strength of the gel. Adding sugar to a cereal starch paste such as cornstarch increases the clarity of the paste.

1. Amylopectin molecules are arranged in branched chains; in what kind of chains are amylose molecules arranged? | Straight lines.

2. What happens to starch granules in the presence of heat and water? | They take up the water and expand forming a gel.

III. MODIFIED STARCHES AND THEIR USE

Corn and wheat starch are modified by hydrolysis (in water and with acids or enzymes) to produce a range of thickeners. Dextrose and other sugars have a number of uses in baked products. Starch modification can be controlled to produce various levels of sweetness and particle size.

Nearly all bakers add gelling or stabilizing agents to pie fillings to improve texture and reduce the amount of liquid soaking into the pie crusts. For maximum translucency, tapioca, rice, or potato starches are selected.

Gums, sometimes in combination, may be used for the same purpose. The gums can be used to replace up to 25% of the starch and help prevent the water in the filling from separating from the gel (syneresis).

Modified starches are also used as stabilizers in puddings and custard cream.

Waxy maize starch and some other special starches are best for sauces that are to be frozen because the sauce will not break down in the freezing process or when reheated. Four ounces of waxy maize starch has the equivalent thickening power of 5.5 oz of cornstarch, 8 oz of cake flour, or 10 oz of bread flour. It gives a very clear, soft paste and is excellent for thickening the fillings of fruit pies. It is as thick when hot as when cold.

3. Wheat starch is flour with the protein removed from it. Would substituting some wheat starch for flour in pastry dough increase the tenderness of the dough? | Yes. If wheat starch is substituted for 30% of the flour in pastry dough, about 20% of the shortening can be left out and the pastry will be more tender. The question is whether enough protein is left to form a continuous dough.

If wheat starch is substituted for 30% of the flour in cookies, the spread of the cookies is increased. Spread in cookies has to do with how much the dough flattens out on the cookie pan during baking.

4. Does substituting wheat starch for flour in cookies make for a more or less tender cookie?	**More.**

Rice starch produces a more tender gel than corn or wheat starch. Potato and arrowroot gels (from root starches) are even more tender.

5. Which gel is more translucent and tender: one made using cornstarch or potato starch?	Potato starch (a root starch).
6. Compared with cereal starches, do root starches gelatinize at a lower or higher temperature, do they produce more tender or more rigid gels, and are the gels more opaque or more translucent?	They gelatinize at lower temperatures, and their gels are more tender and translucent.

Acids break down starch pastes by hydrolysis.

7. The variations often observed in the consistency of lemon pie filling may be because the egg yolks have not completely coagulated. Even so, would it be wise to withhold the lemon juice (an acid) until after the filling has been thickened?	Yes. Allow the gelatinization to complete and then add the acid. Cool quickly because pastes low in pH thin out if cooled slowly.
8. Cross-linked starches have what advantage over those that are not?	They do not become stringy or thin out in the presence of acids. They are preferred for items that are to be frozen because they do not separate when the item is thawed.

Modified or converted starches are changed chemically in processing so that cross-bonding or cross-linking between molecules takes place. Some of the starch molecules are tied to adjacent molecules and in some instances into a cellulose network or matrix.

Cross-linking in starch molecules reduces stringiness in starch paste, increases resistance to thinning in the presence of acid, and helps to prevent separation when the paste is frozen and thawed.

A regular potato starch, for example, is not used for thickening pie fillings because the acids present break it down. A modified (cross-linked) potato starch, however, can be used for this purpose.

Modified tapioca starch is excellent for thickening fruit pie fillings. Sparkling clear and free from the stringy quality of natural tapioca, it does not weep when frozen and thawed or set to a rigid gel.

Starch gels retrograde when frozen or when they stand for a long time. Retrogradation is seen as the separation of water from the starch or as a firming of the gel.

Retrogradation of starch means that the granules try to go back to their original structure before they were cooked. The molecules become less soluble and tend to aggregate and partially crystallize.

9. Is retrogradation a highly desirable or undesirable feature of most starch gels?

Highly undesirable.

IV. INSTANT STARCHES

Precooked starches (also known as *instant* or *pregelatinized* starches) are available. They have been cooked and dried and need no further cooking to absorb water. Instant puddings contain instant starches.

10. In using precooked starches, be sure to mix them with sugar (about one part starch to four parts sugar) before adding liquid. Why?

The precooked starches absorb water so quickly that they lump. The sugar separates the granules, permitting them to disperse in the liquid.

11. Suppose you wanted to make a cherry pie using canned cherries and a prebaked pie shell. Could you finish the pie without further cooking?

Yes, by thickening the cherries with precooked starch and using a whipped cream topping instead of a pastry top.

If frozen fruit is used in "instant" pies, you will need to cook the fruit to inactivate the enzymes present. Once thawed, the enzymes continue to effect changes in the fruit.

12. Can canned fruit be used as the filling in an instant pie?

Yes. Canned fruit has been cooked. In fact, further cooking, as in a pie, causes a loss of quality.

Precooked starch thoroughly mixed with sugar can be used to stabilize whipped cream. The starch gives body, and the whipped cream will not separate for several days if refrigerated.

13. Starch must be mixed with _____ before adding it to a product to avoid lumping.

Sugar.

REVIEW

Starch is the major component of wheat flour and, as such, provides structure and carbohydrates to dough products. Starch from various plants is used as a thickener in pie fillings and puddings. Starch contains two kinds of glucose chains: amylose and amylopectin. As a dough product is baked, the starch granules absorb water that is present and form a gel (gelatinize). The amylose fraction forms an elastic, relatively firm gel. The amylopectin part becomes rigid and is the principle cause of staling. The amylose fraction of the starch is important in that, when acted upon by amylose enzymes, some of the starch changes to malt sugar and dextrins upon which yeast feeds and forms the carbon dioxide that expands the dough.

Starch from various plants such as rice, tapioca, corn, and potatoes is used for thickening purposes. Each has a different granule size and thickening character. Starch chemists have been able to modify starches that, when cooked, have a desired rigidity, translucency, and stability. Instant starches have been pregelatinized (cooked) and can absorb water without further cooking.

CHAPTER 14

THE USE OF GUMS
IN BAKING

I. WHAT ARE GUMS?

II. THE ALGINATES

Selected gums are used in baking as thickeners and stabilizers. Some are used as a dough additive to make softer, more resilient cakes, muffins, quick breads, and biscuits and to add volume to cake. Others produce a smooth, soft texture and body for pastry fillings. Used in bakery icing, some gums counteract stickiness and cracking.

Adding very small quantities of a specific gum or a combination of gums to bakery and pie fillings and bakery jellies improves texture and flavor release. Up to 25% of the starch used in stabilizing pie filling may be replaced by gums.

I. WHAT ARE GUMS?

Chewing gum is an example of a gum. In this case the gum is chicle, collected from the exudate (something that oozes out) of the sapodilla tree in Central America. Gums are hydrophilic; that is, they like water and readily combine with it. Chewing gum quickly becomes chewable when it combines with saliva in the mouth. Another common gum is pectin, found in apples and used in making jelly. For centuries cooks living on the coasts of Ireland and France have used a substance obtained from the sun-bleached fronds of a local seaweed to thicken their blancmange pudding. It is called *carragheen*, from the town of the same name in Ireland, near Waterford.

Traditionally, gums used in food products have been collected from tropical plants and trees. These gums are described as an amorphous exudation from plants that hardens with exposure to air and forms a viscid (resistant to flow) mass with water. Examples of gums collected from plants are locust bean, guar, and tragacanth.

1. How can the addition of a gum improve the quality of a baked product?

> By adding stability to icings and by making softer, more resilient cakes and smoother pie fillings. Specific gums can add volume to cakes.

Today commercial gums continue to be produced from seaweeds and terrestrial plants but are also made by commercial fermentation of microbes, feeding them carbohydrates such as sugar and other growth factors. The Kelco Company lists representative commercial gums and includes several gum derivatives as seen in Table 14–1.

TABLE 14–1
COMMERCIAL GUMS

Marine Plants	Terrestrial Plants	Microbial Polysaccharides	Polysaccharide Derivatives
Agar	Guar gum	Dextran	Carboxymethyl cellulose
Alginates	Gum arabic	Gellan gum	Methyl hydroxypropyl cellulose
Carragheen	Gum tragacanth	Rhamsan gum	Hydroxypropyl cellulose
Furcellaran	Karaya gum	Welan gum	Hydroxyethyl cellulose
	Locust bean gum	Xanthan gum	Propylene glycol alginate
	Pectin		Hydroxypropyl guar Modified starch

Xanthan: Natural Biogum for Scientific Water Control, third edition. Rahway, N.J.: Merck and Co., 1988. (Kelco is a division of Merck and Co.)

Xanthan gum is an example of an artificial gum produced by controlled fermentation. Developed by scientists at the Department of Agriculture's Peoria, Illinois laboratory, very small quantities of xanthan gum cause solutions to be very thick and stable over a wide range of acidities and temperatures. It is produced from the bacteria *Xanthomonas campestris,* first found in a Pennsylvania pond.

Other gums are made by similar controlled fermentation processes. Gellan gum, for example, is made from a fermentation medium of a carbon source, nitrogen sources, and a number of inorganic salts. When the fermentation is complete, the gum is isolated and dried. Locust bean gum, which is obtained from the endosperm of the bean of the carob tree, a Mediterranean species, is used principally to augment the gelling action of the carragheens.

Certain gums can be used as a substitute for most of the shortening in yellow layer cake and muffins, and they are cholesterol free.

2. What is the difference between a **terrestrial** plant gum such as guar gum and a microbial gum such as xanthan?

> One difference is that guar gum is made from the guar plant, whereas xanthan is produced by a fermentation process.

II. THE ALGINATES

Alginates, which are gums, are processed from seaweed. Agar and carragheen are extracted from various types of red seaweed. The giant brown kelp, which grows abundantly along the coast of North and South America, New Zealand, Australia, and Africa, is one of the principal sources of algin.

Like the other gums, the alginates provide stability, soft texture, and a range of gel texture to baked goods. Pastry fillings are given a smoother, soft texture and body. Bakery icings with a small percentage of alginates are less likely to be sticky or crack. Puddings are stabilized and weeping (water formation) is reduced. Bakery jellies and fruit fillings can be given the desired gel texture, color is enhanced, and boil out prevented. The control of the degree that a substance flows (called its *rheological character)* can be changed by adding other gums to alginates.

3. Alginates, like the other gums, can be processed into powder. When added to batters, doughs, pastry fillings, and icings, what functions do they perform?

> Provide greater thickening and stability to the finished product.

4. The addition of a small amount of gum, usually less than 1.5% by weight of the flour, is becoming more widespread in baking cakes and pies and for use in icings and puddings. Will their use grow in popularity?

> Probably, especially in commercial bakeries for use in reduced-fat baked items.

The various gums are used for specific purposes. Some act synergistically with other gums; that is, they combine to complement each other. Xanthan gum, for example, is used with guar and locust bean gum to increase the viscosity (thickness) of their gel at either high or low temperature. Cellulose gum helps to minimize syneresis (weeping) in pie fillings thickened with cornstarch.

5. For what purposes are small percentages of gums being used in pie and jelly fillings?

To make them more stable and less subject to syneresis (water separating out) and to provide smoother and softer textures.

6. What is the source of carragheen?

Various types of red seaweed. It is also called Irish moss.

REVIEW

Gums are present in almost every food and affect structure and texture. They influence water retention, reduce evaporation rates, and affect the viscosity (the resistance to flow of a liquid or porous system).

The term *gum* is applied to all polysaccharides or their derivatives that can be dispersed in water and swell to produce gels or very viscous solutions or dispersions. A little gum goes a long way. It can retard the crystallization of sugar and serves as an emulsifier and stabilizer.

Up to 25% of the starch used in stabilizing pie fillings can be replaced by gums, which improve the body, texture, and clarity of the filling. They also help in preventing syneresis (the release of the liquid from a gel, such as a runny liquid floating on top of an egg custard).

CHAPTER 15

ENZYMES AND BAKING

I. pH AND BAKING

II. THE ROLE OF ENZYMES

I. pH AND BAKING

The degree of acidity or alkalinity of a bakery ingredient, dough, batter, or paste has several effects upon the finished product. First, let's discuss the meaning of pH. It is a measure of the acidity or alkalinity of a solution. The literal translation is from the French *p(ouvoir) H(ydrogene),* or hydrogen powder. The pH is a measure of hydrogen ionization, which translates into the measure of the degree of hydrogen ion concentration and hydroxyl ion concentration. A rise in hydrogen ion concentration equals greater acidity. A taste of vinegar is a prime example of acidity, whereas baking soda is a example of alkalinity. Alkalinity translates into an increase of hydroxyl ions. In 1908, Sorenson, a scientist, suggested the term *pH* to be scaled from 0 to 14. The acidity (or alkalinity) of a solution is compared with pure water, which is the center measure, pH 7. This center is termed neutral; that is, neither acid nor base (alkaline). Each increase or decrease of 1 pH is actually a logarithmic difference, or multiple of 10. For example, a pH of 6 is really 10 times more acidic than pure water. A pH of 5 is 100 times more acidic than pure water, and so forth. Above pH 7, the alkalinity range, a pH of 8 is 10 times more alkaline than pure water. Figure 15–1 shows how acidic and alkaline conditions increase logarithmically as the pH numbers decrease for acidity. Alkalinity increases as the pH rises above pH 7.

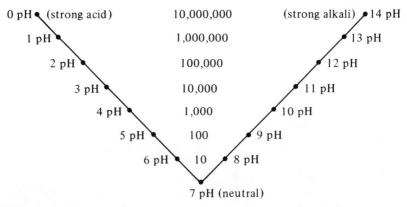

Figure 15–1

1. Looking at the diagram, how much more acidic is pH 4 than pH 5?   1,000 times.

The pH values for typical bakery products and ingredients are as follows:

Lemon juice: 2.2–2.4
Vinegar: 2.4–3.4
Invert sugar: 2.15–4.5
Apples: 2.9–3.3
Strawberries: 3
Blueberries: 3.2–3.4
Cherries: 3.2–4
Peaches: 3.5–4
Prunes: 3.8–4
Bakers' cheese: 4–4.5
Rye bread: 4.3–5.4
Malt syrup: 4.7–5.2
Fermenting dough: 4.7–5.2
Pumpkin: 4.8–5.2
Dextrose: 4.8–6
Molasses: 5–5.4
White bread: 5–5.8
Yeast: 5–6
Egg whites (after aging): 5.5
White bleached flour: 5.7–5.9
Whole-wheat bread: 5.7–6
Evaporated milk: 5.9–6.3

Light Dutched cocoa: 6–6.4
Clear flour: 6–6.4
Bran: 6–6.8
Doughnut flour: 6–7
Rye flour: 6.2–6.6
Egg yolks: 6.3–6.7
Whole eggs: 6.4–8.2
Cookies: 6.5
Cane sugar: 6.5–7
Baking powder biscuits: 6.7–7.3
Distilled water: 6.8–7
Heavy Dutched cocoa: 6.8–7.8
Baking powder: 7
Crackers: 7–8.5
Chocolate cake: 7.8–8
Baking soda: 8.4–8.8
Devil's food cake: 8–9
Egg whites: 9

Source: E. J. Pyler, *Baking Science and Technology.* Merriam, Kansas: Sosland Publishing Company, 1988, p. 251.

Cake batter pH is usually adjusted by varying the amount of either the sodium carbonate or the acid in the leavening agent. More baking soda reduces the acidity. The flavor of the cake is best at a neutral or slightly acid pH, except for angel food cake, which needs a low pH for maximum egg foaming. Chocolate and devil's food cakes are also exceptions because they require an alkaline pH for best flavor and color. These two cakes represent some of the very few finished foods that are alkaline in character.

2. If we raise the pH of a substance from pH 7 to pH 8, what have we done to the alkalinity level? | Raised it 10 times compared with pure water.

3. If we raise the pH of a substance from pH 5 to pH 6, have we increased the acidity level? | No, we have reduced the level by 100 times.

The pH factor affects cake color and texture. Devil's food cake, with pH 7 to pH 7.5, has a light brown color. At a pH of 8.8 to 9, the cake is dark mahogany red, and the texture of the cake tends to become finer as the pH increases. Each type of cake has an optimal pH range for the finished product. These ranges are as follows:

Cake type	pH Range
White layer cake	7–7.5
Angel food cake	5.2–6
Yellow layer cake	6.7–7.5
Chocolate cake	7.5–8
Fruitcake	4.4–5
Pound cake	6.6–7.1
Sponge cake	7.3–7.6

Egg foam development is affected by the pH of the egg whites, which is why the addition of lemon juice to egg whites being beaten into foam tenderizes the egg whites and makes for greater foam development.

Cakes with a very low pH have an acid, biting flavor. Those that are too alkaline taste soapy.

II. THE ROLE OF ENZYMES

Enzymes play a part in baking by increasing bread volume, softness, and shelf life. Products like pizzas and bagels are improved by enzyme action. Enzymes are used in producing high-fructose syrup from starch-bearing grains such as corn, wheat, sorghum, and rice. From the Greek word for "in yeast," enzymes have the remarkable ability to trigger or accelerate biochemical change without themselves being changed.

For example, the enzymes called *amylases* convert a small fraction of the starch in flour to sugar and dextrin as the dough in the oven heats and disrupts the starch granules. The enzymatic action stops as the rising temperature destroys the amylases present.

4. Enzymes are named for the substance on which they act. Amylases act on the starch fractions, amylose. The *ase* at the end of the enzyme name indicates that it is an enzyme.

   What would you know about a *protease*?

Because it ends with *ase,* it is an enzyme and it catalyzes (acts to change) proteins.

Enzymes are important in changing starch into sugars that can be split by yeast into alcohol and gas, carbon dioxide. The carbon dioxide expands, "leavening" (raising) the dough to become a loaf, roll, or other form of raised dough product.

5. Without the amylase, would there be a problem in getting enough sugars needed by yeast for fermentation?

> Yes. Yeasts cannot feed directly on starch.

Several enzymes take part in the fermentation process. Enzymatic action begins when dough is mixed and lasts until the enzymes are inactivated by the oven heat. The amylases convert available starch and dextrins into maltose, which in turn becomes yeast food. Proteolytic enzymes act on proteins in the dough, which are then taken up by the yeast. Together the enzymes soften the dough.

6. Yeast fermentation could not take place without the action of _____ in changing starch and dextrins into maltose.

> Enzymes.

Bakers can add enzymes to their doughs to accelerate fermentation. Several enzyme choices are commercially available. Millers and bakers add enzymes containing proteinases, lipoxygenase, and especially amylose. Fungal amylose is a favored additive; it is made into a powder or tablet from the mold *Aspergillus oryzase.*

Most millers add a minimal amount of malt to the flour, which, when made into a dough, is acted upon by the amylase at dough temperatures between 70 and 104°F (25 to 40°C). The amylases change the malt into malt sugar (maltose), which is directly fermentable. As the oven temperature rises, the enzymes are inactivated.

Other enzymes involved during the fermentation process include carbohydrases, proteases, and lipases.

Enzymes are destroyed by heat at temperatures beginning at about 175°F (79°C). (Some can withstand higher temperatures.) If they are to have an effect, the reaction must take place at temperatures below that at which the enzyme is destroyed.

Enzymes are being genetically engineered. One such available enzyme modifies starch molecules to increase their ability to retain moisture.

7. What would you know about a carbohydrase?

> Because of its ending in *ase,* it is an enzyme; it acts on carbohydrates present.

8. Of the numerous enzymes, which ones are most important in the baking process?

The amylases, because they act to change the amylose starches present to sugars, upon which the yeast can feed, which in turn split the sugars into carbon dioxide, which expands the dough to form loaves, rolls, and other raised dough products.

9. At what temperature are enzymes inactivated?

At approximately 175°F.

REVIEW

The degree of acidity or alkalinity of a substance is particularly important in cakebaking and affects the color and taste of the finished product. The pH of a food (its hydrogen ion concentration) affects a number of reactions that take place in baking as well as the taste of the final product. For example, lowering the pH of egg whites by adding lemon juice tenderizes the egg whites and makes for greater foam development.

Enzymes are another factor in baking and play a part in increasing bread volume, softness, and shelf life. Enzymes are proteins that have the special capacity to trigger or accelerate biochemical change without themselves being changed. There are dozens of enzymes, but the most important ones in baking are the amylases, which change a small part of the starch in flour to sugar and dextrin during dough fermentation. Yeast in the dough feeds upon the sugar and dextrin, splitting sugars present into carbon dioxide which expands the dough to the desired volume.

CHAPTER 16

HEAT AND STEAM IN
BAKED PRODUCTS

I. HEAT IN BAKING

For baking to occur, heat must be transferred from a heat source to the dough or batter or, in the case of frying, from hot fat to the food. Heat makes the product more palatable, digestible, and, in most cases, more attractive in appearance. The nutritional availability of the seven amino acids in wheat is increased when the wheat is milled into flour and made into bread and other baked goods. When eggs are heated during baking, a digestive enzyme necessary to break down some proteins is made available. Starches, when baked in the presence of water, swell and are "cooked," which makes them more digestible and palatable.

1. For baking to take place, there must be the application of _____ to a dough or other food material.

> Heat (or energy).

2. What effect does the baking of dough products have on the nutritional value of the product?

> It makes the protein more available and the starches more digestible. A temperature of about 170°F kills most bacteria and inactivates enzymes.

3. Temperature differentials are created within food, higher temperatures being near the source of heat, which is usually the surface. Will the temperatures tend to equalize even though the food is no longer exposed to the external heat?

> Yes. Equalization continues, and so does some baking.

II. HOW HEAT IS MEASURED

The unit of heat or standard is the British thermal unit (BTU), the quantity of heat required to raise the temperature of 1 lb of water 1°F at or near its point of maximum density. This energy is about equal to that given off by a wooden match when completely burned.

4. If a pound of water is raised in temperature 1°C, is this quantity of heat equal to a BTU?

> No. The BTU is expressed in terms of the Fahrenheit scale.

5. A typical burner on a commercial gas range is rated at 15,000 BTU; that is, the energy it produces in 1 hour is about the equivalent of the burning of _____ wooden matches in an hour.

> About 15,000.

Heat is also measured in calories. The heat of 1 calorie is the equivalent of that heat required to raise the temperature of 1 gram of water by 1°C.

6. Does a cup of water at 100°F contain more or less heat or energy than a cup of water at 101°F?

> Less.

7. Which contains more heat, a cup of water at 100°F or a quart of water at 100°F?

A quart contains four times as much heat because it is four times as large and the temperature is the same.

The BTU unit is measured in terms of the Fahrenheit scale; calories are units measured in terms of the centigrade scale. Most cooking is done using the Fahrenheit scale, but sometimes it is necessary to convert one scale to the other.

On the Fahrenheit thermometer, freezing is at 32°F and boiling at 212°F. Water boiling at sea level is 212°F or 100°C. To convert centigrade to Fahrenheit multiply the centigrade measurement by 1.8 or 9/5 and add 32.

8. To convert Fahrenheit to centigrade, subtract ____ and multiply by 5/9 or 0.55.

32.

9. 194°F is equal to ____ °C.

194 − 32 × 0.55 or 5/9 = 89.

10. 30°C is equal to ____ °F.

30 × 1.8 or 9/5 + 32 = 86.

III. THE NATURE OF CONDUCTION, CONVECTION, AND RADIATION HEATING

Heat is transferred to food from a heat source by three principal methods: conduction, convection, and radiation. (Induction and dielectric heating are also possible but rarely used in baking.)

To understand better what takes place when conduction, convection, and radiation heating are used in baking, consider how they apply to a person in a room sitting in front of a fireplace. The bricks are hot. Heat has been transmitted to the bricks by means of conduction, one brick heating the next; by convection, hot air circulating past the bricks; and by radiation, heat transmitted directly by wave energy. People standing a few feet away from the fireplace still feel warm, even though the air within the room may be cool, because they receive heat directly from the fire by means of radiation, electromagnetic energy transmitted by short waves directly to the body. The electromagnetic waves strike the flesh and are transmitted into heat by agitating the molecules on the surface of the flesh and for a short distance under the flesh, depending on the wave length of the energy.

The room itself is heated mostly by means of convection, air that has been

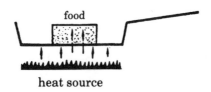

Figure 16–1 *Cooking by conduction.*

heated by the combustion of oxygen with the fuel. The heated air expands and rises, cooler air falls, and air circulation takes place throughout the room.

You have seen radiation heating in action if you have ever gone skiing on a sunny day. Even though the thermometer reads below freezing, you may be quite comfortable being heated by the sun's radiated energy, as long as you stand in the sun and the wind is not blowing. The infrared waves from the sun strike you and turn to heat. (About 60% of the sun's rays are infrared; the balance are visible light and ultraviolet waves.)

11. A room that is heated by a fireplace has heat reflected from the bricks by means of _____.	Radiation.

A. Conduction Heating

To see how conduction heating takes place, apply a lighted match to one end of a small metal rod and hold the other end. Soon the fingers holding the end of the rod will get hot. Heat has been conducted along the length of the rod, molecules having agitated those adjacent to them in passing the "heat" along.

Some metals are better conductors of heat than others. Copper is a metal often used in cooking equipment because of its high conductivity, which is much greater than that of aluminum. (Copper cooking utensils are usually lined with tin or stainless steel because copper reacts unfavorably with some foods and scratches easily.) Aluminum conducts heat about twice as fast as stainless steel.

12. If food sits on the bottom of the deck of an oven in a pan, heat passes through the bottom of the oven into the pan and then into the food by means of _____.	Conduction.

Heat is passed from the stove top up through and around the cooking utensils and on into the food materials. Heat passes by conduction from the surface of the food into the food by conduction. (See Figure 16–1.)

hot   cold

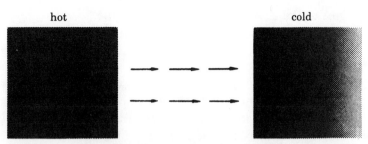

Figure 16–2 *Heat energy flows from a region of higher temperature to that of a lower temperature.*

13. How is heat transferred within the food? | By conduction unless radiated directly into the food.

14. Heat is circulated within the room by means of _____ currents. | Convection.

15. Once the radiated or convected heat reaches a person within a room, heat is carried from the surface of the body inward by means of _____. | Conduction.

Stated in physical terms, heat is determined by the speed of molecular or atomic action within a substance. Heat is a relative term. Rapid action means high heat. Cold is the absence of heat.

16. Does a faster or slower molecular action mean less heat? | Slower.

17. In refrigerated or frozen food the molecular action is relatively _____, but far from being completely stopped. If a substance should reach −459.6°F, it would be at absolute zero, and no molecular action would occur. Otherwise, molecules are in constant motion. | Slow.

When two objects, or different parts of the same object, are at different temperatures, energy is transferred from the region of higher temperature to that of lower temperature. This transfer of temperature (illustrated in Figure 16–2) is called *heat flow*, and the energy transferred is called *heat energy*. Such a flow of heat continues until the two objects attain the same temperature.

18. The greater the _____ between two objects, the greater the flow of energy from the hotter to the colder.

Temperature difference.

19. All food that is baked or cooled involves some heat transference by means of conduction, especially within the food itself. Consider the process of frying. Food is placed in fat or oil. The oil or fat is heated and circulated by means of convection currents. The foods come in contact with the oil and the heat is transferred into the food by means of _____.

Conduction.

20. In simmering, water moves by convection currents and then gives up some of its energy to the food contained within it, again by means of _____.

Conduction.

21. In steaming, the steam surrounds the food and, as it changes from steam to water, gives up its heat to the food by means of _____.

Conduction.

B. Convection Heating

22. *Convection heating* refers to heating that is brought about by _____ of hot liquids or gases.

Movement or circulation.

23. In the usual oven, air is heated by the combustion of gas or by electrical heating elements. The heat circulates throughout the oven by means of convection: Hot air currents rise by means of convection, the heavier cool air drops, and there is circulation within the oven. The hot air surrounds the food that is being baked or roasted and finally the heat is transferred from the hot air to the food by means of _____. (See Figure 16–3.)

Conduction.

To hasten heat transfer in ovens, fans or blowers have been introduced. The fans move air rapidly, passing the hot air over the food being cooked. Forced convection ovens reduce baking time by up to 50%, depending on

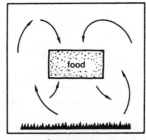

heat source

Figure 16–3 *Convection currents carry the heated air to the surface of the food.*

the food being baked and its position in the oven. In some of these ovens, large temperature variations exist within the oven, and foods bake at different rates, depending on which rack they are placed.

24. The fast movement of air in a forced-convection oven causes more rapid _____ of the air and more rapid conduction of the heat from the air to the food.

Convection.

25. If the fan is turned off, what do you think happens with less air movement?

The oven reverts to a typical conventional oven.

26. In some cases, the fan must be turned off for part of the baking and then turned on. For instance, in some ovens cakes develop rippled tops because of heavy air movement over soft, rising dough. Baffles can help to reduce such airflow. How?

By directing the air off to the sides and not directly over the food.

IV. THE EFFECT OF STEAM

Let's now look more closely at the way steam affects baking. Why is steam so hot (as anyone can testify who has received a burn from steam)? How does the heat get into steam?

At sea level, water boils at 212°F. To change water at this temperature to steam, it is necessary to add 970 BTU to each pound of water. This amount of heat or energy is known as the *latent* heat of steam; it is latent within the steam, ready to be released.

When the steam condenses on food or in a cooking vessel, changing back

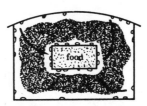

Figure 16–4 *Steam surrounds the food and as it condenses gives off latent heat.*

into water, the same amount of heat—970 BTU—is given off and may be transferred to the food present. (See Figure 16-4.)

27. The principle of physics involved is that energy is given off or consumed whenever matter changes in form. Steam contains 970 BTU of what kind of heat?	Latent.

This latent heat helps to account for the relatively fast cooking action of steam. Steam at about 5 lb per square inch contains six times more heat than boiling water. As steam pressure increases, so, too, does the heat contained in it. Pressure on any gas—and steam is a gas—increases the temperature of the gas.

28. Do high pressures mean a higher or lower temperature?	Higher.
29. Cooking by steam can be accomplished by equipment in which live steam surrounds the food material. It can be free venting, the steam escaping into the atmosphere. In such a case, at what pressure is the steam?	Atmospheric pressure.
30. Another way in which steam is used for cooking is by directing it into a shell-enclosed kettle. Steam-jacketed kettles ranging in capacity from 1 gallon to 200 gallons have an outside shell into which steam can be introduced; the steam changes to water, giving up its ____ heat, and the heat is then conducted through the metal into the food inside the kettle.	Latent.

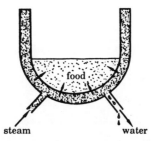

Figure 16–5 *Steam in the jacket changes to water, giving up its latent heat to the food.*

Food within a steam-jacketed kettle is heated by conduction of heat from the shell (where the steam is) to the food. (See Figure 16–5).

31. It is then possible with some steam-jacketed ket-
tles to cool food rapidly by replacing the steam
in the jacket with cold water. Heat then flows
from the food to the _____. | Cold water.

Steam injected into an oven that is being used to bake bread and rolls has the principal purpose of keeping the crust soft during the first part of baking so that the dough can expand rapidly and evenly. Low-pressure steam gives up its heat as it condenses on the bread surface and increases heat penetration into the loaf. Steam injection is not universally used for white bread but is standard practice in producing a glossy surface on hard rolls and rye bread.

Foods baked under pressure bake faster than foods cooked at atmospheric pressure. Why? As pressure increases, so does temperature. Steam under 5 lb of pressure has a temperature not of 212°F but 228°F and contains six times more heat than boiling water.

STEAM PRESSURE AND TEMPERATURE	
Pressure	*Temperature*
5 psi	228°F
10 psi	240°F
15 psi	250°F
20 psi	259°F

32. One reason baking is faster under pressure is that
steam is used. Is steam much hotter or a little
hotter than boiling water? | Much.

V. EVAPORATIVE COOLING

An earthenware jar containing water and sitting in a warm, dry place keeps the water inside cool. The water seeps through the porous walls of the jar and then evaporates, and this process absorbs heat from the water.

Because of evaporative cooling, a glass of water placed in a 400°F oven will never boil; in fact, it evaporates completely, and the water's temperature does not go above 180°F.

33. Does water that evaporates on the surface of food act to cool or heat the food?	Cool.
34. In the example above, if a lid is placed on the glass, would the water boil?	Yes, because evaporative cooling cannot take place.

The creation of steam within or outside food may have the adverse effect of causing evaporative cooling. As the steam forms, it absorbs 970 BTU of heat for every pound of steam formed. This heat is called *heat of vaporization.*

35. Does steam formation act to slow cooking?	Yes. The formation of steam from water in the food requires heat that otherwise might be used to bake bread.

VI. HEAT OF FUSION

Ice in frozen baked goods poses an additional problem, for whenever matter changes form considerable energy is absorbed or given off. For example, 145 BTU are required per pound of ice to change it from ice to water. Thus 144 BTU are absorbed per pound of ice, even though the temperature remains at 32°F. This is known as *heat of fusion.* In cooking food from the frozen state, considerable heat is needed merely to change the ice to water.

36. Conversely, when freezing foods, 144 BTU of energy must be drawn off a pound of water merely to change it to ice. Is it possible to add or subtract heat without changing the temperature?	Yes. Changing ice to water is such a case.

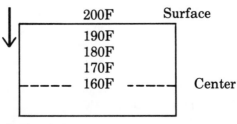

Figure 16–6

VII. BAKING TIME

The thickness of the food material largely determines how long it takes to bake. The thicker the dough, the longer it takes for the heat to move from the surface into the center. Heating the surface of the dough to an excessive temperature burns it.

Temperatures vary as heat penetrates food material in cooking, as shown in Figure 16–6.

The time required to bake food is also a function of *specific* heat, the heat conduction quality—thermophysical or thermodynamic properties—of the food, and the geometric shape of the food. The amount of water in a dough or pie filling and the fat affect the time and temperature required. The specific heat—the number of calories required to raise the temperature of 1 gram of a substance—also varies according to the composition of the food. Ice in frozen food has a different rate of thermal conductivity and specific heat than the unfrozen food around it.

37. Correct baking time depends upon the temperature and what other important factors?

| The thermophysical properties of food, especially the amount of water and the thickness of the food.

Doughs and batters—any food material—can be baked or cooked at a range of temperatures. Time and temperature work together: lower temperatures require longer baking times. For each item, however, there is an optimal combination of baking time and temperature that reflects the amount of liquid, amount of fat, and thickness of the dough or batter. Yeast doughs require time to rise because the yeast needs time to grow and give off carbon dioxide. Quick breads rise rapidly because of the chemical leavening agents.

Lean doughs—those low in fat and sugar, such as French and Italian breads—require slightly higher baking temperatures, about 425°F. Richer doughs are baked at 400°F.

Figure 16–7 shows standard temperatures and some recommendations by specialists for baking. Optimal baking temperatures vary according to the formula, oven, equipment used, and oven conditions.

VIII. MICROWAVE HEATING AND BAKING

Some cake and brownie recipes are produced especially for baking in home-style microwave ovens. Shelf-stable bread and the bread for frozen sandwiches are being baked so that they can be heated or finished off in microwave ovens in the home. Knowing how microwave energy bakes and reheats food items helps in understanding the efficiency and limitations of microwave baking.

Microwaves are electromagnetic wave forms, longer than light waves and infrared waves but shorter than radio waves. They have the unique power to penetrate food materials and to heat them.

The surfaces of some foods, such as bread and rolls, baking in a microwave oven are relatively cool while their interiors are hot. This occurrence is illustrated in Figure 16–8. Two reasons for this strange phenomenon exist: The microwaves pass through the surface and are absorbed in the interior of the bread, and the oven itself, being cool, draws off the surface heat of the food.

38. Is it logical to develop a brown crust on the bread by prebaking it at a higher than normal temperature in a conventional oven to develop a brown crust and then finish baking the interior by microwave?

> Yes. In an industrial bakery this is reasonable and is being done in England in at least one bakery.

A major use for microwave heating is for defrosting foods. Frozen doughnuts and Danish pastry can be defrosted and heated in 10 to 20 seconds per portion. A dozen doughnuts can be heated in about 2 minutes.

Microwaves are extremely fast for defrosting frozen fruits. For example, a consumer pack of frozen strawberries is defrosted by microwave in 3 minutes, which allows the individual berries to be separated for immediate use.

39. Do you think that a few seconds of overheating a filled pastry will boil the filling?

> Yes. Seconds count in microwave heating, especially when single portions of food are being heated. If bread or rolls are overheated, the flavor is the same as occurs in staling.

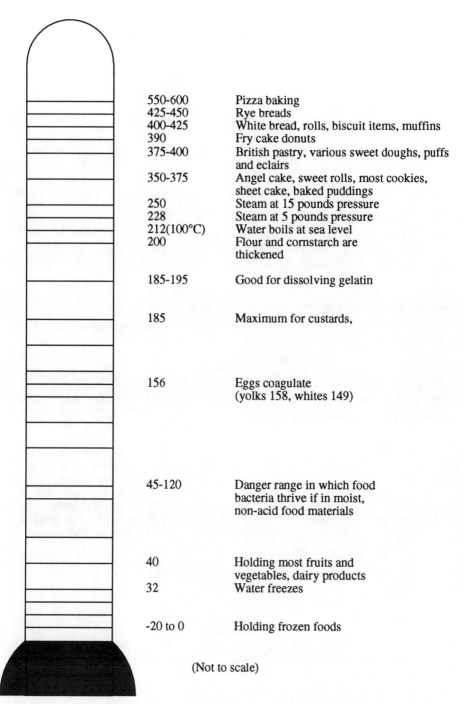

550-600	Pizza baking
425-450	Rye breads
400-425	White bread, rolls, biscuit items, muffins
390	Fry cake donuts
375-400	British pastry, various sweet doughs, puffs and eclairs
350-375	Angel cake, sweet rolls, most cookies, sheet cake, baked puddings
250	Steam at 15 pounds pressure
228	Steam at 5 pounds pressure
212(100°C)	Water boils at sea level
200	Flour and cornstarch are thickened
185-195	Good for dissolving gelatin
185	Maximum for custards,
156	Eggs coagulate (yolks 158, whites 149)
45-120	Danger range in which food bacteria thrive if in moist, non-acid food materials
40	Holding most fruits and vegetables, dairy products
32	Water freezes
-20 to 0	Holding frozen foods

(Not to scale)

Figure 16-7 *Important baking temperatures (in degrees Fahrenheit).*

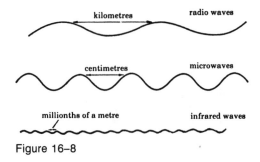

Figure 16-8

Microwave energy strikes food placed in the chamber of the microwave oven. Because the water and fat in the food are nonconductors of this energy, the molecules in the food are driven back and forth (oscillating) at the same frequency of the microwaves (915 million times per second). The result is heat generated because of intermolecular friction.

40. In microwave cooking, energy is transferred to the food by means of radiation and heat is penetrated because of the _____ created.

Intermolecular friction.

Microwave heating occurs at different rates within a food because the different materials absorb microwave energy at different rates. Water is heated at about ten times the rate of ice.

41. Is that part of a frozen food that thaws first cooked much more than a part that thaws later?

Yes. This is one of the problems of cooking frozen foods by microwave. Microwave heating of baked products also tends to toughen them.

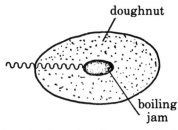

Figure 16-9 *In heating a jam doughnut by microwave, the jam boils while the outside is cool.*

In baking cakes by microwave, cake containers should be made of porous paper. The paper transmits the developing vapors that would otherwise collect and condense on the cake itself as it cools if a glass or other nonporous utensil were used.

42. What's wrong with vapor condensing on a cake?

The texture of the cake surface is undesirable, and the application of the frosting is made difficult.

Items such as cake mixes and brownie mixes that are high in moisture or oil are good candidates for microwave baking. Corn syrup, mono- and diglycerides, and xanthan gum also help hold and disperse liquid so that heat transfer within the batter is more uniform.

Buns that are to be heated by microwave before eating have their formulas changed to include more fat or a combination of more fat and more fiber. The fiber allows greater water dispersion in the dough. Fat dispersion in the dough helps create more even heat transfer.

Another way to produce more uniform heating is to provide susceptors with the product, which are placed in the microwave oven along with the product to be heated or baked. Made of a material that absorbs microwave energy and converts it to heat, the susceptors augment the microwave energy and bake the product's surface.

43. To review: Doughs or batters to be heated or baked by microwave come out tender and moist if they contain increased fat, increased fiber, or both in their formulas. The fiber permits greater water absorption in the dough. What function does the fat serve?

It provides more moisture and, if well dispersed in the batter or dough, aids in uniform absorption of the microwave energy, which eliminates overheating of some parts, hot spots, and toughening of the product.

REVIEW

In baking, heat is transferred from a heat source, such as an oven, to food material, such as dough. At certain temperatures, the heat activates or inactivates yeast and enzymes. It dries the surface to form a crust and chemically changes parts of the ingredients. Pathogens are killed, odors are formed, and ingredients are made more available for nutrition.

Heat is mostly transferred by three methods: conduction, convection, and radiation. All three can occur at the same time. In a gas oven, heat from gas burners is transferred into the oven walls by conduction. Air rises and circulates by means of convection currents and the oven walls transfer some heat to the food material by means of radiation. Convection ovens include fans that accelerate convection heating.

Steam contains latent energy which is transferred to a food material as the steam condenses. Steam is also used to create a crusty surface on dough products. The greater the pressure of steam the more heat it contains.

Baking is a function of time and temperature. Depending upon the amount of water, the thermophysical character of the food material, and other factors (such as time needed for yeast development) each food material bakes optimally within a range of temperatures which could vary during the baking period.

A number of baked items are pre-baked to be finished in microwave ovens in the home, and special containers and formulas are required to reflect the way microwave heating takes place.

CHAPTER 17

BREAD AND OTHER YEAST PRODUCTS

I. TYPES OF DOUGH

1. In its simplest form, bread is wheat flour and water mixed together to form a dough and baked. Bread, as we think of it, is leavened with yeast, and yeast grows and splits the sugars that are present to form carbon dioxide. This expands the dough as the dough bakes; the gluten and starches present in the dough become firm on baking, and we have bread.

Bread, as we usually make it, contains salt, milk, shortening, and sugar and *may* have eggs added to it. The basic ingredients of bread are _____, _____, _____, and _____.

Flour, water, yeast, and salt.

2. Sweet doughs are similar to bread doughs except that flavorings and more sugar have been added. Some sweet dough formulas call for the addition of cake or pastry flour; this results in less gluten being developed and a less chewy product.

Rolls, coffee cake, and Danish pastry are similar to bread in that the basic ingredients are flour, yeast, and water. Dozens of varieties of rolls and breads are possible, all similar in that the basic structure depends upon the flour and water dough.

To make bread products we start with _____ and _____.

Flour and water.

3. Yeast doughs may be divided into rich and lean categories. Both contain flour, liquid, fat, and salt and are leavened by yeast. A conditioner containing sugar may be added, on which the yeast can feed.

The rich doughs contain greater amounts of sugar and fat and sometimes eggs. Doughs to which any amount of sugar is added are called *sweet doughs.*

Lean dough products—bread, rolls, pizza—are characterized by a chewy texture and therefore use what kind of flour?

Hard wheat flour, high in protein and gluten.

4. Flour and water are mixed together to form a smooth mass, to develop the gluten, and to distribute yeast cells uniformly throughout the dough so that they can receive proper nutrition.

Three purposes for mixing dough are (1) to form the dough into a workable mass, (2) to distribute the yeast cells, and (3) to develop the _____.

Gluten.

II. TYPES OF FLOUR

5. The best wheat flours are called *patents* and the poorest *clears*. The patent flour (so named because it was obtained from a patented process) is the finest of the flours (has the smallest particles).

   Soft or winter wheat produces a soft, velvety, powdery flour with more starch and less protein than the hard or spring wheat. A good flour from soft wheat has a clear white color. Soft flours are used for pastry, many quick breads, cakes, and cookies. Hard wheat flour is slightly creamy in color and has a gritty texture.

   We use the hard wheat flours for bread, puff paste, and éclair paste. Soft wheat flour is used for cakes, cookies, and muffins.

   Which flour is likely to be the most expensive?

   The patent flour, which is the most finely ground of the flours and the most highly prized for baking.

6. The amount of water absorbed by a dough is largely related to the amount of protein present.

   Which dough would absorb more water, one made from hard wheat or one made from soft wheat?

   The one from hard wheat, because it contains more protein.

7. Whole-wheat bread is made from 40% to 60% whole-wheat flour and 60% to 40% wheat flour.

   To make regular rye bread, about 20% rye flour is used with 80% white flour, but some rye breads may contain as much as 50% or more of rye flour along with "high-gluten" wheat flour.

   What would happen if we used all rye flour?

   There would be very little volume or structure in the bread because rye flour develops no gluten.

8. Hard, French, Italian, and hearth breads are made with a crisp, chewy crust. To produce such bread, little or no shortening and sugar are used.
   What will happen if shortening is added?

The bread crust becomes tender, which is not desirable in such breads.

III. METHODS OF PRODUCING DOUGH

9. Figure 17–1 lists the basic ingredients of bread and the functions each performs in producing the final product.
   We see that salt, in addition to being a flavoring agent, affects the fermentation process, the gluten, and also the texture and grain of the bread.
   Sugar also affects the fermentation and gives color to the crust.
   Yeast, via the fermentation process, provides volume to the bread and also affects the texture and the grain. Yeast also provides some _____.

Flavor.

Functions	Flour	Sugar	Shortening	Eggs	Leavening	Water
Structure builder (toughener)	X			X		
Bulk builder	X	X				
Dryer	X	X		X		
Tenderizer		X	X		X	
Moistener		X	X	X		X
Flavor (including sweetening)		X		X		
Color builder		X		X		
Lubricant			X			
Creaming agent		X	X			
Binding agent				X		
Lightening agent				X	X	

Figure 17–1 *Reprinted with permission of the publisher from J. Amendola,* The Baker's Manual for Quantity Baking and Pastry Making, *2d edition. Copyright 1956 and 1960 by Ahrens Publishing Company, Inc.*

Straight dough method

A straight dough is one in which all ingredients are put into the mixing bowl and mixed in a single operation. Dough is allowed to rise over a period of time that varies in accordance with the type of dough.

10. Bread is made by using the straight dough method or the sponge method. The straight dough method is one in which all the flour is added to the formula at one time, and the dough is allowed to rise only once.

In the sponge method, about 40% of the flour is added after the dough has risen once. Sponge doughs are punched, given a second mixing, and then given 15 to 25 minutes "floor time" during which some further fermentation takes place. Usually 1 minute is allowed for every 1% of the flour added in this second mixing.

Bread made by the straight dough method is allowed to rise only once; sponge doughs rise _____.

Twice.

11. Straight doughs are fermented from 1½ to 2½ hours, but sponge doughs are fermented longer.

Sponge dough is usually made up by large bakeshops in horizontal high-speed mixers. About 60% of the flour and all of the liquid and yeast are mixed together to form a thick batter. This is allowed to ferment at 77 to 80°F. The dough doubles in bulk and becomes wavy or rippled so that at a slight touch it collapses. It is punched and the remaining flour, all of the salt, sugar, shortening, milk solids, and conditioners are added and mixed.

The second fermentation period then takes place. It is usually referred to as *floor time;* the dough dries out to the point that it can be handled, usually no more than 15 to 25 minutes. The dough rises, but this is *not* regarded as a fermentation.

In the sponge dough process, only about _____ % of the flour is mixed in the first stage.

60.

Sponge dough method

Part of the flour, water, yeast, sugar, and shortening are mixed, forming a dough called the *sponge,* which is permitted to rise and ferment to the desired point. The sponge is then put back into the mixer and combined with the balance of the ingredients: the remainder of the flour, water, sugar, salt, milk, shortening, and yeast. When this is mixed together into a smooth dough, it is again allowed to rise and is then divided into various-sized pieces.

The sponge dough is suitable for larger commercial operations.

12. In the sponge dough method, part of the flour, water, yeast, sugar, and sometimes shortening are mixed, forming a dough called the *sponge.* The sponge is allowed to ferment for 3 to 4 hours and then is "remixed" with the remaining ingredients for final processing.

    In the straight dough method, all of the ingredients are mixed at one time, allowed to rise, and baked. In the sponge dough method, a sponge is made, consisting of _____.

60% of the flour and all of the liquid and yeast.

13. The principal advantage of the sponge dough method is that it allows greater flexibility. Sponges can be held longer without loss of quality in the bread. In contrast, straight doughs must be taken up and baked when ready (ripe). There is little leeway in either direction. If the dough has been fermented too much, it can be used only by adding it, a small portion at a time, to new doughs as they are mixed.

    True or false: The sponge dough method gives the baker a little more flexibility about when the dough must be shaped and baked.

True.

14. With a sponge dough, labor costs are higher because of "double handling." They are partly offset by the fact that about 20% less yeast is needed for a sponge dough than for a straight dough. The sponge dough can give greater volume to the bread and a more uniform desirable texture in grain. For these reasons, are large bakeries likely to use the sponge or the straight dough method of mixing?

Sponge dough method.

IV. DOUGH TEMPERATURE

15. After the dough is mixed, the critical factor in the rate of fermentation is the temperature of the dough. High temperatures speed up the action of the yeast; low temperatures retard the action.

    In making a straight dough, the dough temperature should be between 78 and 82°F.

    In using the sponge dough method, dough temperature is lower, 72 to 78°F, but after the remix, it should be 78 to 80°F—no higher than 81°F.

    Which method of mixing calls for a slower yeast action: the sponge or the straight dough method?

The sponge dough method, because the fermentation time is longer.

16. The big reason why the temperature in doughs cannot be allowed to go above about 82°F is the fact that overfermentation takes place and the doughs become tacky or sticky. Once the dough has become sticky or tacky, it is almost impossible to mold and handle and becomes "bucky."

    Control of the dough temperatures thus becomes one of the most important functions of the baker.

    Is the temperature of dough after it is mixed highly critical or not so very important?

Highly critical.

17. Temperature of the dough continues to rise as it is being mixed; the heat results from the friction caused by mixing. To offset the increase in tem-

perature, cold water, ice, or both are added. Some mixing machines are surrounded by refrigerating coils or brine jackets to accomplish the same purpose.

Why worry so much about dough temperature?

If it gets too warm, there is too much fermentation. The dough becomes very difficult to work.

18. To control the temperature of the dough, one must understand something about heat units. The heat unit used is the British thermal unit (BTU). A BTU is the amount of heat required to raise 1 lb of water 1 degree Fahrenheit.

If we have 25 lb of tap water at 64°F and raise it 1 degree, how many BTU have we introduced into the water?

25 BTU.

19. If we have 100 lb of dough at 79°F and wish to lower the temperature by 5 degrees, how many BTU of energy must be removed from the dough?

Approximately 100 times 5, assuming that 1 BTU raises the temperature of 1 lb of dough 1 degree, which is not quite true.

20. In large bakeries, dough temperature is controlled by refrigeration. The small bakery, however, controls the temperature by adding ice to the water in mixing. The ice and cool water are needed to offset the temperature rise created by the friction of mixing the dough. The longer the mixing time, the higher the temperature rise.

In adding ice, it should be remembered that when ice melts it absorbs 144 BTU per pound of ice, even though the ice water formed is still at 32°F.

Suppose you add 1 lb of ice at 32°F to 1 lb of water at 64°F. Will the resultant temperature be halfway between 32 and 64°F?

No. Much lower, because of the heat absorbed when the ice changes to water.

V. STEPS IN MAKING YEAST PRODUCTS
BREAD AND ROLL DOUGH PRODUCTION STAGES

Raw materials
Weighing of ingredients
Mixing
Fermentation period
Scaling
Rounding
Bench proofing
Molding
Panning
Pan proofing
Baking
Cooling

Many beginners in the baking trade are not enthusiastic about making bread and rolls because they feel the results are not as attractive as pastries and do not produce large profits. The commercial bakeries are doing a fine job in giving the public excellent-quality breads.

There are, in addition to the standard breads, the specialty types of breads and rolls, some of which have the eye appeal and flavor to please the most fastidious gourmet.

Here are a few important rules to follow in making bread and rolls:

1. Maintain absolute personal cleanliness.
2. Use clean utensils, materials, and machinery.
3. Always use ingredients of the very best quality.
4. Keep a dough thermometer on hand for controlling the dough.
5. Read all formulas carefully and scale all ingredients properly.
6. Serve fresh products only, baked daily.

21. Yeast products are made in this sequence of operations: mixing, fermentation, punch, rest, make up, proof, and bake. Before mixing, the ingredients are weighed, "scaled off" as the baker says, and then formed into a smooth paste, and the gluten is thoroughly developed.

    What is the next step?   Fermentation.

MIXING

The three purposes of dough mixing are as follows:

1. To bring about a uniform mixture of ingredients and to form a smooth dough.
2. To develop the gluten in the dough mass in order to promote the elasticity of the dough; the elasticity, in turn, retains the gases formed by the yeast.
3. To distribute the yeast cells uniformly so that they receive proper nutrition.

22. Many things can go wrong in the production of a loaf of bread. The left-hand column of the chart lists these factors. The rest of the chart is concerned with pointing the finger at what could have caused a particular failure. For example, if the bread shows a gray crumb, it could be caused by underproofing of the dough, the dough being too warm, or the proof box being too hot.

A crust that is too thick may be caused by the dough being old, the temperature of the oven being too low, the bread being overbaked, or _____.

Insufficient sugar.

23. If the crust of the bread has not developed a good brown color, this could have been caused by the temperature of the dough being too low, the proof box too hot, too little sugar, or _____.

The dough being too old.

24. Blisters in the crust of the bread can be caused by flour that has not been matured, dough that is too young or too old, or _____.

Improper molding.

FERMENTATION

Fermentation takes place after the dough has been mixed and continues until the oven in which the bread or dough is mixed reaches a temperature of 138°F. At this point the yeast bacteria is dead and fermentation ceases.

BREAD INGREDIENTS AND THEIR FUNCTIONS

Ingredients / Main Functions in Finished Product	Binding agent	Absorbing agent	Aids keeping qualities	Back bone and structure	Affects eating qualities	Nutritional value	Affects flavor	Affects fermentation	Affects gluten	Texture and grain	Imparts crust color	Affects symmetry	Volume	Produces tenderness	Adds quality to product
Bread flour	X	X	X	X	X	X									
Salt					X	X	X	X	X						
Sugar		X	X	X	X	X	X	X			X				
Shortening		X	X	X	X				X	X			X	X	
Milk solids		X		X	X	X			X					X	
Water	X														
Yeast						X			X			X			

Figure 17-2 Reprinted with permission of the publisher from J. Amendola's The Baker's Manual for Quantity Baking and Pastry Making 2nd Edition. Copyright 1956 and 1960 by Ahrens Publishing Company, Inc.

ORDINARY BREAD FAULTS AND THEIR CAUSES

Faults \ Causes	Improper mixing	Insufficient salt	Too much salt	Dough wt. too much for pan	Dough wt. too light for pan	Insufficient yeast	Too much yeast	Dough proofed too much	Dough under proofed	Dough temp. too high	Dough temp. too low	Dough too stiff	Dough too slack	Proof box too hot	Green flour	Dough chilled	Too much sugar	Insufficient sugar	Dough too young	Dough too old	Improper molding	Insufficient shortening	Oven temp. too high	Oven temp. too low	Over baked
Lack of volume	X		X		X	X			X							X			X	X		X			
Too much volume		X		X			X																X		
Crust color too pale										X				X				X	X	X				X	
Crust color too dark											X						X		X	X		X			
Crust blisters															X				X						
Shelling of top crust											X				X			X	X	X					
Poor keeping qualities	X							X	X										X	X	X		X		
Poor texture, crumbly								X					X						X	X			X		
Crust too thick																		X	X	X			X	X	
Streaky crumb																					X				
Gray crumb									X	X				X											
Lack of shred							X												X	X					
Coarse grain	X			X			X			X									X	X	X				
Poor taste and flavor	X								X										X						

Figure 17-3 *Reprinted with permission of the publisher from J. Amendola's The Baker's Manual for Quantity Baking and Pastry Making, 2nd Edition. Copyright 1956 and 1960 by Ahrens Publishing Company, Inc.*

The most favorable temperature for fermentation to take place is from 80 to 82°F. The period of fermentation depends on the amount of yeast used in the dough and the temperature of the room. The lower the temperature, the slower the fermentation; the higher the room temperature, the faster the fermentation takes place.

A dough that is not sufficiently fermented (underproofed) is referred to as a *young* dough; dough that is overproofed is known as an *old* dough.

Punching the dough is a process in which the gases developed during fermentation (carbon dioxide) are forced out of the dough. Punching helps to relax the gluten and equalizes the temperature of the dough.

The time to punch the dough is when it has doubled in size. Insert an open hand into the dough from 4 to 5 inches. If the dough recedes, it is ready for punching. If it springs back when a hand is inserted, longer fermentation is required. After the dough is punched, it must be proofed a second time before being made up into bread or rolls.

25. As fermentation proceeds, the gluten hydrates (absorbs water), and the dough becomes more pliable and smooth.

    Fermentation is considered complete when the dough has doubled in bulk.

    The dough is "taken to the bench young"; in other words, the dough is taken from the container where it is fermenting when fermentation is about three-quarters complete.

    Fermentation causes the dough to rise and become more _____.

    Pliable and smooth.

26. Yeast is used to make bread and sweet dough rise. Yeast action begins during the time the dough is allowed to ferment and ends in the oven when the internal temperature of the dough reaches about 140°F.

    Ethyl alcohol is produced by the action of the yeast on some of the sugars in the dough. The yeast also releases carbon dioxide. The carbon dioxide is the main leavening agent in a yeast dough, although gases from water (steam) and ethyl alcohol may help somewhat in the leavening.

    Carbon dioxide gas is formed by the action of

baking soda, baking powder, and what other common baking ingredient?

Yeast.

PUNCH

27. The next step is the punch. The dough has expanded to a point where the gluten cannot support the structure without the firming action of heat. If it is pushed or "punched," it collapses at that point.

In the punch, the dough is folded over on all sides, causing it to collapse and return to its original bulk. The punch allows the CO_2 formed to escape and redistributes the food available for the yeast so that a vigorous secondary leavening can take place.

Is the term *punch* misleading?

Yes. The dough is actually folded and pressed rather than punched. When folding is complete, the dough is flipped upside down in the container.

REST

28. The make up comes next. The dough is taken to the bench, where it is allowed to rest a short time. It is then divided (cut), shaped, and panned as desired. Rolled-in doughs have shortening spread over them and are folded and rolled at this point.

So far, the dough has been mixed, fermented, punched, had a rest, and _____.

Made up.

MAKE UP

Dough is scaled and formed into various shapes, i.e. bagettes, round, Italian, loaves, etc.

29. Would you guess that small rolls should be docked?

No. Their smaller size produces less spring and, except for hard rolls, their crusts are soft, which permits expansion.

PROOF

30. The next step is the proof. Made-up products are placed in an area where the temperature is about 100°F, and the humidity is high. In a bakeshop a "proofer" or proofing cabinet, in which steam or hot water produces a high humidity, may be used.

    Leavening action increases; the yeast grows quickly, giving off CO_2; and the products swell to at least twice the original make-up size.

    The proof follows what step?

    Make up.

31. Now, finally, the dough is ready to bake. As heat is applied, the final leavening occurs before the heat reaches 140°F and the yeast is destroyed. The steam and CO_2 produced rapidly expand the dough to produce "oven spring." The top crust of a loaf is pushed up because of the spring.

    Would you guess that oven spring might be too vigorous if some of the gases were not allowed to escape?

    Yes. To avoid too much oven spring, hearth and rye breads, which develop hard, unyielding crusts, are "docked", that is, sliced across the top to allow for expansion and to permit some of the gases to escape. If docking is not done, the crusts burst.

32. Baking temperatures are related to size of the product and to richness. Lean rolls and small products bake at 400 to 425°F. Richer products and large, lean ones are baked at lower temperatures.

    Do pizzas, which are a lean, thin product topped with tomato sauce and cheese, require a high or low temperature?

    A high temperature— up to 600°F to dry the tomato sauce and quickly brown the dough.

33. Depanning and cooling of yeast dough products should allow the escape of steam and alcohol developed during baking. Large products may be removed from their pans so that free air circulation can occur.

    Hard-crusted breads and rolls are not wrapped so as to prevent softening of the crusts. Does this mean that hard-crusted bread and rolls will keep longer?

    No. They must be baked daily if a high-quality product is desired.

34. To review, we see that yeast dough products are made in a series of steps: mixing, _____, _____, _____, _____, _____, and _____.

Fermentation, punch, rest, make up, proof, bake.

STORAGE

35. The quality of bread can be properly maintained if bread is wrapped and frozen. However, refrigeration produces more staling than if the bread were kept at room temperature. In hot, muggy climates, refrigeration does prevent mold growth and may be necessary.

    One and one-half lb of unsliced bread that is frozen requires about 3 hours to thaw at room temperature.

    Ordinarily, should bread be refrigerated?

No.

VI. BAGELS

Bagel is a Yiddish term derived from the fact that this hard, glazed, yeast dough product is in the shape of a ring or doughnut. Using a very stiff dough made from a strong, high-gluten flour, the formula is lean (not fat) and inexpensive. Bagels are one of the few baked products to be boiled in water before being baked. The shiny brown crust, almost like a glaze, results from placing the bagels in hot water that is simmering (hot enough to form small bubbles). The bagel dough has been about three-quarters proofed before being placed in the water.

They are allowed to remain in the hot water until rising to the surface. The hot water speeds the yeast action. After removal from the water, the product is dipped in a chopped onion preparation or garnished with sesame or poppy seeds.

36. The traditional bagel is unusual among yeast dough products in that _____.

It is boiled in water for about 2 minutes before being baked.

37. What effect does the addition of malt to the water in which the bagels are boiled have on the surface of the finished product?

The malt, being a sugar, provides a shiny surface to the baked bagel.

Bagel variations include egg bagels, chocolate bagels, pumpernickel bagels, and wheat bagels. Some varieties are not boiled and consequently do not have the hard, shiny crust of the boiled type.

38. One of the reasons bagels are chewy is because of the flour used. What kind of flour is used?	A strong (high-protein) flour.

VII. QUICK BREADS

The person who first named these popular members of the bread family remains a mystery. Why they are so named is obvious: They are easier to make and take less time than the ones made with yeast. What they are requires some special definition, for there are so many of them. They are also called *hot breads*, as well as by the name of the specific recipe used in producing them.

Quick breads can be classified by the type of leavening agent used. For example, biscuits, griddle cakes, scones, and shortcake are leavened by baking powder or baking soda. Popovers and Yorkshire pudding are leavened by steam.

Quick breads can also be grouped according to the thickness or thinness of the batter used to make them. (See Figure 17–4.) There are "pour" batters, "drop" batters, and "soft" doughs that are to be rolled, patted out, or shaped. Popovers and waffles are made with pour batters. Corn bread, loaves, spoonbreads, and dumplings are made from drop batters, whereas some muffins and gingerbread are made from pour batters, and others from drop. Scones, coffee cakes, tea breads, and doughnuts are made from soft doughs, and biscuits can be made from either drop batters or soft doughs.

	Liquid	*Flour*	*Consistency*	*Product Examples*
Pour batters	One part	One part	Pours in a steady stream	Popovers, griddle cakes
Drop batters	One part	Two parts	Forms large drops when poured	Muffins and fritters
Soft doughs	One part	Three parts	Sticky to touch	Bread, biscuits, yeast rolls
Stiff doughs	One part	Four parts	Firm to touch	Pie crusts, cookies, noodles

Figure 17–4 *Reprinted with permission of the publisher from J. Amendola,* The Baker's Manual for Quantity Baking and Pastry Making, *2d edition. Copyright 1956 and 1960 by Ahrens Publishing Company, Inc.*

Although these processes result in completely different breads, all are made of almost the same ingredients. They vary only because of the proportions used and the way they are mixed and baked or cooked.

Further variety in quick breads comes from the diversity of cereal products used: wheat, whole-wheat, rye, and corn flours, bran, oatmeal, and cornmeal. Any of these can be made into muffins, for example, yet each final baked product tastes and looks different.

REVIEW

1. Flour and water are mixed to form a batter or dough. In the mixing, what all-important protein substance is formed?

2. A sweet dough is like bread dough except that more _____ and flavorings are used in the sweet dough.

3. What ingredient in flour absorbs most of the water present?

4. True or false: A good-volume rye bread contains wheat flour as well as rye flour.

5. How could you identify a hard wheat flour by feeling it?

6. Does patent or clear flour have the finest grain size?

7. Which flour—soft or hard—is used for each of these products?

Cakes _____
Bread _____
Muffins _____
Puff paste _____
Cookies _____

8. Do most commercial bakers make bread using the straight dough or the sponge method?

9. What are the advantages of using the sponge dough method?

10. Excessive dough temperature results in a _____ dough.

11. What unit of heat is necessary to raise 1 lb of water 1°F?

12. The more protein in the flour, can it absorb more or less water?

13. Why do doughs rise in temperature when they are mixed?

C H A P T E R 18

BASIC SWEET DOUGH
AND DANISH DOUGH

I. PRODUCTION POINTS

A. Basic Sweet Dough

B. Danish Dough

Basic sweet dough and Danish dough can be used to produce hundreds of varieties of baked goods. Variety can be obtained with these doughs by using cheese, fruit, or almond paste fillings and by varying spices, toppings, shapes, folding, or twisting. No matter how they are varied, these products are popular.

Units of 1 to 2½ oz are referred to as rolls or buns; among these are streusel buns, raisin cinnamon buns, and Philadelphia sticky buns.

Larger units up to 12 oz are referred to as coffee cake varieties; these include almond ring coffee cake, cinnamon ring coffee cake, and meltaway coffee cake.

Today it is more important than ever before to define high-quality ingredients in terms of consumer acceptance. Therefore, select time-proven basic ingredients for your sweet dough from reliable manufacturers. There is no substitute for the best grades of flour, sugar, malt, syrup, salt, shortening, butter, and milk, and the highest-quality frozen eggs, margarine, yeast, and flavors.

I. PRODUCTION POINTS

A. Basic Sweet Dough

Mixing: Now that we have selected top-quality, consumer-accepted ingredients, the method of combining them to form a basic sweet dough is next in importance. To ensure a uniform and thorough distribution of the sugar, shortening, salt, nonfat dry milk, and flavor, it is suggested that they be creamed together thoroughly, but not until light. Next, we add the egg product as fast as the creamed mass will absorb it. All of the water, with the exception of that used to dissolve the yeast, is then added and mixed in to break up the creamed mass. Add the flour and start mixing at slow speed. Immediately after adding the flour, the yeast solution is added and the mixing at slow speed continued until the bulk of the flour has been wetted down.

The mixer may now be advanced to medium speed and the dough mixed until it is smooth and well developed. Should a firm dough be desired, it is suggested that approximately 25% of the flour be held back and added approximately 5 minutes before mixing is completed. This will prevent overheating. Firm doughs usually heat up rapidly and may become too warm before proper dough development has been attained.

Fermentation: Sweet yeast doughs should be given slightly less fermentation than is usually given bread and roll doughs. Slightly underfermented doughs produce more desirable results than fully or slightly overfermented doughs.

Sweet yeast doughs to be retarded should be given less fermentation than doughs that are to be made up in the usual manner. Sweet yeast doughs to be made up into individual units prior to retarding should be given half to three-quarters fermentation. Dough to be cut up into strips and retarded should be given slightly less fermentation, as the larger units require slightly more time for thorough chilling in the dough retarder than individually made-up units.

Makeup: Complete details for makeup are given for the individual varieties. All varieties can be made up as small individual units or as coffee cakes, regardless of whether makeup directions specify one or the other.

Proofing: Sweet yeast dough products should be given full proof at a temperature ranging from 95 to 98°F and a relative humidity ranging from 80% to 85%.

Sweet yeast dough products that have been retarded as made-up units should be allowed to warm up to room temperature before being placed in the proof box to assure a rapid proof and good volume.

Baking: It is suggested that sweet yeast dough products be baked as quickly as possible, yet long enough to ensure a thorough bake.

Finishing: It is recommended that, with few exceptions, all sweet yeast dough products be glazed as they come from the oven; glazing seals them, thus adding shelf life to the product. In addition to adding to the shelf life of the product, the glaze enhances the eating qualities and general appearance of products. Sweet yeast products should be cooled and packaged or placed in display cases as soon after baking as possible.

B. Danish Dough

Naturally, it is important that the ingredients used in making Danish pastry be the best quality obtainable. Also, it is necessary that the formula used be in proper balance to meet the specific plant conditions.

Mixing: Danish pastry doughs should be mixed in the same manner as basic sweet dough, except that mixing should cease as soon as the materials have been thoroughly incorporated. Danish doughs are further developed during the rolling-in process.

Fermentation and rolling-in process: After mixing, scale off strips of an appropriate size and give them a 15- to 20-minute rest or fermentation period, preferably in the retarder.

Then sheet out the dough strips to a thickness of ½ to ¾ inch and in a sheet three times as long as wide. Spot butter or margarine shortening over two-thirds of the length of the dough sheet. Fold the unspotted third over the center third, and then fold the remaining third on top, making three layers of dough and two layers of shortening.

Again roll out to a thickness of approximately ½ inch and fold in thirds (no additional shortening is used). Allow pieces to rest 20 to 30 minutes in the retarder.

Roll out and fold the dough in thirds twice more, with a 20- to 30-minute rest period in the retarder between rollings. The dough must be kept cool during the rolling operation to prevent the margarine from soaking into the dough. Therefore, the amount of time in the retarder between rollings will depend on the room temperature.

After rolling and folding for the last time, it is advisable to allow the dough to rest 4 to 8 hours, preferably overnight, before starting makeup of the individual varieties. The best temperature for retarding is 35 to 45°F.

Make up: All varieties of sweet dough products, with few exceptions, can be made up for greater richness from a rolled-in Danish dough. All varieties can be made up as small individual units or as coffee cakes, regardless of make up directions specifying one or the other.

Proofing: Danish pastry should be proofed at temperatures no higher than 90 to 95°F, and with only sufficient humidity to prevent the units from crusting.

Baking: As in the case of basic sweet yeast dough products, it is suggested that Danish dough products be baked as quickly as possible to ensure a moist, good-eating finished product.

Finishing: It is also recommended that, with few exceptions, all sweet yeast dough products be glazed as they come from the oven to seal them, thus adding shelf life to the product. In addition to adding to the shelf life of the product, the glaze enhances its eating qualities and general appearance. Sweet yeast products should be cooled and packaged or placed in display cases as soon after baking as possible.

Danish pastry is similar to puff pastry, except that yeast is used as a leavening agent. All-purpose or a combination of bread and cake flour is used. Shortening is placed in a thin slab or dotted over the rolled-out dough. The dough is folded over the shortening and rolled several times. Between each rolling, the dough is relaxed in a refrigerator for at least 20 minutes so that it can be better handled.

1. The principal difference between Danish and puff pastry is in the leavening action. Danish makes use of what leavening action in addition to hot air and steam?

    That brought about by the action of yeast.

When Danish has been rolled and folded for the last time, allow it to rest for 4 to 8 hours or overnight before makeup. "Resting" is done in a *retarder* at 35 to 45°F. In resting, the gluten strands relax and the dough can be more easily worked.

2. True or false: The production of Danish pastry is a time-consuming process.

    Indeed it is.

REVIEW

1. What are some ways of adding variety to sweet and Danish dough products?

2. Once top-quality consumer-accepted ingredients have been selected, what is the next important step in making a basic sweet dough?

3. Should sweet yeast doughs be given more or less fermentation than bread and roll doughs?

4. What should be the temperature and relative humidity range for proofing sweet yeast doughs?

5. How should sweet yeast dough products be baked?

6. Why is it recommended that all sweet yeast dough products be glazed as they come from the oven?

7. How does the mixing of Danish pastry doughs differ from that of basic sweet dough?

8. What is the principal difference between Danish and puff pastry?

9. How long should Danish be allowed to rest before make up?

CHAPTER 19

CAKE BAKING

I. CAKEMAKING

II. MIXING

   A. Creaming Method

   B. Two-stage Method

   C. Sponge or Foam-type Mix

III. CAKE MIXES

IV. THE MECHANICS OF CAKE BAKING

However inspired, no written definition of the word *cake* could approximate the glories of sweetened batter, baked, filled, frosted, and made ravishing with edible decorations. Such creations can bring happiness to both our childhood and mature years, for few, if any, people are immune to their charm, and memories of them can lighten the dark corners of life.

The word *cake* comes to us from Middle English and may have had earlier origins in Old Norse. From the earliest days of civilization, people have always considered cake a food for the gods as well as for themselves. The Egyptians made cakes in animal, bird, and human forms for their various gods. Greeks offered honey cakes to their gods, and in the north honey cakes were offered to Thor at the winter solstice to ensure a fruitful year to come.

Few pleasures are greater than turning out a perfect cake. And perfect cakes can be achieved by any cook who is careful and willing to follow recipe directions. Cakemaking is an exact process; the ingredients and their relations to each other are balanced like a chemical formula; in fact, during the baking, a chemical process takes place, transforming the raw ingredients into a delicious new entity.

There are two main classifications of cakes in American fare: those made with fat and those made without.

I. CAKEMAKING

Careful weighing of the ingredients is absolutely essential to obtain uniform results in cakemaking. Every bakeshop must provide a suitable scale, equipped to weigh from fractions of ounces up to several pounds, to permit accurate scaling of ingredients, particularly leavening agents and flavors. Accurate scaling prevents the products from fluctuating from day to day.

II. MIXING

The mixing procedure plays a very important part in good cakemaking, and extreme care should be taken in the handling and mixing of the cake batter. Each type of cake batter should be mixed in accordance with a specific formula, and every phase of the mixing methods carefully observed.

There are three primary ways to mix cake batters: creaming method, two-stage method, and sponge or foam type.

A. Creaming Method

1. Scale all ingredients carefully and keep all of them at room temperature.
2. Sugar, shortening or butter, salt, flavors, and spices are generally creamed together.
3. Add the required amount of eggs gradually in several small portions and continue to cream.
4. Next add liquids—milk or water as directed—gradually and carefully. It is advisable to add only a portion of the milk alternately with the flour in some batters.
5. Add sifted baking powder and flour, and mix until a smooth mixture is obtained.

Throughout the entire mixing process, the sides of the bowl should be scraped down occasionally to ensure a uniform batter.

B. Two-stage Method

1. Scale all ingredients carefully, and have all at room temperature.
2. Place all dry ingredients, such as flour, sugar, spices, baking powder, and salt, in mixing bowl, along with the shortening; add part of the milk; and mix at a slow speed for required amount of time.
3. Take the balance of the milk, beat slightly with the required amount of

egg, and then add this to the above mixture in approximately three parts, scraping the sides of the bowl at intervals while doing so to ensure a smooth batter.

C. Sponge or Foam-type Mix

1. Scale all ingredients carefully, and have all at room temperature.
2. Warm eggs and sugar to approximately 100°F to dissolve the sugar, and then continue to beat until the maximum point is reached.
3. Fold in flour just enough to ensure uniformity.

As we mentioned before, there are variations to these basic methods, and every formula for cakemaking should include complete mixing methods.

III. CAKE MIXES

These are, and will be, increasingly important, as there will be more and more of this type of product on the market. Mixes eliminate the weighing of ingredients and reduce time and a large part of the work involved in cake-making.

1. What is a cake? The ancient Romans served a kind of cake at their wedding meals, a sweetened white bread. Today, we think of a cake as a baked product made using cake flour (made from soft wheat and relatively low in protein), water, and *much* sugar. The batter made from this mixture usually has eggs, some shortening and leavening, salt and flavoring, and perhaps milk powder added to it. Baking powder is usually added as a leavening agent.

   Is a griddle cake a cake?

   Not according to our definition. It has very little sugar.

   Not exactly. It is yeast leavened and is usually made with little or no cake flour. A "sweet dough."

2. Is coffee cake a cake?

CAKE INGREDIENTS AND THEIR FUNCTIONS

Main Functions in Finished Products

Ingredients	Binding agent	Absorbing agent	Aids keeping qualities	Affects eating qualities	Nutritional value	Affects flavor	Adds sweetness	Produces tenderness	Affects symmetry	Imparts crust color	Shortness or tenderness	Eating qualities	Color	Volume	Structure	Grain and texture	Adds quality to product	Brings out flavor
Cake flour	X	X	X	X	X													
Sugar		X	X	X		X	X	X	X	X			X					
Shortening and butter		X	X	X	X						X	X				X		
Salt																	X	
Eggs, whole or yolks				X	X													
Egg whites														X	X			
Flavor and spices																	X	
Leavening agent								X						X	X			
Milk				X											X	X	X	

Figure 19–1 *Reprinted with permission of the publisher from J. Amendola, The Baker's Manual for Quantity Baking and Pastry Making, 2d edition. Copyright 1956 and 1960 by Ahrens Publishing Company, Inc.*

ORDINARY CAKE FAULTS AND THEIR CAUSES

Faults \ Causes	Improper mixing	Batter too stiff	Too much leavening agent	Not enough leavening agent	Batter too slack	Too much heat	Not enough heat	Excessive sugar	Not enough sugar	Improper type of flour	Too much flour	Not enough flour	Cakes scaled too light	Aged baking powder	Over baking	Under baking	Sugar too coarse	Not enough eggs	Fruit not drained right	Not enough shortening	Unbalanced formula	Batter too warm	Not enough liquid
External																							
Crust too dark						X		X															
Cakes too small			X		X	X			X				X							X	X		
Specks on cake																						X	
Shrinkage of cakes	X	X		X										X									
Cake falls during baking												X			X								
Cakes burst on top	X	X			X	X			X	X	X												
Crust too thick							X																
Internal																							
Coarse and irregular grain	X	X	X			X											X			X			
Dense grain			X	X					X											X			
Poor flavor		X																		X			
Cake tough								X	X	X													X
Lack of body in quality	X	X		X		X		X									X			X	X		
Sinking of fruit		X		X					X									X	X	X			
Poor keeping qualities					X				X								X			X	X		

Figure 19–2 Reprinted with permission of the publisher from J. Amendola, The Baker's Manual for Quantity Baking and Pastry Making, 2d edition. Copyright 1956 and 1960 by Ahrens Publishing Company, Inc.

3. A cake is a tender product. Tenderness results partly from the use of cake flour but chiefly from the addition of shortening and sugar.

The use of an oil (or liquid shortening) makes for a more tender cake than the use of a plastic fat. Can you guess why?

When the cake cools, the plastic fat tends to firm. It is not quite as tender as when oil is used.

4. Emulsifier-type shortenings give results superior to other fats in cake baking. These hydrogenated fats include mono- and diglycerides added to give spread to the fat in the batter. The mono- and diglycerides increase the emulsifying property of the fat in the cake batter and produce larger volume, finer grain, improved texture, and tenderness.

Emulsifiers in cake shortenings have what effect?

They spread the shortening out into finer globules, giving a smoother batter and improved texture. Higher ratios of fat and sugar can also be used.

5. The reason shortening tenderizes the cake is that the fat or oil surrounds the gluten strands and "shortens" or untoughens them. The shortening produces a "short break," which means that the crumb breaks clean and does not have to be cut or sheared as when gluten strands are present.

An angel food cake contains no fat whatsoever. Would you expect the crumb to have a short break (break sharply and easily)?

No. It is relatively hard to slice an angel food cake, but the cake is still tender enough to eat because of the egg.

6. Cakes can be classified into:
  1. Fat-type cakes
     a. pound
     b. layer
     c. cup
     d. sheet

  2. Foam-type cakes
     a. angel food
     b. chiffon
     c. sponge
     d. California cheesecake

Fat-type cakes usually include baking powder as a leavening agent. Foam-type cakes do not include baking powder; leavening is achieved by the air whipped into the eggs used.

Fat-type cakes include _____; foam types do not.

Baking powder.

7. Fat-type cakes are developed from batter, which is of the oil-in-water type attained by proper mixing. Creamed into the center of each droplet of fat or oil is a tiny air cell, which acts as a nucleus to pick up leavening gases when they are loosed in the oven by the heat. These cells further expand by as much as 80% when joined by water vapors formed by the heat of the oven.

In the case of pound cakes, enough air volume is initially creamed in so that no baking powder at all is necessary. It is expanded totally by oven-generated water vapor. However, most commercial pound cakes, because they are "leaner" in composition (less fat and eggs), utilize a boost from a greatly reduced "dose" of baking powder.

True or false: Fat-type cakes rely completely on baking powder for their leavening action.

False. Only part of the leavening is a result of the CO_2 formed by the baking powder.

8. Rules governing the formulation of fat-type cakes are simple:
1. The sugar should exceed the flour.
2. The liquid (combined water or liquid milk) and eggs should exceed the sugar.
3. The eggs should exceed the shortening.

Fat-type cakes—pound, layer, cup, and sheet—include shortening, sugar, and eggs. Should they include more or less sugar than flour?

More.

9. Do fat-type cakes include more or less eggs than shortening?

More.

10. In fat-type cakes should there be more or less liquid than sugar?

More.

11. Cakes are made using cake flour made from a soft wheat and relatively low in protein. Can cake flour be leavened by yeast action?

No. The flour is not "strong" enough to support the yeast action. There is not enough gluten to contain the vigorous gas formation from the yeast.

12. Leavening action in cakes results from creaming fat and sugar together, from baking powder action, or from air trapped in beaten _____.

Eggs.

13. Cakes rise because gases in the batter expand when heated. The enlarged bubbles stretch the protein present. During baking, the heat sets the protein and we have a large-volume cake. What gas is involved in the leavening of angel food cakes and pound cakes?

Air.

14. In chemically leavened cakes, what gas besides air is involved?

Carbon dioxide.

15. The volume of many cakes depends largely upon the volume obtained in creaming the shortening, sugar, and eggs. Use shortening that produces good creaming volume. For maximum creaming quality, the shortening should be at about 75°F. Higher temperatures reduce creaming quality. Batter temperatures should be 68 to 72°F.

   Two parts of sugar and one part of shortening result in maximum creaming volume.

   Fine granulated sugar is best.

   Creaming should be done at lower speeds unless the temperature of the fat is below 70°F. Using a higher speed heats up the fat.

   It sometimes takes 8 to 10 minutes to incorporate the maximum amount of air.

   A major purpose of creaming is to _____ the volume of the cake.

Increase.

16. The creaming process may take as long as ____ minutes to attain maximum volume.

8 to 10.

17. Unless the percentage of shortening and eggs is high, 1 oz of baking powder to each pound of flour is used. If a cake formula is low in shortening and eggs, will more or less leavening agent be needed?

More.

18. In mixing eggs and sugar, do you think the size of the bowl has any connection with the amount of creaming action?

The bowl must be large enough to allow maximum incorporation of air. About 3½ lb of eggs and sugar require a 10-quart bowl.

19. Another way of classifying cakes is according to the amount of fat contained in the cake. The old-fashioned pound cake is the richest in fat, containing 80 lb of fat to 100 lb of flour.

The angel food cake, however, contains no fat at all.

Without fat, how can the angel food cake be tender?

The protein filaments are stretched very thinly. Even so, extreme care must be exercised in making angel food cake to prevent its becoming tough.

20. The old-fashioned sponge cake contains no added fat and for this reason dries out quickly. Sponge cake contains some fat because whole eggs are used and egg yolks contain about one-third fat.

Would you develop tenderness in a sponge cake by adding some fat?

Yes.

21. Chiffon cakes are leavened by beaten eggs and some baking powder. They contain oil instead of fat. The large quantity of beaten eggs used gives them the characteristic of sponge cakes. The beaten eggs are folded into the batter at the end of the mixing period so that the eggs will attain volume for leavening.

Would you grease the pans used for baking chiffon cakes?

No, for the same reason that angel food and sponge cake pans are not greased.

22. Cakes can be divided into those that depend upon creaming, those that depend on baking powder, and those that depend upon _____ for their lightness.

Beaten eggs.

23. The precise baker uses different flours for different cakes. The heavy pound cake can use a fairly strong cake flour to advantage.

Cakes leavened with baking powder require flour not quite as strong.

Cakes leavened with beaten eggs use a very soft flour.

If a strong flour were used in a sponge or angel food cake, would the cake tend to be tough or tender?

Tough.

24. Cakes fail—that is, do not achieve their optimal size, appearance, and texture—for a number of reasons. Obviously, if the formula is incorrect— if there is too much baking powder, too much sugar, or too much or too little of any ingredient—the cake *fails*. Excessive baking powder, for example, produces a cake with a coarse grain that dries out rapidly. A pocket forms in the bottom of the cake if there is too much milk. The flour may be too strong or too weak for the cake desired. A cake peaks in the center if there is too little baking powder, too many eggs, or too high a bottom (oven) heat. Too little liquid causes it to "dip."

Aside from an improper formula and the wrong quantities of ingredients, the two principal reasons for failures are the mixing procedure and the control of the heat in the oven.

Three principal reasons for cake failures are improper amount of ingredients, _____, and _____.

Improper creaming.
Improper heat control.

25. If too much air is incorporated into the batter, the cake may dip in the center. The grain is very compact and the cells small.

A baked cake may peak in the center if too many eggs or too much milk is used, or if there is not enough sugar or baking powder.

Another reason for a cake peaking in the center is that the oven has been too hot. Check the bottom of the cake to see if it is overly brown.

Cakes that peak in the center may have the wrong ingredients in them, or the peaking may have been caused by _____.

An oven that is too hot.

26. Cakes can be too tender, falling apart when they are picked up. This can be caused by too much baking powder or sugar, not enough eggs, or improper mixing.

Another reason for excessively tender cakes is that the oven temperature has been too low.

If a cake has too much fat or sugar or if the oven temperature has been too low, the cake is likely to be _____.

Overly tender.

27. Another reason for cake failure is shrinkage; that is, the cake pulls away from the sides of the pan and drops.

Shrinkage can be caused by using too much milk (water) or fat. Another reason for shrinkage is that the oven is too hot. An excessively hot oven causes cracks on the top and a dark bottom crust.

If the oven temperature is too high, the cake is likely to crack on the top, be overly browned on the bottom, and _____.

Shrink.

28. Some ingredients are thought of as tougheners, others as tenderizers. Flour and eggs are structure builders and tougheners. Shortening and sugar are tenderizers.

Therefore, to get a chewy loaf of bread, would you include much, little, or no shortening?

Little or no.

29. To achieve a tender cake, you would include flour that has developed a minimum amount of gluten and include sugar and _____.

Shortening.

30. Most baked items are leavened. A gas such as air, steam, or carbon dioxide expands the dough or batter to produce a larger volume. Doughs are usually expanded by carbon dioxide, which is produced by the splitting of the sugar by the yeast present. Cakes are usually leavened by the use of baking powder, which releases carbon dioxide when mixed with water and in the presence of heat. Baking soda and an acid also release carbon dioxide to produce leavening.

Should the baker know something about what takes place when a dough, batter, or paste is leavened?

Indeed yes. Bakers do not have to be food chemists, but they should know how to control the leavening action.

31. Sugar is added to dough to make sweet doughs. It is added to cakes to add sweetness and to make the crumb more tender. In yeast products, some of the sugar serves as food for the yeast. Some of the sugar is split so that part of it becomes carbon dioxide gas, which leavens the dough. Most of us think of sugar as being only the sucrose we use on the table from cane or sugar beets. However, there are other sugars. Sucrose itself can be split (hydrolyzed) into simpler forms of sugar known as glucose and fructose. Sugars vary in the degree of sweetness that we experience when we eat them. Some sugars, especially those high in invert sugar, hold water better than others; honey, for example.

What ingredient in baked products is split to form carbon dioxide and alcohol?

Sugar.

IV. THE MECHANICS OF CAKE BAKING

32. The mechanics of mixing a cake are important to the final product. If the batter is beaten too long, what happens to the cake?

Excessive gluten is developed and bready texture results.

33. Only the bottoms of cake pans are greased and for a very good reason. The ungreased sides permit the cake to cling to the sides, thereby reducing the chances of the cake falling. The baker's brush is usually used to grease the bottom of the pan.

In baking sheet cakes, fill the pan only half or not more than two-thirds full.

Why not grease the sides of the cake pan?

The cake needs to cling to the sides of the pan for support.

34. Cakes are done when they spring back when touched lightly or when they have pulled away from the sides of the pan. The volume of the cake and the color of the top of the cake are also indicators of doneness.

Is it a good idea to open the oven door from time to time to check on the doneness of the cake?

No. Each time the door is opened the temperature drops sharply.

35. Fast heat penetration is desired in cake baking. What kind of metal pan would be best for baking cake: one made of iron with a dull finish or a bright aluminum pan?

The dull iron one absorbs and transmits heat faster and more effectively than the pan with a shiny surface. Dull pans result in faster browning.

36. Is it reasonable to suggest placing cakes in an oven so that the pans do not touch the sides of the oven or are located directly over one another?

Yes. Allow free air circulation around the pans. If they touch each other or the sides of the oven, the rate of heat transfer is increased where they touch.

37. In that a warm, freshly baked cake breaks easily if handled, would it be wise to allow the cake to cool before removing it from the pan?

Yes. It is recommended that cakes be allowed to cool to 140°F. This may take a long time. At least let them cool for 10 to 15 minutes so that their centers are partially cooled.

38. A sheet cake, baked as a large unit, retains its moisture and freshness longer than the same amount of cake made in smaller units. The smaller units have proportionately more surface area exposed to the air. The sheets can be baked and stored and then cut into a variety of squares, bars, and other shapes.

　　True or false: Sheet cakes are less likely to dry out than smaller cakes.

True, because of the proportionately smaller surface exposure.

REVIEW

1. Cake is a flour and water mixture that always contains much of what other ingredient?

2. Whereas bread products are leavened by the use of yeast, most cakes are leavened by the use of _____.

3. Angel food cake has no leavening agent added, to it; leavening is effected by the action of _____.

4. Which type of cake—fat type or foam type—uses baking powder as a leavening agent?

5. In cakes, is there more sugar or more flour?

6. What would happen to a cake leavened by yeast action?

7. When fat and sugar are creamed together, air is incorporated into the mixture. What happens to this air when the product is baked?

8. If we use a high speed for creaming sugar and fat, what is likely to happen?

9. At what temperature should sugar and fat be for best creaming action?

10. For maximum creaming volume, we want one part of shortening to _____ parts of sugar.

11. Which two ingredients used in baking are tougheners and structure builders?

12. Flour is also a bulk builder. What is another bulk builder in baking?

13. Certain bakery ingredients are thought of as tenderizing agents: sugar, shortening, and the _____ agent.

14. What is the only bakery ingredient thought of as a lubricant?

15. What type of flour—all-purpose, pastry, or bread—is likely to be found in the home?

16. Shortening is fat used in baking. What effect does it have on the gluten?

17. In using bakers' percentages, the formula is always computed as a percentage of the weight of which ingredient?

18. How much shortening is used in an angel food cake?

19. Cakes get their volume and lightness with the action of baking powder, creaming, or the use of _____.

20. What type of flour would you want to use for a sponge cake?

21. Would a pound cake, which is the richest in fat, need a stronger or a weaker flour than a foam-type cake?

22. If a cake peaks in the center when baking, it may be caused by too little baking powder, too many eggs, or _____.

23. What causes a cake to dip in the middle?

24. If excessive baking powder is used, the cake will dry out too rapidly. Will it have a coarse or fine grain?

25. If too much air is incorporated into the batter of a baked cake, will it peak or dip in the center?

26. Would a baked cake peak in the center if there is too much or too little baking powder?

27. Some of the reasons for an excessively tender cake are that the oven temperature is too low or that it contains too much fat or _____.

28. Cake that is cracked on the top, brown on the bottom, and shrinks away from the pan has likely been cooked in an oven that is _____.

29. Does overmixing a batter, which develops too much gluten, result in a tender or tough cake?

30. When mixed with water, does baking powder release carbon dioxide in the presence of an alkali or an acid?

31. To get a moist cake, we might include what type of sugar?

32. When baking, a cake forms a new, larger structure, supported by gelatinized starch and _____.

33. Does the recipe for chiffon cake call for hydrogenated shortening or oil?

34. The tube in the middle of an angel food cake pan serves to pass heat quickly into the batter and to _____.

35. Cake should be allowed to cool before handling; otherwise it is likely to _____.

36. What happens to a cake that is mixed too long?

CHAPTER 20

CAKE FROSTINGS, FILLINGS, AND GLAZES

I. FROSTING

II. FILLING

III. GLAZE

IV. ICING

    A. Fondant

    B. Buttercream

    C. Fudge

    D. Flat

    E. Boiled

    F. Marshmallow

    G. Royal

These sweet decorative coatings are placed between layers or over the tops and sides of the cake to add to the flavor and appearance.

I. FROSTING

Frosting and *icing* mean the same thing. Frostings are both cooked and uncooked.

Cooked frostings, such as white mountain frosting, are made by beating a hot sugar syrup into beaten egg whites. Another method is to cook sugar, butter, and liquid into a candylike frosting, such as in fudge frosting.

Uncooked frostings, such as butter frosting, are made by beating together butter, some liquid, flavoring, and confectioners' sugar. Decorators' frosting is made by beating egg whites with confectioners' sugar.

II. FILLING

Cooked fillings include liquid or fruit thickened with cornstarch, egg, or flour, such as cream filling or pineapple filling.

Uncooked fillings include those made with whipped cream, chopped fruit, jelly, or instant pudding.

III. GLAZE

A glaze is a thin, glossy coating with a firm consistency. It can be cooked or uncooked. Some are baked or broiled onto cakes; others are spread on hot cakes.

IV. ICING

Attractive icings promote the sale of cakes. They have other important functions:

1. Icings improve the keeping quality of cakes.
2. Icings form a protective coating around the cake, trapping in the moisture.
3. Icings improve the taste of the cake and make a most attractive item for sales and eye appeal.

Proper combinations of flavors are imperative. Use only the very best quality of flavoring. There is no saving in poor or cheap flavoring, as it destroys the quality of the entire product.

Use fresh fruit when obtainable for fruit icings.

Be careful not to use food colors in too lavish a manner, which will result in dark icings that are not attractive. Delicate pastel colorings enhance the eye appeal of the icing; too much color destroys the product. Study color combinations carefully and test them out for delicacy. Err on the side of too pale rather than too heavy coloring.

There are seven basic icings:

1. Fondant
2. Buttercream
3. Fudge
4. Flat
5. Boiled
6. Marshmallow
7. Royal

A. Fondant

Fondant icing is a syrup of glucose, sugar, and water cooked to 240°F, then cooled to approximately 110°F, and worked quickly until it is creamy, white, and smooth.

Fondant is a somewhat difficult icing to make and, when required in quantity, it has become customary to purchase a uniform fondant icing from a bakers' supply house. Store the prepared fondant in containers, covering them with a damp cloth or with a small amount of water over the icing to prevent drying out.

When ready to use the fondant icing, take the desired quantity and heat it over a warm bath, stirring constantly, to blood heat (98°F to 100°F). This process thins down the icing and causes it to flow freely.

If the icing is still heavy, a simple syrup may be used to thin it a little more. Fondant icing may be flavored or colored as desired and is used primarily for pouring and dipping.

Do not heat fondant icing above 100°F. It loses its glossiness and creates a dull finish for the product. Fondant may be used as a base for other icings such as buttercream by creaming the butter or shortening with the fondant to create fluffier icings.

B. Buttercream

Buttercream is made by creaming the icing sugar, butter or shortening, and eggs, which are added to give the icing the desired consistency. The amount of creaming depends upon the lightness required in the finished product. Buttercream may be colored and flavored as desired. When not in use, store this icing in a cool place with a waxed paper covering. Buttercream is generally used for layer cakes and decorated cakes.

C. Fudge

Fudge icing requires cooking the sugar into a syrup in order to obtain the smoothness required in the finished icing. When the hot syrup is added to the balance of the ingredients in the formula, it creates a rather heavy body. Before applying the icing to the cake, fudge icing should be heated slightly in a water bath. When fudge icing is not in use, it should be properly stored and covered to prevent spoilage and drying. Fudge icing is generally used on cupcakes and layer cakes.

D. Flat

Flat icing or plain water icing is a simple icing. Mix well all basic ingredients—water, icing sugar, corn syrup, and flavor. Before applying flat icing to coffee cake or danish pastry, heat it to 100°F and apply by hand or pastry brush to the product. Flat icing is usually white and flavored with vanilla or lemon. Coloring may be used, but very sparingly. Store icing properly when not in use and be sure to keep it covered.

E. Boiled

To make boiled icing, cook a syrup of sugar, water, and glucose. Add to beaten eggs while hot. Heavier syrup produces a heavier icing. Thinner icing is produced by thinner syrup. This icing should be applied generously and left in peaks on the cake. Boiled icing breaks down if stored overnight and should be made only in needed amounts each time.

F. Marshmallow

Marshmallow icing is a variation of boiled icing that has a stabilizer, usually gelatin and confectioners' sugar, added to it. It is applied in the same manner as boiled icing.

G. Royal

Royal or decorating icing is a fairly simple icing to make. Beat together icing sugar, egg whites, and an acid agent until a smooth consistency is obtained. Royal icing is used primarily for decorating and flower making. It is often used to make cake "dummies." It is seldom used on stable cakes as it tends to become hard and brittle. Royal icing can be colored as desired and should be covered with a damp cloth when not in use.

1. Cakes are coated with frostings or icings to enhance appearance, to extend the shelf life by forming a protective coating, and to hold in the moisture and increase the flavor of the cake.

   Frostings or icings are divided into cooked and uncooked categories. A buttercream frosting, for example, is made by merely beating together butter (shortening), some liquid flavoring, and confectioners' (powdered) sugar of the ultrafine type (confectioners' 10X).

   Why should we coat cakes with frosting?

   To enhance appearance, to extend shelf life, and to increase the flavor.

2. Decorating frosting is made by beating egg whites with confectioners' sugar.

   Why confectioners' sugar?

   Confectioners' sugar is ground into tiny particle size and will not be tasted as granular (will not be gritty).

3. Fondant icing is a syrup of glucose, granulated sugar, and water cooked at 240°F, cooled to about 110°F, and worked quickly until it is creamy, white, and smooth.

   The rate of formation of the sugar crystals in the fondant determines whether the fondant is smooth and free of a gritty or grainy texture (large sugar crystals).

   A fondant is a creamy mixture of granulated sugar, glucose, and water. Are the sugar crystals tiny or large?

   Tiny.

4. Fondant can be purchased already made.

   Would it be wise for the bakeshop to purchase prepared fondant?

   Most of the larger shops do because of the time involved in making fondant and the possibility of large sugar crystals forming in it if made in the shop.

5. Icings can be divided into those that are cooked and those that are uncooked. Fondants, fudge, boiled, and marshmallow icings are cooked.

   Buttercream, flat or plain, and royal or decorating icings are uncooked.

The simplest icing is flat or plain icing, which is merely a mixture of water, sugar, corn syrup, and flavoring. It is heated to 100°F so that the sugar goes into solution and the icing can be applied by hand or with a pastry brush.

Royal or decorating icing is used primarily for decorating and flower making. It tends to become hard and brittle.

All icings are basically sugar and water, sometimes with egg whites. Buttercream is the only icing to which an appreciable amount of fat is added.

Icings are applied to cake to add flavor and enhance the appearance. What other important function does an icing perform for a cake?

It holds in the moisture and extends the shelf life of the cake.

6. Frostings, icings, and glazes are sugar and water mixtures, some of which have egg whites added to them. The purposes of these coatings are to add flavor, enhance the appearance, and help hold in the moisture of the cake.

Would you expect a frosted cake to be moister than an unfrosted one?

Yes. The frosting helps to keep the cake from drying out.

7. In some types of boiled icings, gelatin and egg whites are added to impart body and structure to the icing.

Glucose, invert sugar, and malt syrup are also sometimes added because they are moisture-retaining agents that aid in keeping the icing soft and fresh. Another reason for adding invert sugar is that it interferes with the formation of large sugar crystals and produces a smoother icing.

To keep an icing moist, malt syrup, invert sugar, or _____ may be added.

Glucose (a form of sugar).

8. In damp weather, icings that ordinarily would have a dry surface may become sticky. To overcome this, a small amount of flour or other drying agents, such as dried milk or gelatin, is added.

Sometimes moisture-retaining ingredients are added to a boiled icing; at other times drying agents such as flour, gelatin, or _____ may be added.

Dried milk.

9. To get a soft, glossy surface on the icing, from 5% to 25% of the amount of sugar used in the icing may be added in the form of shortening. The fat particles help disperse the tiny sugar crystals and produce a smooth, light icing.

Various ingredients are added to icings for particular purposes. Gelatin and egg whites give the icing more body. Glucose, invert sugar, and malt syrup keep the icing moist. To dry out icing, flour, dried milk, and gelatin may be added.

What is likely to be added to make a very smooth, flat icing?

Shortening, 5% to 25% of the amount of sugar used.

10. Creamed icings made by whipping air into fat and sugar have considerable bulk and increase the volume of the cake. Adding beaten eggs also increases the volume and the foamy character of the icing.

What is it that gives a creamed icing its volume?

The air that has been whipped into the mixture makes it lighter and fluffier.

11. A further word about the sugars used in baking, especially those used in icings: The usual household sugar is sucrose made from sugar beets or sugar cane.

Molasses is also sucrose, but it contains 20% to 25% water, 2% to 5% mineral matter, and 15% to 30% invert sugar.

Invert sugar occurs naturally in honey and molasses, and it can be made by the action of an acid or an enzyme, invertase, acting on sucrose.

The usual granulated sugar that is used in the bakeshop is _____.

Sucrose.

12. Invert sugar, relatively new to the bakeshop, has certain advantages over sucrose, the ordinary granulated sugar. It has a remarkable ability to hold or retain moisture. Because of this fact it

delays the staling of cake or other baked goods, which have a tendency to dry out too rapidly.

Invert sugar helps prevent the formation of large sugar crystals, which are experienced as graininess. In this way it promotes a desirable smoothness in many icings.

Invert sugar is sweeter to the taste than sucrose.

Invert sugar helps produce a rich brown color on the crust of baked products.

Invert sugar used in icings prolongs the freshness and adds smoothness. Is it just as sweet as or sweeter than sucrose?

Sweeter than (about 130% as sweet).

13. Commercial glucose, more commonly known as *corn syrup*, also has the ability to hold moisture and helps produce a glossy surface on the icing. Like invert sugar, commercial glucose also prevents formation of large crystals of sugar and graininess.

The addition of shortening, egg whites, or invert sugar to a sugar–water mixture interferes with the formation of large sugar crystals and prevents graininess. What other sugar does the same thing?

Corn syrup.

REVIEW

1. Volume in an icing is created by the _____ action.

2. Besides adding invert sugar to an icing to produce a smooth, light icing, what other ingredients might be added?

3. Is fondant icing a cooked or uncooked icing?

4. Is a buttercream frosting cooked or uncooked?

5. Flat or plain icing is a mixture of water, sugar, flavoring, and _____.

6. What type of sugar would be added to an icing recipe to help retain the moisture in the icing?

7. Besides retaining moisture, does invert sugar help produce a smooth or coarse icing?

8. Which is sweeter: invert sugar or sucrose?

CHAPTER 21

COOKIES

I. WHAT ARE COOKIES?

At one time, what we now call a *cookie* was referred to as a *small cake* or *sweet biscuit.* We must thank the Dutch for providing us with a special name for it. It is derived from *koekje* or *koekie,* meaning a "small cake." The word *cookie* is an American usage; in England what we know as cookies are called *biscuits.*

There are more varieties of cookies than of any other baked product because there are so many different shapes, sizes, textures, and flavorings possible. To the basic ingredients, often the same as those used in cakes, all kinds of flavorings may be added: extracts, spices, nuts, and fruits. Decorations of every sort are always in order.

Cookies are usually classified according to the way in which the dough is shaped. The six classifications are bars and squares, drop cookies, rolled cookies, spritzed or bagged cookies, sheet cookies, and ice box or refrigerator cookies. Bar and drop cookies are made with soft dough that has a comparatively high percentage of liquid. The other varieties call for stiff dough, usually less sweet and often higher in fat content than soft dough.

Cookies are one of the most profitable items produced by bakers. A most important factor in their production is the use of high-grade ingredients. Butter is the preferred shortening in making cookies. Careful selection of the purest of spices, molasses, and flavorings assures delicious cookies.

Cookies should be baked fresh daily if possible. When it is necessary to bake ahead, a week's output can be prepared in advance and properly stored.

Flour used for cookies is typically of the long patent or straight grade, with a protein content of 9% to 10%. The flour usually comes from soft white or soft red wheat varieties. Chlorinated flour is used for those cookies where less spread of the cookie is desired. Higher levels of chlorination result in less *spread* (the cookies are smaller in diameter and thicker).

1. Chlorination of cookie flour makes more or less spread in the baked cookie?	Less spread.
2. The cookie baker must find a balance of ingredients that will give the desired structure and tenderness. Which of these ingredients provide strength and structure: eggs, flour, sugar, shortenings, starch?	The eggs and flour are strengtheners. Sugar, shortening, and starch are tenderizers.
3. Would you expect a cookie batter rich in sugar and fat to produce more or less spread than a cookie batter rich in eggs and made with a high-protein flour?	Eggs and the high-protein flour will result in less spread because both are strengtheners that restrict spread.

II. COOKIE MIXING METHODS

A. The One-stage Method

1. Place all the ingredients into a mixing bowl and mix until all are smoothly blended.
2. Allow 2 or 3 minutes at low speed for the mixing.

B. The Creaming Method

1. Place sugar, shortening or butter, salt, and spices in the mixing bowl and cream together.
2. Add the eggs and liquid.
3. Add last the flour and leavening agent.

III. TYPES OF COOKIES

A. Rolled

1. Roll on a flour bag; it is easier to handle if chilled first.
2. Roll out $1/8$-inch thick.
3. Cut in desired shape and size with a cookie cutter.
4. Place on baking sheets and bake.

B. Ice Box or Refrigerator

1. Scale dough at 1 lb, 8 oz, and roll into bars 18 inches long.
2. Roll onto waxed paper, and place rolls on sheet pans.
3. Refrigerate overnight.
4. Slice into $1/2$-inch strips and bake.

C. Spritz or Bagged

1. Put mixture into pastry bag with desired size and shape tube.
2. Press directly onto sheet pans.
3. Garnish with cherries, nuts, or other items and bake.

D. Bars and Squares

1. Scale the dough into 1-lb pieces, and roll out to the length of the sheet pan. Place on the sheet pans, leaving a space between the strips.
2. Place three strips on the pan.
3. Flatten with the fingers and shape into uniform 1-in. strips.
4. Egg wash and bake.

E. Sheet

1. Spread the cookie mixture onto sheet pans.
2. Wash or sprinkle with nuts, and bake.
3. Cool and cut into squares or oblongs.

F. Drop

1. Drop mixture onto sheet pans with a spoon or by hand.
2. Press or flatten out with a weight or special cookie die.
3. You can also cut a strip of dough into $1/2$-oz pieces.
4. If the dough is rich, it will spread by itself; do not press or flatten.

ORDINARY COOKIE FAULTS AND THEIR CAUSES

Faults \ Causes	Improper mix	Insufficient sugar	Too much sugar	Flour too strong	Too much flour	Insufficient leavening	Too much leavening	Too much baking soda	Not enough baking soda	Insufficient eggs	Too much shortening	Insufficient shortening	Over baked	Too low baking temperature	Too high baking temperature	Pan insufficiently greased	Dough too slack	Insufficient liquid	Poor quality ingredients	Unbalanced formula	Cookie pans unclean & uneven
Spreading	X							X						X			X				
Crumbly	X	X	X				X			X	X										
Tough	X		X	X	X																
Hard				X								X	X	X				X			
Dry				X	X							X	X	X				X			
Pale in color	X	X			X		X							X						X	
Lack of flavor																			X	X	
Sticking to pans	X		X													X					X
Sugary crust	X		X				X													X	
Lack of spread	X	X		X		X			X						X	X					

Figure 21–1 Reprinted with permission of the publisher from J. Amendola, The Baker's Manual for Quantity Baking and Pastry Making, 2d edition. Copyright 1956 and 1960 by Ahrens Publishing Company, Inc.

1. At one time, what we now call a *cookie* was referred to as a *small cake* or *sweet biscuit.* We must thank the Dutch for providing us with a special name for it. It is derived from *koekje* or *koekie,* meaning a "small cake." The word *cookie* is an American usage; in England what we know as cookies are called _____.

   Biscuits.

2. There are more varieties of cookies than any other baked product because there are so many different shapes, sizes, textures, and flavorings possible. To the basic ingredients, often the same as those used in cakes, all kinds of flavorings may be added: extracts, spices, nuts, and fruits. Decorations of every sort are always in order.

   Cookies are usually classified according to the way in which the dough is shaped. The six classifications are bars and squares, drop cookies, rolled cookies, pressed cookies, molded or shaped cookies, and refrigerator cookies. Bar and drop cookies are made with soft dough, which has a comparatively high percentage of liquid. The other varieties call for stiff dough, usually less sweet and often higher in fat content than soft dough.

   Name six classifications of cookies.

   Bars and squares, drop cookies, rolled cookies, pressed cookies, molded or shaped cookies, refrigerator cookies.

3. Cookies are one of the most profitable items produced by bakers. A most important factor in their production is the use of high-grade ingredients. Butter is the preferred shortening in making cookies. Careful selection of the purest of spices, molasses, and flavorings assures delicious cookies.

   _____ is the preferred shortening in making cookies.

   Butter.

4. Cookies should be baked fresh daily, if possible. When it is necessary to bake ahead, a week's output can be prepared in advance and properly stored.

   If possible, cookies should be baked _____.

   Fresh daily.

5. Cookies that are too crumbly may have insufficient eggs, too much leavening or sugar, or too much _____.   Shortening.

6. Excessive spread in cookies could be caused by a baking temperature that is too low, a dough that is too slack, too much sugar, or too much _____.   Baking soda.

REVIEW

1. What do the English call cookies?

2. What are six classifications of cookies?

3. In which classifications is a soft dough used?

4. What is the preferred shortening in making cookies?

5. Name the two cookie mixing methods.

6. Give two reasons why cookies may stick to the pans in which they are baked.

7. Lack of spread in cookies can be caused by too much flour or flour that is excessively strong. What are some other causes?

8. Give some reasons why cookies may be too hard.

CHAPTER 22

PUDDINGS AND CREAMS

I. WHAT ARE PUDDINGS?

II. SAUCES FOR PUDDINGS AND ICE
CREAMS

A. Cream Sauce

B. Fruit Sauce

C. Hard Sauce

III. PASTRY CREAMS OR CUSTARD CREAMS

IV. PASTRY CREAM (CRÈME PÂTISSERIE)

I. WHAT ARE PUDDINGS?

The word *pudding* is used to describe a wide variety of baked, boiled, or steamed soft foods, either savory or sweet, served hot or cold, as main dishes, side dishes, or desserts. *Pudding* is also another name for blood sausage.

The chief types of puddings are (1) unsweetened boiled or baked dishes, usually with a cereal base and a texture resembling custard, such as corn pudding; (2) sweetened boiled or baked dishes of a soft, spongy, or thick creamy consistency, such as chocolate pudding; and (3) suet-based or suet-custard dishes, such as plum pudding, which were originally boiled in a bag but are now often baked or steamed.

There seems to be no end to the variety of puddings, both savory and sweet. Puddings have had a long culinary history, and there has been time for cooks to develop all sorts of recipes. The name itself may be related to old Germanic words meaning "sausage" or "swollen." Certainly blood puddings such as haggis, that Scottish conglomeration Robert Burns called the "great chieftain o' the puddings race," are swollen. Also swollen and encased like a sausage are the early English "puddynges" of the 14th century. These were often suet crusted, such as the now popular steak-and-kidney pudding. Steamed within a bag or cloth in a huge kettle along with the rest of the dinner, they became swollen. The bag or cloth took the place of the sausage casing.

Sweet dessert puddings are relatively modern. Only when sugar became available in the late 18th and early 19th centuries did sweet puddings come into their own. The sweet puddings were of such great variety that Englishmen now often use the word to mean "dessert."

Americans inherit the English enjoyment of puddings. The early settlers of New England ate their puddings as a first course. It may have well been an Indian pudding, made with the cornmeal the Indians introduced to the colonists. The early Americans used native ingredients to build on the foundations of English pudding cookery. Hasty pudding, for instance, was quickly made in England with wheat flour. Here, where wheat flour was not available, the colonists used cornmeal or a mixture known as *rye 'n Injun*. Sweetened with maple sugar, the New England hasty pudding was and is a delight.

Today, in addition to the almost endless number of puddings to be made from scratch at home, there is available a wide variety of canned puddings and packaged pudding mixes.

Puddings are very popular, economical, and profitable. The careful preparation of puddings is imperative to obtain a good result. All too often puddings are prepared haphazardly, which results in a mediocre finished product. As in all good products, method and recipe go hand in hand, and an attractive manner of serving the item is also of importance.

There are five basic methods of preparing puddings:

1. Boiled
2. Baked
3. Chilled
4. Steamed
5. Soufflé

The boiled, baked, and chilled puddings are the most popular in commercial food operations.

The steamed pudding is generally served during the cold season as it tends to be heavy and is usually served with a hot sauce. This pudding can be served very attractively if care is taken with the final preparation.

The soufflé is adaptable to à la carte service. It must be made just before service to secure lightness and fluffiness, or it will become heavy and soggy. Thus, one can see that soufflés are not a good choice for the cafeteria.

II. SAUCES FOR PUDDINGS AND ICE CREAMS

There are three basic sauces from which a great many varieties may be made by the addition of various ingredients.

A. Cream Sauce

First and most popular is the cream sauce developed from milk, sugar, eggs or egg yolks, and water cooked to a very soft custard, flavored, and served either hot or cold.

B. Fruit Sauce

Fruit sauce is made from fruit or fruit juices, boiled with water and flavored. Lemon juice is then added and the whole reduced or thickened, as the case may be, with a small amount of starch, then cooked until it becomes a thin gel-like sauce.

C. Hard Sauce

Hard sauce consists of powdered sugar and butter creamed lightly, sometimes thinned down with cream or egg and flavored. Hard sauce is always served cold on hot puddings or apple dumplings.

III. PASTRY CREAMS OR CUSTARD CREAMS

Custard creams, milk custards, cream fillings, and the like must always be carefully made and handled, but precautions are especially important during the summer months. In many instances, alleged food poisoning attributed to various bakery cream products has been detrimental not only to the individual foodservice operation but also all quantity operations.

With the approach of warm weather, increased caution and care must be the watchword in the production and distribution of cream goods. Creams and custards are a perfect medium for bacteria contamination and growth.

1. Do not use wooden or composition containers for mixing or storing cream goods. (Never store in copper containers.)
2. Do not use hands for stirring. Hands must never come in contact with custard cream.
3. Do not use leftover custard creams.

4. Do not expose custard to shop dust; keep covered while cooling.
5. Do not cool slowly as creams become easily contaminated.
6. Do not use day-old or leftover cream puffs, éclairs, or other cream goods.

Many state health departments have passed laws and adopted regulations governing, the manufacture and sale of bakery goods. Some of these regulations prohibit the sale of cream goods for a defined period during the summer months; others require refrigeration.

Check your state and local food and health laws and protect yourself by following such laws as may be in force. If these laws are difficult to follow, it would definitely be to your advantage to discontinue the sale of cream goods during extremely hot weather.

1. It is important that all employees handling cream goods and custards are clean, tidy, and careful about their hygiene.
2. Use only metal containers that have been thoroughly sterilized for preparing and cooking.
3. Use sterile shallow pans plus refrigeration for quickly cooling custard.
4. Use a sterile wooden spoon or spatula for stirring. Also use a sterile filling machine for cream puffs and similar items.
5. Destroy leftover custard cream and day-old or leftover finished products.
6. Just because day-old creams have a pleasant, sweet, palatable taste does not mean that they are satisfactory; the various harmful bacteria do not always impart an unpleasant or distinguishable taste to the product.
7. If you run a takeout operation, educate customers to the fact that cream and custard items are perishable and that refrigeration in the home is necessary.

IV. PASTRY CREAM (CRÈME PÂTISSERIE)

Pastry cream is a cream filling that plays an important part in the making of many desserts. It is one of the basic necessities all students should know how to make, and it is very important that it should be made well.

Smoothness and flavor are especially important; therefore, great care should be taken during the mixing and boiling processes. The milk should be boiled with one-half of the sugar. The eggs or egg yolks should be well beaten with the rest of the sugar, flour, and cornstarch.

When the milk boils, a part of the milk should be mixed with the egg mixture. Then this milk–egg mixture should be mixed into the boiling milk.

These are then boiled together while you stir continuously with a whip to prevent the cream from burning or scorching and at the same time to ensure a thorough mixing and to obtain a smooth cream. Add butter and flavor last.

Caution: Never allow your sugar and eggs to stand without mixing. If you do, your sugar will curdle or burn the eggs, causing small, hard lumps to form. Then you will have to strain your mixture before using it, thus losing some of the value of the eggs and making the cream grainy instead of smooth.

1. Pudding is used to describe a wide variety of baked, boiled, or steamed soft foods, either savory or sweet, served hot or cold, as main dishes, side dishes, or desserts. *Pudding* is also another name for blood sausage.

   Puddings come in a wide variety, but they are all _____.

   Soft.

2. The chief types of pudding are unsweetened boiled or baked dishes, usually with a cereal base and a texture resembling custard, such as corn pudding; sweetened boiled or baked dishes of a soft, spongy, or thick creamy consistency, such as chocolate pudding; and suet-based or suet-custard dishes, such as plum pudding, which were originally boiled in a bag but are now often baked or steamed.

   Three chief types of puddings are: unsweetened, sweetened, and _____.

   Suet-based.

3. Sweet dessert puddings are relatively modern. It was only when sugar became widely available in the late 18th and early 19th centuries that sweet puddings came into their own. The sweet puddings were of such great variety that Englishmen now often use the word to mean "dessert."

   The availability of _____ was responsible for the popularity of sweet puddings.

   Sugar.

4. Puddings are very popular, economical, and profitable. The careful preparation of puddings is imperative to obtain a good result. All too often puddings are prepared haphazardly, which results in a medio-

cre finished product. As in all good products, method and recipe go hand in hand, and an attractive manner of serving the item is also of importance.

To obtain a good result, _____ is imperative. | Careful preparation.

5. The boiled, baked, and chilled puddings are the most popular in commercial food operations.

The three most popular puddings in commercial food operations are boiled, baked, and _____. | Chilled.

6. The steamed pudding is generally served during the cold season as it tends to be heavy and is usually served with a hot sauce. This pudding can be served very attractively if care is taken with the final preparation.

Steamed pudding is generally served during the _____ season. | Cold.

7. The soufflé is adaptable to à la carte service. It must be made just before service to secure lightness and fluffiness, or it is heavy and soggy. Thus one can see that soufflés are not a good choice for the cafeteria.

If not made just before service, a soufflé will become _____ and _____. | Heavy. Soggy.

8. There are three basic sauces from which a great many varieties may be made by the addition of various ingredients: cream sauce, fruit sauce, and hard sauce.

The three basic sauces are cream sauce, fruit sauce, and _____. | Hard sauce.

9. Custard creams, milk custards, cream fillings, and similar foods must always be carefully made and handled, but precautions are especially important during the summer months, as creams and custards are perfect media for bacterial contamination and growth.

Creams and custards are perfect media for _____ contamination and growth. | Bacterial.

10. Pastry cream is a cream filling that plays an important part in making many desserts. Smoothness and flavor are especially important; therefore, great care should be taken during the mixing and boiling processes.

To obtain smoothness and flavor, great care should be taken during the _____ and _____ processes.

Mixing. Boiling.

REVIEW

1. What are two requisites for making good puddings?

2. What are five basic puddings?

3. Which three are the most popular in commercial food operations?

4. Why are soufflés a poor choice for a cafeteria?

5. What are the three basic sauces for puddings and ice creams?

6. How is hard sauce always served?

7. Why must custard creams and the like be carefully made and handled, especially during the summer months?

8. Name five precautions to take in connection with cream goods.

9. In connection with the mixing process for pastry cream, why is it most important that sugar and eggs should never be allowed to stand without mixing?

CHAPTER 23

THE NUTRITIONAL VALUE
OF BAKED PRODUCTS

I. THE "HEALTHY" BAKED PRODUCT

II. COMPLETE PROTEINS

III. CHOLESTEROL AND SATURATED FATS

IV. HOW IS NUTRITIONAL VALUE
     MEASURED?

I. THE "HEALTHY" BAKED PRODUCT

Bakers are responding to consumers' increasing concerns about the amount of calories, carbohydrates, protein, total fat, saturated fat, cholesterol, sodium, and fiber each "serving" of a baked product contains. The U.S. Department of Agriculture handbook, 8-1 to 8-21, gives food values of portions of commonly used foods, such as a hamburger bun or a slice of cake. Several software programs contain databases of prepared foods and raw materials.

1. Would a baker be wise to hire a nutritional firm to make a nutritional analysis of a portion of a product the baker wishes to sell?

The cost would be prohibitive and it is unnecessary because the nutritional information is already available for nearly all of the ingredients used. For mixes and bases the supplier provides this information.

Some computer programs include an ingredients database of more than 6,000 foods, including gums, starches, oil fractions, and concentrates. One such program contains information on the comparison of polyunsaturated fat to saturated fat and the amounts of cholesterol present in some 2,500 food items. Another program lists 15 macronutrients, 18 vitamins, 18 amino acids, and 23 fatty acids present in 4,000 food items.

By reference to U.S. Department of Agriculture handbook, 8-1 to 8-21, or to computer nutrition databases. If the government publication does not include the specific information needed, there is a relatively inexpensive means of securing the information for specific bakery formulas. The Computerization Inc. telephone service, (800) 222–4458, reports the total nutrients per formula, nutrients per typical serving, the percent of the U.S. recommended daily allowance per serving, and nutrients per 100 grams. The answers for 20 nutrients, including vitamin and cholesterol content, come back the next day.

2. The Food and Drug Administration wants to make sure that all food labels are accurate and not misleading. A baker who wishes to produce products with reduced calories, cholesterol, fat, or sodium must be sure that the ingredient list is accurate and that the product is indeed as stated. How can this be done?

II. COMPLETE PROTEINS

Nutritionally, proteins must contain eight so-called essential amino acids, and they must be in balance for the protein to be most beneficial in the human diet. The nine essential amino acids are lysine, tryptophan, phenylalanine, leucine, isoleucine, threonine, methionine, and valine. Another amino acid, histidine, is essential for infants but not adult humans. Any protein that lacks one or more of these essential amino acids is partially deficient as a nutrient.

3. Could a protein contain all essential amino acids and still be an "incomplete" protein?

Yes. Wheat protein contains all needed amino acids but lacks sufficient lysine to be complete.

Even so, bread made of wheat flour is one of the best and least expensive food sources in much of the world. To make wheat flour even more nutritious, soy flour or isolated soy protein can be added to the flour; the soybean contains an abundance of lysine that improves the amino acid balance of wheat flour. When up to 3% of soy flour is added to wheat flour, it significantly increases the nutritional value of the flour. Adding nonfat dried milk and other milk products to wheat flour is another way of improving the amino acid balance and adding complete protein to the flour.

4. Bread, called in the Bible "the staff of life," can be nutritionally enriched by adding up to 3% of which kind of flour to the wheat flour?

Soy flour.

III. CHOLESTEROL AND SATURATED FATS

The two nutritional villains in foods—especially found in cakes, pies, and cookies—are cholesterol and saturated fats. Egg yolks, butter, lard, and whole milk contain large amounts of cholesterol. Animal fats such as butter and lard are also high in saturated fat. Coconut and palm oil contain 49% to 86% saturated fats and should also be avoided in producing "healthy" bakery products.

It is quite possible to produce high-quality baked items by using ingredients without cholesterol and large amounts of saturated fats. Nonfat milk products are used instead of whole milk; egg whites replace egg yolks. Modified starches, gums, and sweetener substitutes have enabled bakers to produce a variety of products with reduced calories and cholesterol that have taste and mouth feel similar to products rich in fat and calories.

According to the Food and Drug Administration definitions, some fat can be included in "fat-free" products. If the product contains less than 0.5 grams of fat per serving, it can be labeled with 0 grams fat and be called *fat-free*. Products with fewer than 2 grams per serving are considered "low-fat."

Health authorities urge consumers to restrict their consumption of fat to 30% of total calories. Overweight people at risk for heart disease should reduce fat consumption even more.

The search is on for ingredients that can be used to replace fat in baked goods and that will provide the same fatlike properties of lubricity, mouth feel, body, moisture retention, and shelf life. In other words, fat substitutes are wanted that give the eater the feeling of eating fat but without the 9 calories per gram of fat.

Carbohydrates, if modified, can mimic the eating characteristics of fat and give the perception of moistness, creaminess, and smoothness of a fatty product. Tapioca, rice, corn, oats, pectin, and several fruit-based products made from pears, figs, prunes, and raisins are being modified so that when included in a baked product they produce a physiological effect in the mouth that resembles that of fat, yet the calories are sharply reduced. Carbohydrates contain but 4 calories per gram compared to the 9 calories contained in fat. Also, some of the fat substitutes can carry more water, which further reduces the calories in a serving.

How are these carbohydrates modified to resemble the feel of fat in the mouth? Starch is modified by chemically cross-linking the hydroxyl groups in two different starch molecules or on two adjacent branches of the same molecule. The hydrogen bonds within the molecule are reinforced to control how the starch swells in hot water, its gelling characteristic.

Cornstarch is modified by acid treatment so that in water it resembles a smooth cream that can substitute for fat in cakes and ready-to-spread frostings. Citrus peel, a source of pectin, is sheared into small gel particles that mimic the physical and sensory characteristics of fat globules in food products created by emulsification.

5. The big reason for the use of fat substitutes in baked goods is _____.

To meet the growing demand for products that taste as if they contain fat but in fact have 4 calories per gram instead of the 9 calories per gram in fat.

One way to fool the mouth and disguise the feel of the carbohydrates being eaten is to make them into very tiny particles—3 microns or less in diameter—so small that the tongue and taste buds perceive them as a smooth cream rather than as a particle.

So, we have fooled the mouth but we have not fooled the smell receptors in the nose, the organ that is mainly concerned with identifying aromas, so important in the enjoyment of food.

Just how important the nose is in flavor reception can be seen by closing your nose with your fingers while you are eating freshly baked bread. The aroma and flavor are lost.

6. Some fats such as butter are flavorful. What can be done to replace the flavor of fats that are normally used?

Flavors can be added.

IV. HOW IS NUTRITIONAL VALUE MEASURED?

7. To find the nutritional value of a baked product, look at its ingredients: How much fat, how much and what kind of protein, how much sugar, how much starch, and how many vitamins are present?

   Carbohydrates (starches and sugars) produce 4 calories per gram of energy for the body.

   Fats, however, produce 9 calories per gram.

   True or false: Fats produce more than twice as much energy per gram as do carbohydrates or proteins.

True.

8. Calories are only one measure of nutritional value. An adult eats between about 2,000 and 6,000 calories a day, depending upon size and energy output. The usual adult can do with fewer than 2,000 calories a day, whereas the huge professional football player may consume 6,000 calories. (U.S. Military Academy at West Point allows for 4,200 calories per day per person.)

   Nearly all baked products contain large amounts of calories.

   4-in. cut of apple pie—330 calories
   1 doughnut—136 calories
   1 sweet roll—178 calories
   1 plain roll—120 calories
   1 slice ½-in. white bread—63 calories

1 slice ½-in. whole-wheat bread—55 calories

True or false: It is safe to say that most baked products are high in calories.

True, although a few contain little fat and, therefore, fewer calories.

9. A graham cracker contains 27 calories, and a 2-in. saltine cracker contains 12 calories. Why would such comparatively small pieces of food contain so many calories?

Both are high in fat.

10. Calorie count is only one aspect of nutrition. Calories provide only energy. Living tissue, however, needs to replace itself and to grow. For this it needs protein. In addition to containing carbon, hydrogen, and oxygen, protein also contains nitrogen.

Most baked goods are a good source of protein in that the flour used contains about 6% to 15% protein.

For example, white bread is about 9% protein. Angel food cake, rich in eggs, contains about 7% protein. Most cakes run about 4% to 5% protein.

Compared with flesh foods (meat, fish, poultry), baked products have a little less than half as much protein present.

True or false: Most baked goods are fairly high in protein.

True for dough products. Dessert products, which contain much more fat and sugar, are not especially good sources of protein.

11. The quality of proteins varies considerably, depending upon how much of the essential amino acids the protein contains. The essential amino acids are needed by the human body each day for best nutrition.

Nearly all cereals, including wheat, are deficient in one of the amino acids, lysine.

Because of this deficiency, protein from wheat does not have the same value to the body as proteins from animals, such as meat, fish, poultry, and dairy products.

True or false: Although flour contains a fair amount of protein, the protein is not of the same value to the body as are proteins from animals.

True.

12. To overcome the lysine deficiency in flour, some bakers add 0.5% to 1% lysine to their flour. This greatly increases the protein value of the flour. Adding soy flour also increases the value of the wheat protein. The soybean has more than enough lysine in it. The soybean is a remarkable plant in that its beans contain 30% to 50% protein.

Wheat flour is deficient in what essential amino acid?

Lysine.

13. Proteins are the raw materials for the growth of new body cells or their replacement. They are complex molecules containing nitrogen. Proteins, like all food materials, are made up of molecules. In proteins, molecules are grouped together to form amino acids.

When we eat bread, the proteins in the gluten and the other proteins present break down into amino acids in the digestion process. They are then reassembled by the body to build or replace the body cells.

Whereas starch and fat are used principally to provide energy for the body, protein is necessary to _____.

Build or replace body cells.

14. Flour contains about 70% by weight of starch. In the diet it is the source of energy and, if not burned as energy, is converted into fat. During the baking process, when the starch is heated in the presence of water, some of the starch soaks up water and swells (gelatinizes). On drying it helps to form the bulk of the baked dough.

Along with gluten, _____ helps to give a baked product its bulk and structure.

Starch.

15. Interestingly enough, starch can be broken down (hydrolyzed) into simple sugars. Both sugars and starches are of the same overall class of food materials called *carbohydrates.*

Carbohydrates are principally used by the body to provide energy or body fat. Are nearly all baked goods high in carbohydrates?

> Yes. Name one that isn't.

16. Another aspect of the nutritional value of a food is its vitamin content. Vitamins are essential in small amounts to regulate the metabolic processes of the body.

The whole wheat grain is high in the B vitamins (thiamin, niacin, and riboflavin). The wheat germ, containing fat, is high in vitamin A.

True or false: The whole grain of wheat is a good source of vitamin A and the B complex of vitamins.

> True.

17. When flour is made from the whole wheat kernel, most of the A and B vitamins are removed in the germ and the bran. The iron present is lost.

Since 1941, millers and bakers have "enriched" flour by adding back, and then some, the B vitamins and iron. Today the federal government, most states, and Puerto Rico require that flour be enriched. About 90% of all commercially baked standard white bread is "enriched."

Enriched flour has been "enriched" by adding back to the flour the _____ vitamins and iron.

Some flour is further enriched by the addition of calcium and vitamin _____.

> B.

18. What are the B vitamins?

> Thiamin, niacin, and riboflavin.

19. According to the nutritionists, we should cut out eating all fat.

> False. The body needs about 10% to 20% of its total calories in the form of fat.

20. Which types of fat, saturated or unsaturated, should be eaten if we are concerned about the buildup of cholesterol in the blood system?

About 1.5 to 2 times more polyunsaturated fats should be eaten than saturated ones.

21. Many baked products are high in fat. Puff pastry is layers of fat and high-gluten dough. Pastry shells are about one-third fat. Here are some other high-fat baked products:

> Yeast-raised doughnuts—27%
> Danish pastry—23%
> Assorted cookies—20% or higher
> Chocolate cake icing—14%
> Devil's food cake—12%
> Apple pie—11%
> Coffee cake—10%

Where there is fat, there are calories, maybe more than are needed by the person eating the food. But fat tastes so good and produces such a delectable texture in such items as cream puffs and napoleons!

Would you guess that all baked goods are relatively high in fat?

Many have little or no fat; angel food cake and Italian bread are examples.

22. Name two bakery products that contain more than 20% fat.

Puff pastry, doughnuts, and Danish pastry.

23. Some fat is needed by the body. The problem is how much and what kind. Fat eaten by North Americans may run as much as 40% of the total calories taken in. Fat should constitute about 10% to 25% of the total calorie intake.

Much of the fat eaten is "hidden." It is part of foods not ordinarily thought of as high-fat foods. Examples are hamburgers, nuts, cheese, and avocados.

Can we say that all baked goods are fattening?

Some are, some are not. It depends on the number of calories they contain.

24. Depending on the number of double-bond carbon linkages, fats are known as *saturated, unsaturated,* or *polyunsaturated.* Saturated fats contain only single-bond carbon linkages and are the least active chemically.

$$
\begin{array}{cc}
H & H \\
| & | \\
-C & - C - \\
| & | \\
H & H
\end{array}
$$

Monounsaturated fats contain one double bond.

$$
\begin{array}{cc}
H & H \\
| & | \\
-C & = C - \\
\end{array}
$$

Some fats are naturally saturated, which means that they have their full complement of hydrogen atoms. At room temperature such fats are likely to be plastic; oils are usually less saturated and are liquid at room temperature.

Whether a fat is saturated, monounsaturated, or polyunsaturated depends on the number of double bonds it contains. If no double bonds are present, the fat is known as _____.

Saturated.

25. If only one double bond is present in a fat, it is known as a _____.

Monounsaturated fat.

26. If more than one double bond is present in a fat, it is known as a _____.

Polyunsaturated fat (*poly* means "many").

27. Vegetable oils are likely to be polyunsaturated; animal fats are likely to be saturated.

To make vegetable oil more plastic for use in baking, some hydrogen is added to the oil. Then it becomes more saturated.

Oils are likely to be polyunsaturated, whereas hydrogenated fats and animal fats are more likely to be _____.

Saturated.

28. Too much polyunsaturated fat can be harmful. Nutritionists who are studying the problem of fat and the formation of cholesterol in the body say that we should take in about 1.5 to 2 times more polyunsaturated fats than saturated ones. Apparently, the unsaturated fats allow the cholesterol to pass through the intestinal walls and out of the body. If we eat only saturated fats and do not exercise enough, cholesterol can build up in the blood system and deposit inside the blood vessels.

About 10% to 25% of the total calories we eat should be in the form of fat. Should we have more or less polyunsaturated fat than the saturated types?

More polyunsaturates.

29. Do baked products that use only butter as the shortening contain a polyunsaturated or saturated fat?

Saturated fat; butter is an animal fat.

30. Does bread contain predominantly saturated or unsaturated fats?

The fat in bread that has fat added is usually hydrogenated and, therefore, saturated.

31. Many baked products contain sugar. Sugar does nothing for the body except provide energy. It contains no vitamins and does not replace or build tissues. Sugar that is not burned as energy in the body is converted into fat and stored. Is sugar good for us?

It depends on whether it is needed and how much of it you consume. Some nutritionists believe that sugar can be a cause of high blood pressure and heart disease.

32. Generally speaking, baked dough products are highly nutritious and are likely to contain vitamins A, B complex, and sometimes D. Dough products are a good source of the calcium needed for bone growth. They are a good source of protein.

All baked goods are a good source of energy. Are baked products fattening?

Any food is fattening if it contains large amounts of calories or if eaten excessively and in amounts in excess of what the body needs. No food is fattening if taken in a quantity that is needed by the body.

33. When we remove the bran and germ from the wheat kernel, we remove most of the B vitamins, the iron, and vitamin A.

   The yellow pigments called the *carotenoids* contain what is used to make vitamin A in the body. Would you expect white flour to contain vitamin A?

No. The yellow pigments are removed or bleached out, and wheat germ, which contains most of the vitamin A, has been removed.

34. Many people on diets feel that baked products are something they should avoid completely in their diet. Is such a belief justifiable?

They should avoid those items that are high in fat. The rest of the baked items are no higher in fat than other foods and are highly nutritious.

35. Are baked products economical from the point of view of the nutritional value purchased?

Some are, some are not. Items that require much labor to produce cost more. Flour itself, at about 15 cents a pound, is one of the cheapest foods we can buy.

REVIEW

1. Three broad classifications of food materials from the point of view of nutrition are fats, proteins, and _____.

2. Each gram of fat introduces _____ calories of energy.

3. Each gram of protein or carbohydrate produces _____ calories per gram.

4. True or false: All baked goods are fattening.

5. Is bread a good source of protein?

6. Which cake is the highest in protein?

7. Wheat would be an excellent source of well-balanced protein except that it is deficient what amino acid?

8. What can be added to flour to be used in making bread to increase its effectiveness as a source of protein?

9. Of the principal food ingredients—protein, carbohydrates, and fats—which is absolutely necessary for the replacement of tissue?

10. Would you say that bread is a good source of vitamin A?

11. What has been added to enriched flour?

12. True or false: "Enriched" bread is high in vitamins A and C.

13. When flour is milled, the bran is removed. With the bran goes some of the vitamins. To replace these lost vitamins, flour is enriched by the addition of thiamin, niacin, iron, and riboflavin. Thiamin, niacin, and riboflavin are part of the B complex of vitamins. Thiamin is also known as vitamin B_1. Riboflavin is also known as vitamin _____.

14. "Enriched" flour has had B vitamins and _____ added to it.

15. Vitamin B_1 is also known as _____.

16. Because most of the vitamins have been removed in the milling process, would you think that white bread is less nutritious than whole-wheat bread?

17. Is rye bread more nutritious than white bread?

C H A P T E R 24

PIE MAKING

Any dish of fish, flesh, fowl, or fruit covered on top with a crust of some sort is a pie. In America, pies are more often than not dessert pies, baked in a shallow pan with a bottom crust. In England, this type of pie is known as a *tart*. There are many kinds of crusts used for pies: crumbs, meringues, and biscuits, as well as regular pastry. There are even pies such as shepherd's pie, whose "crust" consists of mashed potatoes. Many pies are, in fact, not covered with a crust at all, but rather baked in a pastry shell with the top exposed. There seem to be as many varieties of pie as there are people of many nations who bake pies.

Americans inherit their love of pies from the English. In the 14th century, London was full of cookshops selling deep-dish meat pies with a heavy crust. The famous English mince pie, the Christmas pie that Little Jack Horner ate in his corner, evolved from these early meat pies. An old English tradition claims that eating twelve mince pies, one each day from Christmas until Twelfth Night, will make the eater happy for 12 months of the year.

When the colonists came to this country they brought with them their love for the English meat pies and dessert tarts. Until the Revolution, women continued the custom of baking pies in deep pastry shells covered with a top or "coffin." Sometime after we declared our Independence, a thrifty New England housewife realized that flat pies, or "tarts," needed less filling, and now the traditional American pie is a flat one.

Several pies are particularly associated with the United States. There is the pumpkin pie, a refinement of the first pumpkin pies that were merely hollowed-out whole pumpkins; the molasses-flavored shoofly pie of the Pennsylvania Dutch; and, most famous of all, American apple pie. In the days before refrigeration and freezers; the apples were picked, peeled, quartered, and hung on cords in the kitchen. The dried quarters of apple were used to make pies all through the winter. New Englanders ate them for breakfast.

"What is pie for?" asked Emerson when challenged on the custom. In 1902 the *New York Times* blasted an English suggestion that pie be eaten only twice a week. This, said the *Times*, was "utterly insufficient . . . as anyone who knows the secret of our strength as a nation and the foundation of our industrial supremacy must admit. Pie is the American synonym of prosperity, and its varying contents the calendar of the changing seasons. Pie is the food of the heroic. No pie-eating people can ever be permanently vanquished."

I. PIE CRUSTS

There are two basic types of pie crust: flaky pie crust and mealy pie crust. Although the crusts may contain identical ingredients in the same proportions, the results may be quite different.

When a flaky crust is desired, rub the flour and shortening together until they become nuggets the size of walnuts before adding the liquid and salt.

When a mealy crust is desired, rub the flour and shortening until there is a finer distribution of the shortening throughout the flour.

A. Ingredients for Pie Crust

Always use a soft wheat flour, such as pastry flour, for pie crust. If a stronger flour is used, it must be worked with a higher proportion of fat, which is why pastry flour is recommended.

Shortening or fats used in making pie crust must be of plastic consistency. Lard is a good choice, but many people object to the taste. Thus the most popular fat is vegetable shortening. A proportion of butter greatly improves the flavor and should be used if the cost factor does not become too serious. Water must always be very cold when used for making pie crust. The salt is usually dissolved in the water.

Thus the essential ingredients that go into making good pie crust are as follows:

Pastry flour
Vegetable shortening, some butter when possible
Salt
Cold water

In some formulas other ingredients such as vinegar and baking powder are suggested. These ingredients do not improve the pie crust.

Note: Pie dough should not be *overmixed.*

B. Pie Trimmings

When pie crusts are rolled out, care should be taken to keep the size of each piece as close as possible to the size of the pans, thus keeping pie trimmings to a minimum. Pie trimmings should not be used to make up more than 50% of the piece of dough and should be used for bottom crusts only.

C. Pie Washes

Milk, cream, eggs and milk, melted butter, and water are the various kinds of pie washes used to improve the eye appeal of pie crusts. The type used depends on the finish required on the particular product.

II. THICKENING AGENTS

Starches and flours are used as thickening agents in pie fillings. Starches are used more often because they do not have a tendency to discolor and become gummy.

The amount of starch used varies and depends upon the gelling quality of the starch, the amount of liquid in the filling, and the desired consistency of the finished pie. From 2 to 5 oz of cornstarch per quart of liquid (juice plus water) is the approximate amount used in preparation of the different fillings.

Care should be taken to cook the starch until the mixture is transparent and shiny. The mixture should be removed from heat when it starts to boil.

III. PIE FILLINGS

There are five main types of pie fillings:

1. Fruit pie
2. Cream pie
3. Chiffon pie
4. Soft pie
5. Specialty pies

A. Fruit Pies, Preparation

The most popular fruit pies are apple, cherry, blueberry, pineapple, apricot, peach, raisin, prune, etc. The fruit used may be fresh, frozen, canned, dried, or as prepared pie filling.

Among the many methods used in filling pies today, the following three are the most generally accepted:

1. COOKED JUICE METHOD
1. Drain juice from fruit and bring to a boil.
2. Thicken with proper amount of dissolved cornstarch.
3. Bring back to a boil to clarify or assure proper setting of the starch.
4. Add granulated sugar, salt, spices, butter, or other flavoring agents, and stir until dissolved.
5. Pour over drained fruit, stir carefully, and do not crush the fruit.
6. When the filling is cold, it is ready for the pies.

This method is generally used for cherry, apple, blueberry, apricot, and peach pies.

2. COOKED FRUIT AND JUICE METHOD

1. Bring juice and fruit to a boil.
2. Add the amount of dissolved cornstarch needed to bring juice and fruit to a proper consistency. After the cornstarch is added, always bring the filling back to a boil so that it will clarify.
3. Add the desired amount of sugar, and stir until thoroughly dissolved. Care should be taken when cooking the fruit to stir occasionally to prevent the possibility of scorching.
4. When the filling is cold, it is ready for the pies.

This method is generally used for raisin, pineapple, and also, if the fruit is unusually hard, apple.

3. HOMEMADE METHOD

1. Mix the fruit with spices, flour, and sugar.
2. Fill the unbaked pie shells.
3. Place a lump of butter or margarine on top of the filling.
4. Cover the pie and bake as usual.

This method is very simple. However, the flour in the filling has a tendency to remain uncooked. Therefore, the consistency is not as easily controlled as in the preceding two methods.

B. Cream Pie Filling

Vanilla, chocolate, butterscotch, banana, and coconut are the most popular cream pies. Care should be taken to acquire a smooth cream with a delicate flavor. This cream filling is always placed into pre-baked pie shells.

The cream pie method is as follows:

1. Place milk with part of the sugar in a round-bottomed pan and scald.
2. Mix egg yolks, balance of sugar, starch, and flavor into a paste. Add to this part of the milk to make the mix into liquid form.
3. When part 1 is near the boiling point, add part 2 and continue to stir until it reaches a boil; then remove from the heat.
4. Add necessary flavor to batter and stir.

5. Place in pre-baked pie shells.

6. After cooling, top with meringue or whipped cream.

C. Chiffon Pie Filling

Chiffon pies are mixed in a manner similar to the fruit pie method 2 or the cream pie filling method. Meringue is folded into this mixture.

Both cream pies and fruit pies may be converted into chiffon pies.

Prepare chiffon pies as follows:

1. Place in a pan the fruit, sugar, flavor, color, salt, and water or milk, and bring to a boil on top of the stove.
2. Dissolve the starch in juice or water, mix with part 1, and continue to boil.
3. Remove from heat.
4. Make meringue with egg whites and sugar.
5. While the first mixture is still hot, *immediately* fold in the meringue.
6. Place mixture into pre-baked pie shell. Remember to fill the shell generously. Pyramid the filling into the shell with a spatula.
7. Allow to cool and top with whipped cream.

D. Soft Pie Filling

Pumpkin, sweet potato, squash, custard, and pecan pies are soft pies. They require a deep pie plate with an additional fluted pie crust rim.

Soft pies are made with an unbaked crust.

An uncooked filling is made, which is set during the baking process. The filling contains eggs, which help to coagulate the filling during baking.

E. Specialty Pie Filling

Nesselrode, ice cream, and Boston cream pies are specialty pies. They are made with a combination of the foregoing methods.

1. The broad definition of *pie* is any dish of meat or fruit covered with or baked in a dough crust. In the bakery we are concerned with dessert pies baked in a shallow pan with a bottom crust and often with a top crust. Crusts are made from crumbs, meringues, and biscuits, but the one with which we are concerned is a short pastry dough.

    When we say *short*, we mean what?

The dough contains a relatively high proportion of fat.

2. A common way of classifying pies is according to the filling used. Fillings can be divided into fruit, cream, chiffon, soft fillings such as pumpkin or custard, and fillings for specialty pies such as ice cream pie. A chiffon pie is similar to a fruit or a cream except that beaten egg whites and sugar have been folded into the filling to "leaven" it.

How would you classify a strawberry chiffon pie?

> As a chiffon pie, because it is a foamy filling created by folding in the beaten egg whites.

3. Pies can also be divided into those that have the shell and the filling baked together and those for which the shell and filling are prepared separately. Chiffon, cream, lemon meringue, and most specialty pies use pre-baked shells. These shells are best made from a mealy crust.

Soft pies such as pumpkin, custard, and pecan are baked crust and filling together. The bottom crust should be "mealy." The richer in shortening, the less likely that bottom soakage will occur.

Most fruit pies are baked crust and filling together.

True or false: Pie crusts are usually baked separately for chiffon, cream, and specialty pies.

> True.

4. Why not bake the filling and the crust together when making a chiffon pie?

> The chiffon filling containing beaten egg whites would be overcooked while the shell was still baking.

IV. PIE DOUGHS

5. Pie dough is usually made from pastry flour (medium protein content), a plastic shortening, salt, and cold water.

Fat constitutes from 25% to 40% of the pie crust formula.

When baked, pie dough is a relatively compact (unleavened) dough (unlike cake or bread) that breaks easily when eaten.

What ingredient in pie dough makes the crust tender?

> The fat.

6. Pie crusts are of two basic types: flaky and mealy. They both may contain exactly the same ingredients, but the method of mixing is different.

Flaky crust is made by mixing the flour and half the shortening into a complete blend and then adding the rest of the shortening and mixing into pea-sized or larger balls of fat surrounded by the flour–shortening blend. Water is added, and the mixing completed. When the dough is baked, the fat melts, and the steam generated separates the layers. The resulting crust is layers of dough, separated by the fat.

Mealy crust is well mixed. The shortening is distributed throughout the flour. (Mix half of the flour with all shortening, then the rest of flour, and then the water.)

Differences between a mealy and a flaky crust are normally the result of the method of _____.

Mixing.

7. Lard at one time was the popular shortening for use in pastry. Today vegetable shortening, despite its higher cost, is used more frequently. Some butter or margarine may be added for flavor or color.

From what you know, what would happen to a pie dough if we use bread flour?

The crust would be tough because too much protein is present. You would have to add more shortening to tenderize the gluten strands.

8. In mixing pie dough, develop the gluten only to the point where it will hold the dough together when rolled. If overmixed, too much gluten is developed. There is excessive shrinkage when the crust bakes. The crust is likely to be _____.

Tough.

9. Very cold water—usually ice water—is used when mixing pie dough so that the gluten development is depressed during mixing. The cold water allows enough mixing to distribute the water evenly without making for a tough dough. Salt and any dextrose used is dissolved in water so that it will be evenly distributed in the dough.

What would happen if no water were used?

There would be no gluten development, and the dough would not roll out. You would have a roux (fat and flour mixture).

10. Can we successfully use cake flour for making pastry?

No, because there is not sufficient gluten development to hold the dough together for proper rolling.

11. Some bakers feel that to make a flaky crust it is necessary to hand-mix the flour and the fat, which takes too long, is costly in labor, and is not particularly sanitary. A special dough-mixing machine, Artifax, was developed in Sweden and is available in this country. The mixing arms scoop up the dough in a manner similar to what would be done in mixing the dough by hand. Small commercial batches can be successfully mixed on low speed in a regular upright mixer with a paddle.

The key to making a flaky crust is to avoid overmixing the flour and fat and to stop when the balls of fat and flour are of the size desired.

True or false: A flaky crust can be made only by hand-mixing the fat and the flour.

False.

12. Fat used in making pie dough should be at about 70°F. If the fat is appreciably colder, it is apt to be too hard and will break and tear the gluten strands. If too hot, it becomes oily and over-blends with the flour.

Once water is added, mix as little as possible. What happens if pastry dough is overmixed?

It gets tough because too much gluten is developed.

13. Excessive water in a pastry dough causes tough-ness, possibly because the gluten takes on too much water and because it requires more mixing to develop the dough to the point where it will be "workable." Most water in a pie dough is ab-sorbed by the gluten, not the starch. Butter con-tains up to 20% water. If butter is used, should some allowance be made for the water in the butter?

Yes. More butter than vegetable shortening is needed to do the same shortening job.

14. The use of ice water for pie dough prevents the gluten from developing as fast as it would in a warm dough.
    True or false: We want plenty of water in a pie dough.

False. Just enough to form a dough that will roll.

15. Leftover dough can be used for making a mealy dough (commonly used for bottom crust). The mealy dough is preferable for use in making cream and custard pies. Why?

The dough is more densely packed and does not become soggy as quickly as a flaky pastry.

16. A flaky dough becomes what kind of dough when mixing is continued?

Mealy and tough.

17. In rolling out dough, the dough is sometimes rolled thin, and then allowed to relax or rest. The gluten strands have been stretched excessively. During the relaxing period, the gluten strands shorten somewhat, but not back to their original length. The dough can then be rolled again and stretched farther. Strudel dough, which is stretched to paper thinness, must be relaxed between rollings and uses bread flour for maximum gluten development.
    A dough is relaxed for what reason?

To allow it to adjust to the new, extended length of the gluten strands.

V. PREVENTING A SOGGY BOTTOM CRUST

18. If a flaky crust is wanted for a pre-baked shell, fill the shell only a short time before serving the pie. Why?

So that the crust will not be soaked.

19. To minimize soakage in the bottom crust of a fruit pie, would it be a good idea to bake the pie on the bottom shelf of the oven?

Yes. The bottom is hotter and the crust will bake more quickly, sealing out the juices.

20. Use of a shiny pie tin may result in a soggy bottom crust. Why?

A shiny surface reflects heat and retards baking time. Some frozen pie bakers used to "ink" the outer bottom of the "tin." Some still employ a dark metal for the bottom.

21. To prevent the bottom crust from soaking, dry cake crumbs can be put in the bottom of the pie before filling it. The crumbs absorb excess liquid from the fruit that would otherwise soak into the crust. High shortening content is a good deterrent to bottom soaking.

 To avoid soggy bottom crust in a pie, bake the pie in the bottom of the oven, use a mealy crust, or _____.

Put some dry cake crumbs in the bottom of the pie before filling it, or use more shortening for the bottom crust.

VI. OVEN TEMPERATURES

22. Temperatures vary within the oven; they are hotter near the bottom and cooler at the top. Some electric ovens have both top and bottom heat sources, and the temperatures vary according to the heat produced at the top and bottom.

 In a gas oven, why does the temperature vary within the oven?

Heat is applied at the bottom of the oven, creating a higher temperature near the bottom.

23. Oven temperatures are not always what is read on the temperature control knob (the thermostat). Check the thermostat by placing a mercury thermometer in the oven. The thermostat and the thermometer should read the same. If not, calibrate (change) the thermostat to read the same as the thermometer.

 Do not use a spring thermometer; it will lose its accuracy with the slightest jar.

 What is used to check the accuracy of the thermostat (the control knob)?

A mercury thermometer.

24. Suppose an oven is too hot at the bottom. A sheet pan placed on the lowest oven rack will even out the temperature. Most bakeries put pies in sheet pans to bake, a practice known as *panning.* If the bottom heat is still too high, they may "double pan." Also, it makes a big difference if the sheet pan is new and shiny, or blackened by "ink." If heat is applied from both bottom and top, reduce the bottom heat.

Would you expect a convection oven (one with a rotor fan in the back) to have a more even temperature throughout the oven?

> Yes, but temperatures in them also vary within the oven chamber.

25. The kind of filling used in a pie determines the oven temperature to use. Fruit pies are usually baked at 400 to 425°F for 25 to 30 minutes. Some bakers prefer 350 to 375°F for 45 minutes.

Custard pies and others using a quantity of milk and eggs must have special handling. Custard pies baked directly in the shell are baked for 10 minutes at 450°F. Then the temperature is reduced to 300°F and the baking continued for 45 to 50 minutes to cook the custard.

What will happen to an egg and milk filling if the high heat is continued?

> The custard will become too firm and tough, and the water will separate from the protein.

26. Why not use microwave ovens for baking pies?

> These ovens produce energy so fast that the inside of the pie is overcooked before the crusts become barely warm.

27. Remember, the fruit in baked pies is already cooked. The problem is to bake the crust to a golden brown and reheat the filling. This usually takes 45 to 55 minutes using a 425°F oven.

What would happen if you bake such pies longer than an hour?

> At 425°F the filling is likely to be overcooked and the crust too dry and perhaps burned.

VII. STARCH THICKENERS

28. Starches are widely used in the bakery for thickening pie fillings and also for thickening custards and puddings in the bakeshops of restaurants.

There most widely used starch in this country is that of corn. There are two types: regular cornstarch and that made from waxy maize, a special type of corn.

Regular cornstarch has a high thickening power, but its gel is relatively cloudy or opaque.

Would you want to use regular cornstarch for fruit pies?

> No. The fruit would not usually be seen, and the gel is too rigid.

29. Would regular cornstarch be suitable for cream or lemon pies?

> Yes. It is the most commonly used starch.

30. Figure 24–1 shows granules of waxy maize starch magnified 500 times.

Waxy maize and other cornstarches are modified by cross-linking the molecules of starch. As a result of this cross-linking, the granules are more resistant to breakdown in the cooking and handling processes.

The modified waxy maize starches produce pastes that are water-clear, viscous, and cohesive. After cooking and cooling, they form weak gels.

Modified waxy maize starches are excellent for use in thickening fruit pie fillings.

Regular cornstarch that has been cooked and cooled forms a _____ gel, whereas modified waxy maize starch forms a _____ gel.

> Cloudy. Clear.

31. Some bakeshops are using pre-cooked starches, also known as *instant* or *pre-gelatinized starches*. They have already been cooked and have been dried. When water is added, the water is immediately absorbed by the starch granules.

Although pre-cooked starches cost more, they

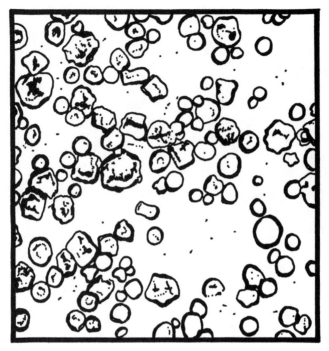

Figure 24–1

save the time usually taken in cooking, cooling, and handling the usual starch.

The natural flavor of the fruit is protected in the preparation of fruit pie fillings, and the fruit tends to retain its natural shape and appearance because it is cooked only once.

Pre-cooked starches would likely be used in thickening what kind of pies?

Fruit pies, especially those like strawberry pie in which it is desirable to retain the appearance and form of the fruit.

32. In using pre-cooked starches, the starch must be blended with sugar and other dry ingredients before liquid is added. Otherwise the starch will lump when water is added.

"Instant pies" can be made by using pre-cooked starch and pouring a filling into baked pie shells.

True or false: Instant starch has already been cooked and dehydrated.

True.

33. Pre-cooked starch can be used to stabilize whipped cream. The whipped cream will not separate for several days if it is refrigerated.

Would you guess that the pre-cooked starch would have to be blended with sugar before being added to whipped cream?

Yes. The pre-cooked starch soaks up water very fast and will lump if not separated by the sugar.

34. Pre-cooked starch can also be substituted for part of the flour in cakes to improve eating quality or to help retain moisture.

Why is pre-cooked starch a good stabilizer for whipped cream?

The starch granules soak up and retain moisture.

35. When heat is applied to starch and water, the granules begin to swell and take up the water. This process is called *gelatinization.* The larger granules swell first at lower temperatures; the smaller granules gelatinize at a higher temperatures. Regular cornstarch begins to gelatinize at about 147°F, but complete gelatinization does not take place until the solution reaches about 200°F.

The technical name for the thickening of a starch and water solution is _____.

Gelatinization.

36. Regular cornstarch completes its thickening at about 200°F. As it cools, it thickens further and forms a gel that is more rigid than the paste formed during the initial thickening. This is a disadvantage in that the baker cannot tell for sure how rigid the gel will be until it has cooled and set.

Waxy maize starch has no second thickening; therefore, its consistency can be better controlled by the baker.

Which starch is more easily controlled as regards final consistency: waxy maize or regular cornstarch?

Waxy maize.

37. Overcooking of a starch causes the granules to rupture, which thins out the solution. Many a pie filling has been ruined because of overcooking the starch. Excessive stirring of a starch solution during cooking also ruptures the starch granules and causes the paste to thin out.

Two practices to avoid in cooking starch are _____ and _____.

Overcooking.
Overstirring.

38. Acid ingredients in the pie filling destroy the thickening power of the starch and prevent it from setting.

To avoid this, add the acid ingredients after the starch has thickened. Then cool the solution as quickly as possible because slow cooling of paste solution with a high pH also makes a runny solution.

In making a filling for a gooseberry pie (low pH), would you cook the starch separately and then add it, or cook the starch with the gooseberries?

Cook the starch separately so that the acid does not interfere with the gelatinization.

39. Too much sugar also interferes with gelatinization. To avoid such interference, add the sugar to be used in two stages. Add only part of the sugar to the starch-water solution and cook it. After the gelatinization has taken place, the other sugar can be added.

Other ingredients such as fat, salt, eggs, and dry milk solids weaken a starch gel.

When large amounts of sugar, fat, or dry milk solids are called for, does the recipe need more or less starch to achieve a particular thickening level?

More.

40. Pie fillings and puddings thickened by starch sometimes weep after setting a while. Water that has been only partially absorbed by the starch separates from the starch, and the gel may collapse or lose its consistency. This is usually caused by failure to cook the starch solution completely so that the water is firmly bound into the starch granules.

Weeping is likely to be caused by _____.

Undercooking the starch and water solution.

41. Puddings and pie fillings thickened with starch that are to be frozen should be made with the waxy maize starches or other starches that have been specially modified and will withstand freezing without separating.

Numerous starches have been tailored for the bakeshop, and the baker is well advised to purchase those that are recommended for particular pie fillings and puddings, even though they cost somewhat more than regular cornstarch.

True or false: As bakery ingredients are improved and new ones are developed for specific uses in baking, the baker should at least try them out rather than only using "tried-and-true recipes and ingredients."

Very true, because many of the new items available, such as invert sugar and the modified starches, produce superior baked products.

VIII. AVOIDING BLISTERS IN THE SHELL

42. Blisters tend to form in a crust that is baked in a pie pan. To avoid these, holes are made in the dough before baking, a process called *docking.*

Another way of avoiding blisters is to double pan the dough. An empty pie tin is placed on top of the dough in the pan. Double panning holds the crust in place.

To avoid blisters forming in a pie shell, double pan or _____ the dough before it is baked.

Dock. Blisters also form because of excessive moisture in the dough.

43. Double panning is the recommended way to make pie shells, the single bottom crusts. By placing a pan inside the shell while the crust bakes, the crust is held in place and the proper shape is held.

Double panning helps to avoid blisters in the shell and also holds the _____ of the shell while it bakes.

Shape or form.

IX. HANDLING FROZEN PIES

44. Frozen pies are raw crusts containing a cooked filling that is frozen solid. The problem is to bake the crust without overcooking the filling. This is why directions call for baking from the frozen state.

Usually crusts will bake and the filling reach the boiling in about 45 to 55 minutes, provided a pre-heated oven is used at 425°F.

In what part of the oven would you place a frozen pie if the bottom crust is not browning sufficiently before the top crust is done?

On the bottom rack, where the temperature is highest.

45. Can a fruit filling be damaged by overcooking?

Yes. The fruit becomes mushy and loses its identity.

46. The temperature of the frozen pie determines in part the necessary time for cooking or baking it.

Which pie takes longer to bake: one held at 0 degrees or one at −15°F?

Obviously the colder pie takes longer to heat and bake. Best temperatures to hold frozen pies are 0 to 5°F.

47. How about thawing out a frozen pie before baking it?

Not recommended, because the crust may burn before the pie is done. Store frozen pies in the freezer, not the refrigerator.

48. Frozen pumpkin pies may require 10 to 15 minutes longer to bake than fruit pies. The added time dries excess moisture and allows the filling to set.

Is more time needed for baking an oven full of pies than for one or a few pies?

Yes. Each pie requires a certain number of BTU to bake. The oven is limited in the number of BTU it can generate.

49. Figure 24–2 shows that many things can go wrong in making a pie crust.

If we put in excessive water, the crust will shrink up and be _____.

Tough and solid.

ORDINARY PIE FAULTS AND THEIR CAUSES

Faults \ Causes	Over mixed	Insufficient shortening	Too much shortening	Improperly mixed	Insufficient liquid	Too much liquid	Improper flour	Over working of dough	Baking temp. too low	Baking temp. too high	No bottom oven heat	Excess acidity in filling	Hot filling used	Lack of opening, top crust	Improperly sealed crusts	Filling too thin	Wet pie plates	Boiling over of filling	Too much sugar	Insufficient sugar	Watery egg whites	Not beat firm enough
Pie dough																						
Stiff	X					X																
Crumbly	X	X	X	X																		
Tough	X	X	X			X																
Baked crust																						
Shrinkage	X	X			X	X	X															
Solid crust	X	X			X	X		X														
Too light in color									X													
Tough	X	X			X	X	X															
Two crust pies																						
Unbaked crust bottom									X		X					X						
Boiling of filling during baking									X	X	X	X	X	X	X			X				
Crust sticking to pans		X								X					X		X					
Crust soaked on bottom			X						X		X	X	X		X		X	X				
Meringue																						
Watery or weeping									X										X		X	X
Tough										X									X			

Figure 24-2 Reprinted with permission of the publisher from J. Amendola, The Baker's Manual for Quantity Baking and Pastry Making, 2d edition. Copyright 1956 and 1960 by Ahrens Publishing Company, Inc.

50. A crumbly pie may be caused by overmixing the dough, excessive shortening, or insufficient _____.

Liquid.

51. If a pie crust sticks to the pan, it may be because of insufficient shortening in the dough, the filling may have boiled over and stuck to the bottom of the pan, there may not be not enough bottom heat, or the pie plates may have been _____.

Wet.

REVIEW

1. A short crust is one that is high in _____.

2. A chiffon pie has some leavening taking place because of the presence of what ingredient?

3. Should a soft pie have a flaky or mealy bottom crust?

4. With more shortening in a crust, is it more or less tender?

5. True or false: A flaky crust always has more shortening in it than a mealy crust.

6. Is a pie crust that shrinks away from the pan when baked likely to have too much or too little gluten in it?

7. Is a principal reason for using ice water in mixing pie dough to retard or increase gluten development?

8. True or false: To get a flaky crust, it is necessary to hand-mix the dough.

9. At about what temperature should the shortening be for mixing into pie dough?

10. What ingredient in dough soaks up most of the water in mixing?

11. Dough that has been thoroughly mixed would be preferably used for which crust: the top or the bottom?

12. True or false: Always use shiny pie tins for baking pies.

13. The purpose of "double panning" of pies is to _____.

14. Ordinarily, what type of starch is used for thickening a cream or lemon pie?

15. Which starch is better for any filling that will be frozen: regular cornstarch or waxy maize?

16. Are cross-linked starches more or less stable than those that have not been modified?

17. When a starch and water solution is heated and the starch granules absorb much of the water, the process is known as _____.

18. Which of these starches, regular cornstarch or waxy maize, has two thickening periods when it is cooked and cooled?

19. If a starch is overcooked, is the resulting solution thicker or thinner than usual?

20. Does too much sugar or the presence of acid interfere with or encourage gelatinization?

21. Does weeping in a pie suggest that the filling has been undercooked or overcooked?

CHAPTER 25

PASTRY

I. WHAT IS PASTRY?

The term *pastry* refers to baked items made mostly with a smooth mixture of flour, water, and fat that is more viscous (flows) than a dough. The mixture is called a *paste*. The term *pastry* has been extended to include a number of baked items that are made from doughs rich in fat. Pies, Danish pastries, strudel, and phyllo products may be called pastries.

Pastry flours are made from soft wheat and range in protein content from about 6% to 9%; they are used in pie doughs, some cookies, biscuits, and muffins. Several pastry items, however, need strong flour such as bread flours so they can withstand the stretching that occurs in cream puffs and éclair shells, puff pastry, and strudel.

Éclair paste is an example of a basic pastry that, when baked, puffs up and becomes cream puffs, éclair shells, and profiteroles (small cream puffs). Éclair paste is also known by its French name, *pâte a choux* (pronounced *pat-a-shoo),* which means "cabbage paste" because cream puffs made from the paste look like little cabbages.

Items made from the paste expand rapidly when exposed to high oven heat (425°F or 220°C) because the moisture in the paste turns to steam, which expands the paste. Éclairs and profiteroles are leavened the same way.

They are usually filled with whipped cream or pastry cream. Pastry cream is made with whole eggs, egg yolks, sugar, and butter. Its cornstarch thickening provides stability. It is also used as a filling for cakes and cream pies and as a pudding. Pastry cream is also known by its French name, *crème pâtisserie.*

1. Why is it necessary to use bread flour in making éclair paste?

When heated, the paste is rapidly expanded by steam, which greatly stretches the paste to form éclair shells. A weak flour would tear.

2. If pastry cream is not thickened with cornstarch or another thickener, what might happen to the eggs at high temperature?

They would be likely to curdle and lump.

II. ÉCLAIRS AND CREAM PUFFS

A cream puff in an oblong shape is called an *éclair.* The name is French and literally translated means "lightning." Although cream puffs and éclairs are made from the same ingredients, éclairs are considered more festive and elegant than cream puffs; why, no one knows.

Éclairs are made with a chou (pronounced *shoo)* pastry, filled with cream fillings, whipped cream, or ice cream, and glazed with chocolate, vanilla, or coffee icing. They can be frozen, but most devotees prefer fresh éclairs.

Chou or cream puff pastry is made by adding flour to boiling water and butter and cooking the mixture until a thick paste is formed. Then the eggs are beaten in, one at a time. The eggs make the paste, which is nothing but a thick sauce, puffed up during cooking. When finished the puffs are cut open and filled with either sweet or savory filling.

A cream puff is an airy little cream-filled cake, brother to an éclair. Cream puffs are round; éclairs are oblong. They are of French origin and made by an entirely different method from other pastries.

Cooks should rid themselves of the idea that cream puffs are hard to make. As a matter of fact, they are one of the easiest pastries. They are also extremely useful because they make all sorts of delightful desserts or, if the filling is not sweet, elegant appetizers and garnishes.

3. Éclair paste (also called *chou paste)* is between a batter and a dough consistency. It is made of bread flour, butter or shortening, eggs, water, and salt.

   The paste is used for making cream puffs and éclair shells, their small cousins the profiteroles, and French doughnuts (also called *French crullers).*

   Popover batter is similar except that it is thinner in consistency than chou paste and without fat. It must be beaten well to develop the gluten so that when steam explodes the batter the new form will hold.

   a. Éclair paste is also known by its French name, ——.

   b. What do you suppose gives éclairs their yellow color?

   > Chou paste. The eggs contained in the paste.

4. The leavening agent in puff paste, chou paste, and popover batter is steam. Steam develops in the areas where fat exists, between the sheets of dough in the puff paste, and causes flaking. In the chou paste and popover, the steam formed inside pushes the paste of batter up or out, making a large hollow inside. Continued baking causes the shell around the hollow to form from coagulation and gelatinization. Baking must continue until this wall is quite firm and will not collapse when the product is removed from the oven and the steam pressure subsides. Actually the shell is partially dried out in the baking to give it strength.

   What do you think oven temperatures would be in products such as this that are leavened by steam: High or low?

   > High to start (450°F is used for some items to secure rapid steam development before the product sets; then when full expansion has occurred, the temperature is dropped to complete baking).

III. PUFF PASTE

Puff paste or *blatterteig,* as it was originally called by the bakers of Germany where this delicacy originated, is made by alternately rolling and folding a fat into a previously made dough. The result after the series of rolling and folding stages is a sheet of dough with alternating layers of dough and fat.

The making of perfect puff pastry products is an art that can only be learned by close observation and practice.

A. Refrigeration Aids Production

For making puff pastry, it is necessary that the materials be cold; therefore, the paste should be made up in a cool place. Modern mechanical refrigeration makes it possible to make up all the puff pastry products required for several days by placing the made-up pieces into the refrigerator and baking off quantities as needed so that the product can be brought oven-fresh to the salesroom. This practice gives the retail baker the advantages of high quality and freshness.

Puff pastry lends itself exceptionally well to refrigeration for two reasons: first, because of the solidifying nature of the fats, of which there is a great abundance; second, because the dough has no leavening agent added, such as yeast or a gas-producing leavening agent, as is the case with sweet yeast-raised dough or baking powder cakes.

B. Leavening

The leavening action of puff paste comes from three sources:

1. *Vaporization of moisture* in the dough and fat layers.
2. *Enclosed air.* When the dough is first rolled, it contains very little air. However, each time it is folded in the rolling process, a certain percentage of air is enclosed with it. These air cells expand during baking, thus assisting in the leavening of the product.
3. *Bubbling of fats.* When subjected to baking temperature, the fats form air bubbles and boil. These bubbles assist in raising the dough.

Acids such as cream of tartar, lemon juice, or vinegar are not, in a sense, added as leaveners, yet they do contribute to the leavened condition of the finished products by causing the protein or gluten of the flour to become more elastic, thus enabling it to stretch rather than break.

The addition of one egg for each pound of flour also increases the leavening power, this power coming principally from the egg whites. The yolks add richness and color to the product.

Many bakers prefer not to use acid in a puff paste dough when it is to be held in the refrigerator either in dough form or in shaped units and baked off over a period of time as needed. Products made from retarded puff paste dough have less volume when an acid is added than is the case when the acid is omitted.

C. Flour and Fats

The flour should be a good bread flour, or a blend may be used of two-thirds bread flour and one-third cake flour in the event the bread flour should prove too strong.

The fat should be of a tough nature. There are many good margarines on the market made specifically for puff paste and these margarines give the finished product an appearance that excels that of a product in which butter alone is used. In combining a portion of each, the baker is able to have both flavor and appearance.

To begin rolling in the fats, dust the table and the dough with flour, and roll out an oblong sheet three times as long as it is wide to a thickness of one-half inch. Care must be taken that corners are square. Brush off excess flour.

Place the fats in small pats or discs over two-thirds of the area. Now fold the bare or uncoated part over half of the coated part, and then fold this over the remaining coated dough so that there are two layers of fat and three layers of dough. Press down the ends and sides with rolling pin to seal in the fats. This now forms an oblong or square. Lift this sheet or block around lengthwise carefully.

Dust again with flour and begin rolling out carefully with not too great a pressure on the pin (at no time should the rolling pin be borne down upon) to a sheet of not less than one-half inch thick and the same length as the sheet was before the folding process. Corners must be rolled square. Brush off excess flour and fold the sheet in three. Place on cloth-covered pan or board, cover with moist cloth or greased paper, and permit to rest for at least 15 minutes in refrigerator or another cool place.

Care must be taken that the dough does not remain refrigerated too long in the early stage of rolling and folding, which would cause the fat to solidify as it is still somewhat in pats, having received only one roll. Should this happen, then at the next rolling stage these solidified fat particles would thrust through the layers of dough. The result is very undesirable. After the second roll, the fats have commenced to be sheeted and the danger of breaking through is lessened.

After the dough has rested for the required length of time, the rolling and folding process is repeated until a total of five rollings and foldings, including the original one, have been made.

It is essential to allow the 15-minute rest period between each rolling and folding stage because, immediately after rolling, the dough is quite tough and elastic. If you were to roll and fold right in succession, the dough would be so tough and elastic that great pressure would have to be put onto the rolling pin. This would not only be very hard to do, but the layers of fats and dough would have a tendency to crush into each other, causing breaks. In resting, the dough becomes soft and pliable, enabling the baker to continue rolling and folding with ease and lessening the danger of crushing the layers into one another.

Practice and observation will determine if one more turn or fold-in-two is required. As a rule, if the fats run out during baking, then one more half-fold may be given; if the goods made from the paste bake out too tight or heavy, then the dough has been worked too much and should have received one rolling and folding less. If you are not quite certain that the dough has received sufficient rolling and folding, a small piece may be baked off in a pie plate to test it.

Because the original shape of puff paste from the first rolling and folding stage is oblong, there is a tendency to roll the dough throughout the entire process of rolling and folding in one direction; namely, lengthwise. This causes the formation of strands that naturally flow in the direction in which the rolling was done. This condition is objectionable and to prevent it the rolling-in should be done in two directions—lengthwise and breadthwise—or roll in the direction of the length of the bench and alternate by rolling at a right angle to the bench length, in a crisscross manner.

After the final rolling stage, the dough should rest at least 1 hour before it is made up into shapes, and the shaped units should be allowed to rest at least 30 minutes before baking.

5. Puff pastry consists of many layers, usually more than 1,000. It is high in fat and leavened completely by steam and hot air. It is made by incorporating a large amount of fat into a dough and by repeated foldings and rollings (usually at least three or four rollings) the many layers are formed. It is used for making patty shells and their big brothers, the vol-au-vent, for crème horns, crème slices, turnovers, for napoleons, and for top crusts when a high-rise, short crust is wanted. The baked puff pastry is delightfully crispy, many layered, and tasty.

What leavening agent is used in puff pastry?

None is added. Steam and hot air expand the many layers of dough.

6. In the Continental kitchen, puff paste is known as *feuilletes,* which means "many leaves." This is an apt description because the identifying characteristic of puff pastry is the fact that it is made of a thousand or more layers of thinly rolled dough and is therefore tender.

   To get the thin layers required, what kind of flour would you think would be used?

   > We need high gluten development and therefore bread flour. Some of the older recipes still call for a weaker flour. If weaker flour is used, the product has fewer layers but is more tender.

7. Modern puff pastry formulas call for bread flour, fat, eggs, water, and salt. The eggs also help in forming the layers.

   Many recipes call for 0.75% cream of tartar, which helps to tenderize the gluten and make a whiter dough.

   Often the fat used in modern formulas is a special puff pastry shortening. It comes in sheets ready to be laid over the rolled dough.

   Why the name *puff pastry?*

   > Because the dough puffs or rises rapidly when exposed to high temperature.

8. No other baked product is quite like puff paste. It contains no sugar or leavening agent, yet it can rise to eight times its original size. A ¼ in. of puff pastry dough may rise to over 2 in. in thickness.

   Puff pastry is thin strands of gluten and eggs separated by fat and leavened by _____.

   > Hot air and steam.

9. Getting the shortening into the dough can be done in two ways, but is usually accomplished by "rolling in," spreading the fat evenly on the rolled surface of the dough.

   The dough and the shortening should be at about the same consistency so that the shortening will not break into and rupture the walls of the dough when rolled.

   Care must be taken that every bit of fat is evenly distributed through the dough.

   If the room is warm, the dough must be kept refrigerated after it has been rolled. The fat must not be less than 60°F, or it will puncture the dough walls.

In making up puff pastry, the temperature of the dough must not be too high or the dough will puncture; the temperature of the fat must not be too high because it will become oily and will not spread.

Temperature of the fat must not be too low because _____.

It will be too hard and puncture the dough.

10. After fat is rolled into the dough, the dough and fat are allowed to rest for at least 20 to 25 minutes under refrigeration to allow the gluten strands to adjust to the new length and to keep the dough and fat at the same temperature. The dough is rolled and rested several times.

   Is making up puff pastry a time-consuming and costly process?

Yes. This is one reason why puff pastry is often purchased already made, ready to be formed and baked.

REVIEW

1. Is puff pastry made from a stiff dough that is high or low in fat?

2. Why add cream of tartar to a puff pastry formula?

3. What leavening agent is contained in a puff paste formula?

4. Why is it important to keep puff pastry comparatively cool?

5. What happens to the fat used in puff pastry if it is too warm?

6. Some puff pastry formulas call for the inclusion of eggs. Why?

7. Danish pastry and puff pastry are alike in that layers of dough are formed. They are different in that one of them is yeast leavened. Which?

CHAPTER 26

REVIEW SECTION

I. INTRODUCTION TO BAKING

II. BAKING PROCESS

I. INTRODUCTION TO BAKING

1. What is baking? The application of heat to food in an "oven." More exactly, as used in this book, baking refers to the application of heat to doughs, batters, and certain dessert mixtures. To bake food, _____ is applied to certain mixtures in an oven.

Heat.

2. By definition, baked products are those items produced in a bakeshop. They include breads, rolls, cakes, pies, and other pastries. They also may include a number of baked desserts such as puddings and meringues. When we think of baked products, we usually think of products that include a large percentage of wheat flour and that are cooked in an _____.

Oven.

3. Doughs and batters are usually mixtures of wheat flour and water to which salt is added. Milk, eggs, sugar, shortening, flavorings, and a leavening agent are often added. The ingredients most common to baked products are _____.

Flour and water.

4. Each common ingredient in a baked product adds a particular character and performs a particular function in producing the finished product. Listed below are the various functions performed by each ingredient.

Functions	Flour	Sugar	Shortening	Eggs	Leavening	Water
Structure builder (toughener)	X			X		
Bulk builder	X	X				
Dryer	X	X		X		
Tenderizer		X	X		X	
Moistener		X	X	X		X
Flavor (including sweetening)		X		X		
Color builder		X		X		
Lubricant			X			
Creaming agent		X	X			
Binding agent				X		
Lightening agent				X	X	

Figure 26–1 *Reprinted with permission of the publisher from J. Amendola,* The Baker's Manual for Quantity Baking and Pastry Making, *2d edition. Copyright 1956 and 1960 by Ahrens Publishing Company, Inc.*

5. From the chart we see that flour acts to dry the product, provide bulk, and add _____.

Strength.

6. Is sugar a tenderizer or a toughener?

Tenderizer.

7. Are eggs tenderizers or tougheners?

Tougheners.

Flour and liquid mixtures can be classified according to the proportion of liquid added to the flour.

8. Bread dough would be classified as _____.

Soft.

9. Is a muffin mixture classified as a drop batter or a soft dough?

Drop batter.

10. A pie crust is an example of a _____ dough.

Stiff.

BREAD INGREDIENTS AND THEIR FUNCTIONS

Ingredients	Binding agent	Absorbing agent	Aids keeping qualities	Back bone and structure	Affects eating qualities	Nutritional value	Affects flavor	Affects fermentation	Affects gluten	Texture and grain	Imparts crust color	Affects symmetry	Volume	Produces tenderness	Adds quality to product
Bread flour	X	X	X	X	X	X									
Salt					X	X	X	X	X						
Sugar		X		X	X	X	X	X			X				
Shortening		X		X	X		X		X	X			X	X	
Milk solids		X		X	X	X			X		X			X	
Water	X														
Yeast						X			X			X			

Figure 26-2 Reprinted with permission of the publisher from J. Amendola's The Baker's Manual for Quantity Baking and Pastry Making 2nd Edition. Copyright 1956 and 1960 by Ahrens Publishing Company, Inc.

11. A popover mixture would be an example of a
    _____.   Pour batter.

12. Some mixtures are classed as pastes, somewhere
    between a soft dough and a batter in consistency.
    Examples are éclair paste and puff paste. Éclair
    paste, also known as chou paste, is made by
    cooking flour, shortening, and water. The batter
    is cooled to 150°F and eggs are added. The end
    product is a smooth, velvety paste, thick enough
    to retain its shape when placed in a pan.

    Pastes can be shaped by forcing them out of a
    pastry tube. Paste has a consistency somewhat
    less than that of _____.   Soft dough.

13. What ingredients added to a dough tend to make
    the dough into a paste?   Eggs and shortening.

14. Flour and liquid mixtures can be classed as bat-
    ters, doughs, and _____.   Pastes.

15. What is preferred in a baked item is largely a matter
    of food habit, what the eater has learned to like. In
    this country, white bread, for example, with a fine,
    even crumb and large volume is most popular.
    Many people, however, like a tough, chewy crust
    like that found in Italian or French bread. Others
    like a coarse loaf with some bran included in the
    flour. Cakes with a high proportion of sugar and
    eggs and a tender texture are most popular.

    In speaking of the quality of a baked item, we
    must always relate the term to whatever the eater
    expects in the product.

    True or false: Baking standards and formulas
    must be in terms of what the eater expects or wants.   True.

16. To make the product desired, the baker has a wide
    range of ingredients and formulas to choose from.   Probably not. Rather,
    True or false: The baker should choose those   the baker should
    formulas that produce a product that the baker   make the item that is
    personally likes best.   most pleasing to
                                                        customers.

17. The baker has a choice of flours to use. To get the desired final product, the baker must understand what each flour will do to the product. Flours are usually classified as cake, pastry, all-purpose, and bread. Most home kitchens use an all-purpose flour, which is somewhere between pastry flour and bread flour in its characteristics. To get optimum results, however, the baker must use a flour that is right for the product that is to be produced. For example, the protein content of flour for use in an angel food cake should be lower than that used in a loaf cake, and both would be lower in protein than flour used for making a pie crust.

   True or false: The baker must understand the differences in various flours and their effects upon the final product.

   Very true.

18. Fats used in most baking are known as *shortening*. They are used for reasons other than the fact that most people like the taste of fats. Shortening surrounds gluten in dough and makes it less continuous and the product more tender.

   When a batter or dough is baked, the fat globules entrap gas and expand.

   Shortening has a "lubricating" effect on doughs that makes them easy to chew and to swallow.

   Is it reasonable to expect the baker to know something about fats and what effects they have on the finished baked item?

   Yes. All craftsworkers understand their tools and products.

19. Pastry includes a wide variety of products made from doughs containing medium to large amounts of fats. Sweet rolls, for example, contain a medium amount of fat and are leavened with yeast. Danish and other rolled-in sweet doughs have butter, margarine, or shortening spread between layers of dough, and puff paste contains so much fat that a portion of it is also folded or laid into the dough. Pie crust contains 40% to 75% as much shortening as flour.

Are pastry doughs identified by the fact that they contain more or less fat (shortening) than other doughs?

More fat.

20. Bakers have developed for themselves a unique system for calculating formulas for all types of baked products that is simple, effective, yet un-involved. Instead of formulating on the basis of true percentages that in each case must add up to 100%, he does so on the basis of so many pounds of any ingredient involved to 100 lb of flour (the baker's basic ingredient). If he uses 2 lb of eggs to 10 lb of flour, he is using 20% eggs. If 12 lb sugar are used to 10 lb flour, it is 120% sugar.

This system is known as *baker's percentages*. It simplifies formula variation because it provides a simple means of varying one ingredient at a time without having to recalculate the percentage rela-tionship of the other ingredients to this change.

Suppose a formula calls for 30% shortening and 10 lb of flour are used. How many pounds of eggs are needed?

3 lb.

21. If a formula calls for 20 lb flour and 20% sugar, how many pounds of sugar are needed?

4 lb (20% of 20 lb).

II. BAKING PROCESS

22. The baking process takes place in an oven as heat is applied to doughs or batters. The process can be broken down into these steps:

1. Gases are formed and expand.
2. The gluten and eggs present are stretched to form a new structure. These become firm (coag-ulate) and provide chewiness in the product. They both are tougheners.
3. The starches present take on moisture and be-come firm (gelatinize).
4. Some of the water evaporates.

5. Shortenings present melt and release air bubbles that in the case of batters help to leaven the batter. The oil (melted shortening) then deposits around cell walls and makes them less tough.

6. Flavors develop and brown colors appear because of the caramelization of sugar and browning of the milk, gluten, and egg proteins.

7. A crust forms as water is driven off by the heat, a process that occurs first on the surface. The baking process involves heat, gas formation, coagulation of proteins, gelatinization of starches, vaporization of water, melting of shortening, development of flavors and color, and the formation of a _____.

Crust.

23. During the baking process, what is it that raises the dough or batter to create a new and large form that is of lighter density than the dough or batter?

The gases that are formed. These include steam, hot air, and carbon dioxide, depending on what leavening agent is used.

24. What ingredients are mainly responsible for giving a dough product its chewiness or toughness?

The gluten and eggs present.

25. When a starch is heated in the presence of moisture and expands (swells) and then becomes firm, this is known as _____.

Gelatinization.

26. What is it that tenderizes a dough or batter product?

The shortenings or oils present. Sugar also acts as a tenderizing agent.

27. Let's look at the baking process step by step, first the gas formation and the leavening action.

Depending upon the leavening agent used in baking, the gases formed are hot air and steam, carbon dioxide, and, when baking ammonia is used, ammonia bicarbonate. Some items such as éclairs, pound cake, and angel food cake are leavened by hot air and steam only.

Most cakes are leavened by the carbon dioxide

gas formed from baking powder. A few products are leavened by baking soda and an acid as in some cookies and chocolate cakes.

Leavening of a baked product involves the expansion of a _____.

Gas.

28. Baked dough products rise or are leavened by the action of a gas—usually carbon dioxide—which expands the dough. CO_2 is formed by the action of yeast, which breaks down sugar to CO_2 and alcohol and by the action of an acid or heat on soda, which releases CO_2. Baking powders contain soda plus an acid ingredient that reacts with the soda when moistened and the product is heated. Double-action baking powders are called this because they release from a fifth to a third of their gas while at room temperature when moistened. The remainder of the gas is given off during the baking process; hence the baking powder acts twice and is named *double-acting*. A single-acting baking powder gives off all of its gas in the cold stage when moistened. This makes it difficult to handle in high-quantity baking.

What gas is responsible for most of the leavening action in baked dough products?

Carbon dioxide gas.

29. Double-acting baking powders give off CO_2 twice—when first mixed into a product and at what other time?

During the baking when heat is applied.

30. In using soda alone as a leavening agent, we may add an acid such as sour milk, molasses, or buttermilk. Soda that develops carbon dioxide alone in a product without an acid ingredient to react with it (by heat alone) may leave a soapy flavor in the baked product. Sometimes we add an excess of soda to a chocolate cake so an alkaline action is developed, and this causes the chocolate to turn a nice reddish color. However, we do this at the expense of the flavor, for we may get this soapy flavor in such a cake.

Baking soda and acid produce leavening by the formulation of what gas?

Carbon dioxide.

31. Still another leavening agent used, but not widely, is baking ammonia (ammonium bicarbonate). In the presence of moisture and heat, baking ammonia changes to carbon dioxide and ammonia gas. It is used in making cookies and chou pastry (for making the shells of cream puffs, éclairs, and the small cream puffs known as profiteroles). Ammonia does not discolor the dough as would baking soda. The word *choux* means "cabbage" in French; the chou pastry probably takes its name from the fact that some of the pastries look like little cabbages.

   Would you think that in using ammonia as a leavening agent the residual gas would be dangerous?

Most of the gas escapes; when the shells are opened so that the fillings can be inserted, any gas that is left escapes.

32. To achieve a leavened product, we need (1) a gas acting on the dough, paste, or batter and (2) the presence of what substance in the dough that stretches and forms the structure for the raised product?

Wheat flour containing gluten.

33. In the leavening action, the gas, whatever it is, expands into cells already in the dough or batter (by creaming or mixing), stretching and enlarging them. The cell walls that are expanded are made up of gluten and starch.

   Which ingredients in a baked product are absolutely essential if the product is to rise?

Gluten or egg protein, because they alone will stretch under the pressure of the expanding gas.

34. Carbon dioxide performs what task in a baking powder biscuit?

The gas that is released from the baking powder or soda expands with heat, stretching the gluten, which coagulates and firms, giving the biscuit its shape and texture.

35. Steam and hot air are other gases that also expand dough. When water changes to steam, its volume increases 1,600 times. This accounts for almost all of the leavening action in the baking of popovers, cream puff shells, crackers, and pie crust.

Is it necessary for carbon dioxide gas to be present for a dough to rise?

No. Air and steam also act to expand the dough.

36. Yeast is used to make bread and sweet dough rise. Yeast action begins during the time the dough is allowed to ferment and ends in the oven, when the internal temperature of the dough reaches around 140°F.

Ethyl alcohol is produced by the action of the yeast on some of the sugars in the dough. The yeast also releases carbon dioxide. The carbon dioxide is the main leavening agent in a yeast dough, although gases from water (steam) and ethyl alcohol may help some in the leavening.

Carbon dioxide gas is formed by the action of baking soda, baking powder, and what other common baking ingredient?

Yeast.

37. Yeast is also used to leaven such items as baba au rhum, English muffins, and crumpets. Sourdough and old-fashioned hotcake batter are "started" by use of an old dough or batter in which fermentation is quite complete. Such a starter is highly acid or sour, hence the name *sour dough*. The gold prospectors of Alaska carried bits of this dough in their pockets, keeping the yeast or bacteria alive to be used at their next campsite.

A *sourdough* refers to an individual who uses sourdough as his yeast product, but it also refers to the dough that has been well _____.

Fermented.

38. The leavening action of yeast is most interesting. Gases are formed in the process known as *fer-*

mentation. The fermentation we are talking about is splitting sugar by the action of yeast enzymes to form carbon dioxide and alcohol. The ancient Egyptians knew about the leavening action of yeast but did not understand what was taking place.

True or false: Yeast as it grows gives off the carbon dioxide that raises the dough.

> Not quite. The yeast gives off an enzyme, zymase, that splits some sugars into alcohol and carbon dioxide.

39. During fermentation, enzymes in the yeast known as *zymase* change the sugars, dextrose, and levulose into carbon dioxide and ethyl alcohol:

$$C_6H_{12}O_6 + \text{yeast } 2\ CO_2 + 2\ C_2H_5OH$$

Dextrose or levulose	Carbon dioxide	Alcohol
100 parts	48.9 parts	51.1 parts

Temperatures of about 78 to 90°F are best for fermentation. Above 110°F yeast action is slowed, and at about 138°F yeast is destroyed.

Enzymes in the yeast act on simple sugars to produce _____ and alcohol, which cause the dough to rise. This is the fermentation process.

> CO_2.

40. Yeast is in the air practically everywhere. *Saccharomyces cerevisiae* is the yeast that is responsible for splitting sugar into carbon dioxide and alcohol and is the yeast wanted for fermenting dough products. In fact, *saccharomyces* means "sugar splitter."

Commercial bakers' yeast is purchased as compressed yeast or active dry yeast. Compressed yeast can be bought in 1-lb or 5-lb blocks. If refrigerated, it keeps its fermentation power up to 4 to 5 weeks. If frozen, it can be stored for months. Compressed yeast is about 70% water.

If most of the water is taken out of compressed yeast, we have active dry yeast.

Bakers' yeast can be bought in compressed or dry form. Is the dried form the same as or different from the compressed form with the water removed?

Same as.

41. Dry yeast can be used interchangeably with compressed yeast. Only 40% as much of the dry yeast is needed.

   Compressed yeast should be stored between 30 and 45°F. Dry yeast can be stored at room temperature. When the temperature rises and moisture is present, the yeast comes to life and begins to grow.

   Yeast action varies with the temperature:

60–70°F	Slow reaction
80°F	Normal reaction
90–100°F	Fast reaction
138°F	Yeast dies

   Looking at the chart, what do you think happens to yeast during the baking process?

When the heat approaches 138°F, the yeast dies.

42. In small-quantity baking, yeast is conditioned by being placed in warm water. Compressed yeast is sprinkled into water that is about 100°F. Dry active yeast is sifted into water at about 110°F. Both are allowed to stand about 3 minutes before stirring.

   To get yeast ready for use in small-quantity baking, we condition it by placing it in _____.

Warm water (in large-scale baking, yeast is mixed directly into the dough).

43. Because yeast is a living one-cell plant, it needs food, as does any other living plant or animal. Besides the food found in the flour and water, many bakers add yeast foods, which cause the yeast to be more active and give a larger volume of a dough product. The yeast foods also reduce the time required for the dough to rise (proof). Yeast foods contain bromate, ammonium chloride, and gypsum.

   Because these foods are minerals, would a yeast food tend to offset the undesirable effects of using soft water?

Yes. A certain amount of minerals is desirable for tightening the gluten. Soft water lacks such minerals. The yeast food makes up for their absence.

44. Much of the characteristic aroma of bread and similar baked items comes directly from the activity of the yeast.

The yeast in bread, in addition to being the principal cause of the leavening action, also adds _____ to the bread.

Flavor.

45. The flavor of baked goods is developed from a variety of factors, among them the sugar, fat, and flavorings present. What baking action also adds flavor and some color?

The browning of the sugars, milk, and proteins.

46. When starch gelatinizes, it helps give the baked product some firmness and most of its bulk.

Starch together with _____ gives the product its structure and bulk.

Coagulated protein.

REVIEW

1. During the baking process, dough is leavened (raised) by the action of expanding _____.

2. The gases press against the dough, stretching _____ present.

3. The proteins present become firm and are largely responsible for the structure of the product. Are gluten and eggs considered tougheners or tenderizers?

4. Name two tenderizers.

5. Where does the carbon dioxide that is made available by the fermentation process come from?

6. Is yeast used in baking dead or living?

7. At what temperature is yeast killed?

8. The best temperature for fermentation that takes place before baking is about _____.

9. Do yeast foods make the yeast more or less active?

10. If yeast activity is speeded up, is proof time (fermentation time) longer or shorter?

11. True or false: Soft water is best for proper gluten development.

12. Éclairs are leavened by what gases?

13. The technical term for the process that takes place when starches are cooked is _____.

14. When acted upon by the yeast enzyme zymase, sugar splits into _____ and _____.

RECOMMENDED READINGS

Gisslen, Wayne, *Professional Baking.* New York. John Wiley & Sons, 1985.

Sultan, Wilham J., *Practical Baking Fifth Edition.* New York. Van Nostrand Reinhold, 1990.

For the person who wishes to seriously delve into the physics and chemistry of baking:

Pyler, E.J., *Baking Science & Technology Third Edition,* Volumes I & II. Merriam, Kansas. Sosland Publishing Company.

For a list of baking books, some old, some new, and some highly specialized, such as *The Italian Baker, Professional French Pastry,* and *Yeast Technology,* write to:

Culinary & Hospitality Industry Publications
Golden Bear Lane
Kingwood, TX 77339

GLOSSARY

Alpha-amylase: Added to bread dough to convert some starch to sugar and dextrose.

Ascorbyl palmitate: Added to shortening, it reacts with oxygen to prevent reactions with unsaturated fats that cause rancidity.

Arteriosclerosis: The gradual blocking of arteries with deposits of lipid, smooth muscle cells, and connective tissue. Contributes to most deaths from cardiovascular disease.

Average flour value: Value composed of four factors: color of flour, loaves per barrel, size of loaf, and quality of bread as applied to any given shipment of flour.

Baba au rhum: French sweet dough cake soaked with rum.

Bacteria: Numerous microscopic organisms, various species of which are involved in fermentation and spoilage.

Bag out: To press product out of a conical canvas (or plastic disposable) bag onto baking pans in the desired forms.

Bake: To cook by dry heat in a closed space, as in an oven.

Baked Alaska: Cake layer topped with firm ice cream, completely covered with meringue, and then delicately browned in a very hot oven.

Bake-off: A bakery operation that concentrates on finish-baking frozen doughs supplied from a central bakery or purchased from a manufacturer.

Baking ammonia: A leavening ingredient that releases ammonia gas and carbon dioxide.

Baking or bicarbonate of soda: A sodium salt of carbonic acid with the ability to combine with acid to produce carbon dioxide. It is alkaline in nature.

Baking powder: A chemical leavening agent composed of baking soda, dry acid, and usually cornstarch to absorb moisture; when wet, carbon dioxide (a gas) is given off to raise the batter.

Batter: A pourable mixture containing flour or other starch, used for the production of such products as cakes and breads and for coating products to be deep-fried.

Beat (or whip): To whip air into a liquid mass such as eggs, sweet cream, or gelatin solution until the desired lightness is obtained.

Bench: A worktable for product make-up.

Benzoyl peroxide: A powder that, mixed in very small amounts with flour, bleaches the flour.

Biscuit: Small roll made with yeast, soda, or baking powder. In British usage, a kind of crisp or hard bread that is thin, flat, and made without leavening.

Biscuit tortoni: Mousse containing and sprinkled with macaroon crumbs and frozen in individual paper cases.

Blanch: To remove the skins from various nuts and other foods by scalding.

Blancmange: An English pudding made of milk, sugar, and cornstarch; or a French dessert made of milk, cream, almonds, and gelatin.

Bleeding: Term applied to dough that has been cut and left unsealed at the cut, thus permitting the escape of air and gas.

Blend: To fold or mix two materials together to obtain equal distribution.

Bloom: Of chocolate, a whitish coating caused by separated cocoa butter; of a bread-crust, a rich or lustrous appearance. *Sugar bloom* is a white-speckled appearance on icings and coatings caused by sugar crystallization.

Boil: To bubble, emitting vapor, when heat is applied. Boiling temperature for water is considered as 212°F at ordinary altitudes, but it varies with other liquids and other altitudes.

Boiled icing: Made by boiling sugar and water to thread stage (238°F) and then adding it to beaten egg whites and confectioners' sugar.

Bolting: Sifting of ground grain to remove the bran.

Boston brown bread: A dark, sweet bread (not yeast-raised) containing cornmeal and molasses; it is steamed and not baked.

Bouchée: Literally "a mouthful." A small, baked pastry shell or a small tart.

Bowl knife: A spatula or flexible, dull-edged knife used to scrape batter or dough from bowl sides.

Bran: The hard outer covering of kernels of wheat and other grains.

Bran flour: Flour to which bran flakes have been added.

Bran muffin: Sweet muffin containing a large percentage of bran.

Bread: 1. The accepted term for food of flour, sugar, shortening, salt, and liquid made light by the action of yeast. 2. A staple food made from flour or meal mixed with a liquid, usually combined with a leavening agent and kneaded, shaped into loaves, and baked.

Bread dough: The uncooked mass of ingredients used to make bread.

Bread faults: Deviations from standards of perfection; used to determine wrong factors in the process of production of bread.

Bread flour: A flour with 11% to 13% protein content. Usually made from hard winter wheat. A strong flour, such as patent flour.

Bread schedule: List of exact periods of dough fermentation; also shows times needed for completing the baking process.

Bread scoring: Analysis of finished loaf to determine quality.

Breaking down: Overcreaming of ingredients, causing weakened products that collapse.

Brioche: A soft, light-textured roll or bun made from eggs, butter, flour, and yeast.

Bucky dough: A dough that is hard to handle.

Buns: Small cakes of bread dough, sometimes slightly sweetened or flavored.

Buttercream frosting: Rich, uncooked frosting containing powdered sugar, butter and/or other shortening, and egg white.

Butter horns: Basic sweet dough cut and shaped like horns.

Butter sponge: Sponge cake batter to which shortening is added. Used for torten and French pastry.

Butylated hydroxytoluene (BHT): An antioxidant added to prevent oxidation and rancidity in baked products.

Cacao: An evergreen tree, native to tropical America, from which chocolate is obtained. Large quantities are grown in West Africa.

Cake: A leavened and shortened sweet product containing flour, sugar, salt, egg, milk, liquid, flavoring, shortening, and a leavening agent.

Cake faults: Deviations from standards of perfection for the type.

Cake flour: A fine, white flour made from soft wheat.

Calcium propionate: Added to baked goods (principally bread and roll dough) to prevent the growth of mold and certain bacteria.

Caramel: A brown compound formed when sugar or starch is heated. Sugars are sometimes added to baked goods so that they will turn brown (caramelize) when heated.

Caramel icing: Cooked icing of brown sugar, shortening, and milk.

Caramelized sugar: Dry sugar heated, with constant stirring, until it melts and darkens in color; used for flavoring and color.

Carbohydrates: Includes starches, sugars, fiber, and pectin. Most baked products contain large amounts of carbohydrates, which are important in providing the body with the materials for energy.

Carbonated ammonia: Leavening agent made of ammonia and carbonic acid.

Carbon chain length in fatty acids: Partly determines the melting point of a fat. The longer the chain, the higher the melting point. Coconut oil, which is almost 90% saturated fatty acids, has a low melting point because it has a high proportion of relatively short-chain fatty acids.

Carbon dioxide: A colorless, tasteless, edible gas obtained during fermentation or from the combination of soda and acid. Important for its leavening action in baked products.

Cardamon: Angular, aromatic seeds of an herb grown in India and Ceylon, having aniselike taste. Used whole or ground in pickling, breads, cookies, and many Scandinavian desserts.

Carragheen: Extracted from Irish moss, a type of seaweed named after Carragheen, Ireland, and used as a stabilizer in desserts, milk puddings, and a number of other foods. Like gelatin, it can form a gel.

Casein: The principal nitrogenous, or protein, part of milk.

Celsius scale: The metric system of temperature measurement, with 0°C set at the freezing point of water and 100°C set at the boiling point of water.

Centi-: Prefix in the metric system meaning "one-hundredth."

Cheesecake: Cake made of sweet or short dough base with a filling of cheese combined with eggs and milk.

Chemical leavener: A leavener such as baking soda, baking powder, or baking ammonia that releases gases produced by chemical reactions.

Chiffon method: A cake-mixing method involving folding whipped egg whites into a batter made of flour, egg yolks, and oil.

Chocolate liquor: Unsweetened chocolate, consisting of cocoa solids and cocoa butter.

Cholesterol: A building block for cells and hormones. In the bloodstream it is known as serum cholesterol and can be a factor in the harmful buildup of plaque in the arteries and heart disease.

Chou pâte: Paste used in making éclairs, cream puffs, and French doughnuts.

Cinnamon: The aromatic bark of certain trees of the laurel family, which is ground and used as a spice flavoring.

Citron: The sweetened rind of the citron fruit.

Clear flour: 1. Flour made from middlings after patent flour is taken. 2. A tan wheat flour made from the outer portion of the endosperm and used mainly as part of the flour for making rye bread.

Cleave or round: To shape a piece of dough into a smooth special form.

CMC (cellulose gum): Made from cellulose and acetic acid, it is sometimes used in bread doughs to hold moisture and increase volume. In pie fillings it prevents the fruit from settling or floating to the top.

Coagulation: The process by which proteins become firm, usually when heated. Also, transformation of a liquid into a semisolid or solid mass.

Cocoa: 1. A powder made from chocolate minus most of its cocoa butter. 2. The dry powder that remains after cocoa butter is pressed out of chocolate liquor.

Coffee cake: Sweet bread in various shapes, with fillings and toppings.

Combination bakery: An operation that combines frozen dough, mixes, and scratch products.

Confectioners' sugar: Sucrose that is ground to a fine powder and mixed with a little cornstarch to prevent caking.

Corn flour: Coarse flour ground from corn; it is finer than meal.

Cornmeal: Granular form of corn somewhat coarser than corn flour.

Corn syrup: Made by "digesting" cornstarch with acids or enzymes. It contains dextrose, maltose, and dextrin. Some of the dextrose can be converted to fructose, a sugar sweetener, by enzymatic action to form high-fructose corn syrup. These syrups can be used to sweeten baked products, retard crystallization of sugar in icings, and prevent loss of moisture from cakes, cookies, and whipped foods.

Couverture: Natural, sweet chocolate containing no added fats other than natural cocoa butter; used for dipping, molding, coating, and similar purposes.

Cream: The fat part of cow's milk; or a thickened, cooked mass of sugar, eggs, milk, and a thickener used for pies and fillings.

Creaming: The process of beating fat and sugar together to blend them uniformly and to incorporate air.

Cream of tartar (Potassium bitartate): Used as a leavening agent in baked goods.

Cream pie: One-crust pie with cream filling and topped with whipped cream or meringue.

Cream puff: Baked puffs of cream puff dough (chou pâte) that are hollow; usually filled with whipped cream or a cream filling.

Crème: Cream or cream sauce.

Crème Anglaise: A light vanilla-flavored custard sauce made of milk, sugar, and egg yolks.

Crème caramel: A custard baked in a mold lined with caramelized sugar.

Crème Chantilly: Cream whipped with vanilla and sugar.

Crêpe: A very thin French pancake, often served rolled around a filling. A crêpe suzette is served in butter sauce flavored with orange, lemon, and curaçao and then flamed in brandy.

Crescent rolls: Hard-crusted rolls shaped into crescents, often topped with seeds.

Croissant: A flaky, buttery yeast roll shaped like a crescent, made from a rolled-in dough, and usually served at breakfast.

Crullers: Long, twisted baking powder doughnuts.

Cupcakes: Small cakes of layer cake batter baked in muffin pans.

Custard: A liquid that is thickened or set by the coagulation of egg protein; a sweetened mixture of eggs and milk that is baked or cooked over hot water.

Danish pastry: A flaky yeast dough with butter rolled into it and filled with almond, cheese, jam, or other fillings.

Deci-: Prefix in the metric system meaning "one-tenth."

Deck oven: Containing separate shelves. Product can be heated either in or out of pans.

Developing dough: Making dough smoother by mixing so that proteins are properly hydrated and the gluten is stretched and relaxed. A dough is "developed" when it pulls away from the sides of the mixing bowl.

Dextrin: Made by the action of heat, acids, or enzymes in starch. It is used as a thickening agent and to prevent sugar from crystallizing in candy.

Dextrose: see *Glucose.*

Diastase: An enzyme that can convert starches into dextrin and maltose (a simple sugar). Found in flour and in diastatic malt.

Disaccharide: A complex or "double" sugar such as sucrose.

Docking: Piercing or perforating pastry dough before baking in order to allow steam to escape and to avoid blistering.

Doughnut: A round cake, usually with a center hole, made of yeast or baking powder dough and cooked in hot deep fat.

Doughnut screens: Screens used to lift doughnuts from fat or for keeping them under the fat surface during cooking.

Dough temperature: Temperature of dough at different stages.

Drained weight: The weight of solid canned fruit after draining off the juice.

Dredge: To sprinkle thoroughly with sugar or another dry powder.

Drop batter: A batter that is too thick to pour but will drop from a spoon in lumps.

Dry yeast: A dehydrated form of yeast.

Dusting: Distributing a film of flour on pans or a workbench.

Dusting flour: Flour spread on workbench to prevent sticking.

Dutch process cocoa: Cocoa that has been processed with an alkali to reduce its acidity.

Éclair: A long, thin shell of the same paste as cream puffs.

Éclair paste: A paste or dough made of boiling water or milk, butter, flour, and eggs; used to make éclairs, cream puffs, and similar products.

Egg wash: A mixture of eggs and water (or milk) in equal parts brushed on an unbaked product to produce a glazed effect and to give the product a rich brown color.

Emulsifier: Provides stability to an emulsion and widely used in bread and rolls for antistaling, softening, dough conditioning, stabilizing, and aerating.

Emulsify: To make into an emulsion. The shortening (fat) is kept from separating, which allows the mixture to contain more sugar.

Emulsion: A suspension of small globules of one liquid in a second liquid, with which the first will not mix. A dispersion of liquids that are immiscible (incapable of mixing or attaining homogeneity). Milk, mayonnaise, ice cream, and icings are examples.

Endosperm: The starchy inner portion of grain kernels.

Enriched bread: Bread made from enriched flour or containing federally prescribed amounts of thiamin, riboflavin, iron, and niacin.

Enzyme: A minute substance produced by living organisms that can bring about changes in organic materials.

Evaporated milk: Unsweetened canned milk from which water has been removed before canning.

Expansion of dough: The stage of dough production when the most air has been assimilated.

Extract: Essence of fruits or spices used as a flavoring.

Extraction: The portion of the grain kernel that is separated into a particular grade of flour, usually expressed as a percentage.

Fat: Predominantly esters of acids and glycerol, commonly called *triglycerides.*

Fermentation: The chemical reaction of the ingredients used in making dough that causes the forming of a gas, carbon dioxide, which in turn causes the dough to expand.

Fiber: Two types of fiber, soluble and insoluble. Both types are present in whole grains, raw fruits, and vegetables. Insoluble fiber provides little or no nutrition. Both types are important for providing bulk to the human diet. Soluble fiber such as that found in oat and rice bran is believed to be helpful in reducing serum cholesterol.

Fillings: Sweet creams, jams, or similar substances baked between cake layers, in cake rolls, or shaped into yeast-raised goods.

Flavor: An extract, emulsion, or spice used to produce a pleasant taste or the taste of a finished product.

Fleurons: Garnitures made from light puff paste cut into oval, diamond, or crescent shapes and served with meat, fish, or soup.

Floor time: Time allowed for additional fermentation to take place.

Flour: Finely ground meal of grain (wheat, rye, corn, etc.).

Flour scales: Large platform scales used to show the weight of flour when delivered and when used in order to detect losses by shrinkage.

Foam: Mass of beaten egg and sugar, as in sponge cake, before adding flour.

Fold: The method of lapping dough over on itself after it reaches the right fermentation, as in making yeast-raised sweet goods.

Folding: Gently incorporating or mixing flour into the mix.

Folding or punching: Forcing the gas out of dough by folding one part of the dough over the other.

Fondant slab: Marble slab on which fondant is worked until creamy.

Fondant: A type of icing made of boiled sugar syrup that is agitated so that it crystallizes into a mass of extremely small white crystals; an icing of boiled sugar and water, without egg white.

Formula: In baking, a recipe giving ingredients, amounts to be used, and the method of combining them. Amounts are usually given by weight.

Free fatty acids: Uncombined fatty acids present in a fat. Prolonged use of a fat in frying builds up the amount of free fatty acids and produces unfavorable flavors.

French bread: An unsweetened crusty bread baked in a narrow strip and containing very little or no shortening.

French doughnuts: Doughnuts made of chou paste.

French knife: A long knife with a pointed blade used in cutting cakes, doughs, and nuts.

French pastry: A variety of small, fancy cakes and other pastries, usually in a single-portion size.

Fritters: Doughnuts made from cream puff paste and fried in hot deep fat; fruit-filled drops of heavy cake batter fried in deep fat; a deep-fried item made of or coated with a batter or dough.

Fructose: Constitutes one-half of a molecule of sucrose (cane or beet sugar); glucose (corn sugar) makes up the other half. It is made chemically by splitting sucrose into its two component sugars and then separating out and purifying the fructose. In some foods it tastes almost twice as sweet as sucrose, so less of it can be used to achieve the same sweetening effect as sucrose.

Fruitcake: A cake containing large amounts of dried fruits and nuts with only enough batter to bind the fruit together.

Frying: In the baking industry, cooking in hot deep fat.

Fumarate: Chemical added to bread dough to strengthen it so that it can withstand the mechanical punishment received from breadmaking machinery.

Gâteau: French for "cake."

Gaufre: French for "waffle."

Gelatin: Obtained from collagen, the major constituent of tendons, ligaments, and skin. When dissolved in hot water and then allowed to cool, the molecules of gelatin react weakly to form a tangled, three-dimensional network of long, thin molecules forming a weak gel.

Gelatinization of starch: Formation of jellylike substance when moistened starch is cooked. The starch granules absorb water and swell in size.

Génoise: A sponge cake made with a batter containing melted butter.

Germ: That part of the seed (such as in grain) from which the new plant grows.

Glacé: Sugar treated to look like ice.

Glaze: 1. A transparent coating, such as syrup, applied to a food. 2. To make a food shiny or glossy by coating it with a glaze or by browning it under a broiler or in a hot oven.

Gliadin: A protein in wheat flour that combines with another protein, glutenin, to form gluten; the part of gluten that gives it elasticity.

Glucose (dextrose): A simple sugar made by the action of acid on starch (corn syrup).

Gluten: The protein part of wheat flour that gives structure to bakery products by enabling flour to expand around air or gas and to hold the texture so formed; the determining quality factor. It is added to specialty breads to provide more strength.

Glutenin: The part of gluten that gives it strength.

Graham flour: Unbolted wheat meal.

Gram: The basic unit of weight in the metric system; equal to about a twenty-eighth of an ounce.

Greasing: Spreading a film of fat on a surface.

Guar gum: The endosperm of the guar plant, used to increase resilience of doughs and batters.

Gum arabic: A gum obtained from a species of acacia tree found in the Middle East.

Gum paste: A white modeling substance of gum tragacanth of gelatin, water, and sugar.

Gum tragacanth: A gum from a Middle East bush used as a thickening agent in acidic foods.

Hardness of water: An indication of mineral salts in greater amounts than are found in soft water.

Hard wheat: Wheat high in protein.

Hearth: The heated baking surface or floor of an oven.

Hearth bread: A bread that is baked directly on the bottom of the oven, not in a pan.

High ratio: Term referring to cakes and cake formulas mixed by a special method and containing more sugar than flour, the mixing method used for these cakes, or certain specialty formulated ingredients used in these cakes, such as shortening.

Hot-cross buns: Sweet, yeast-raised buns with raisins added, marked on top with a cross in dough or frosting; a Lenten favorite.

Hydrogenated oil: Oil to which hydrogen had been added to give a type of shortening; hydrogenation of oil creates additional saturation of fat molecules.

Hydrogenation: A process that converts liquid oils to solid fats (shortenings) by chemically bonding hydrogen to the fat molecules. A process by which some of the unsaturated fatty acids present light upon a hydrogen atom and become saturated. If an oil is completely hydrogenated, it becomes a hard, brittle solid at room temperature. Hydrogenation changes oil from a viscous form to a plastic form and reduces its susceptibility to oxidation and rancidity.

Hydroxylated lecithin: Manufactured by treating soybean lecithin with peroxide, it is used as an emulsifier and antioxidant in baked foods.

Hygrometer: An instrument to determine the degree of humidity.

Hygroscopic: Able to draw moisture from the air.

Ice: To frost or put on as icing or frosting; frozen water.

Icing: A frosting or coating for cakes made by mixing confectioners' sugar with water and other ingredients.

Inversion: A chemical process in which a double sugar splits into two simple sugars.

Invert sugar: A fifty-fifty mix of glucose and fructose, it is sweeter and more soluble and crystallizes less readily than sucrose (ordinary table sugar). Invert sugar forms when sucrose is split in two by an enzyme (invertase) or an acid.

Jelly: A combination of fruit juice and sugar stiffened by the action of the sugar on the pectin in the fruit.

Kernel paste: Ground apricot kernels and sugar.

Kilo-: Prefix in the metric system meaning "100."

Knead: To work into a mass or to develop dough by added mixing.

Lactose: The sugar of cow's milk.

Lard: Rendered hog fat.

Lean dough: A dough that is low in fat and sugar.

Leavening: The production of gases in a baked product to increase carbon dioxide and to produce shape and texture; raising or lightening of dough by air, steam, or gas (carbon dioxide).

Leavening agent: An ingredient (or ingredients) used to introduce carbon dioxide, such as yeast, baking powder, or baking soda plus sour milk.

Lecithin: Commercially obtained from soybeans, it is used as an antioxidant in shortenings and oils to retard spoilage and rancidity. It also acts as a strong emulsifier by lowering the surface tension of water. In baked goods lecithin helps shortening mix with other dough ingredients, retards the crystallization of starch, and stabilizes air bubbles in cake batter. The end result is bread and rolls that are more tender and stay fresh longer, as well as fluffier cakes.

Levulose: Better known as *fructose*, a simple sugar found in honey and fruits.

Liter: The basic unit of volume in the metric system; equal to slightly more than a quart.

Locust bean gum (carob seed gum, St. John's bread): From the endosperm of the carob tree bean, a Mediterranean species. It is used to improve the texture of pie filling and to make softer, more resilient cakes and biscuits.

Low-density lipoproteins (LDL): Carried in serum cholesterol and associated with increased risk of heart disease.

Macaroon paste: A combination of almond and kernel paste.

Macaroons: Small cookies of nut paste (such as almond), sugar, and egg white.

Make up: Method of mixing ingredients or handling dough. After mixing, it includes scaling individual ingredients and shaping for final proofing.

Malt extract: A syrupy liquid obtained from malt mash.

Malt syrup: A type of syrup containing maltose sugar, extracted from sprouted barley.

Marrons (chestnuts) glacé: Chestnuts preserved in syrup or candied; used in making fancy desserts.

Marzipan: A paste or confection made of almonds and sugar and often used for modeling, masking, and making torten.

Masking: Act of covering with icing, frosting, or a sauce.

Meal: Coarsely ground grain; unbolted wheat flour.

Melting point: The temperature at which a solid becomes liquid.

Meringue: A thick, white foam made of whipped egg whites and sugar.

Meter: The basic unit of length in the metric system; slightly more than a yard.

Metric system: A system of weights and measures baked upon multiple units of ten; used in the baking industry chiefly for flour analysis.

Middlings: Coarse particles of ground wheat consisting of the endosperm fragments with some mixture of bran particles and germ. It is made during the rolling of the grain in flour mills.

Milk bread: White bread in which all liquid is milk or that contains not less than 8.8 parts (by weight) of milk solids for each 100 parts of flour (by weight). This federal standard is rigidly enforced.

Mix: A mixture of ingredients that usually requires only the addition of water and/or yeast to produce a batter or dough.

Mixing: The blending of ingredients.

Mocha: A flavor combination of coffee and cocoa.

Molasses: Light to dark brown syrup obtained in making cane sugar.

Molder: Machine that shapes dough pieces for various shapes.

Mono- and diglycerides: Make bread softer and prevent staling by preventing the starch from crystallizing and make cakes fluffier by helping to generate and trap air bubbles.

Monosaccharide: A simple or single sugar such as glucose or fructose.

Monosaturated fats: Fats with fatty acids that contain a large percentage of carbon-to-carbon links with only a single double bond.

Monounsaturated fatty acids: A fatty acid that contains one double bond. Olive, corn, and canola oil are high in monounsaturated fatty acids. A diet high in mono-unsaturated fatty acids may conserve HDL in the form of cholesterol in the blood and be considered a protection against coronary heart disease.

Mousse: A frozen dessert lightened by the addition of whipped cream, egg whites, or both.

Muffins: Small, light quick bread baked in muffin pans.

Napoleon: Delicate French pastry made with puff paste in layers with a cream filling between and thin frosting or powdered sugar on top.

Nesselrode pie: Rum-flavored Bavarian cream pie filling with mixed preserved fruits and chestnuts in a flaky pie shell and topped with shaved chocolate.

No-time dough: A bread dough made with a large quantity of yeast and given no fermentation time except for a short rest after mixing.

Nougat: A confection made from almonds, pistachio nuts, and sugar.

Oatmeal: Meal made by grinding oats.

Old dough: A dough that is overfermented.

One mix: A cake mixing method where all ingredients are combined and beaten at one time.

One-stage method: A cookie-mixing method in which all ingredients are added to the bowl at once.

Oven spring: The rapid rise of yeast goods in the oven due to the production and expansion of gases caused by the oven heat.

Parker House rolls: Folded buns of fairly rich dough.

Pasteurized: Heat-treated to kill bacteria that might cause disease or spoilage.

Pastillage: A sugar paste used for decorative work that becomes very hard when dry.

Pastry cream: A thick custard sauce containing eggs and starch.

Pastry flour: A weak flour used for pastries and cookies.

Pâte a chou: Éclair paste.

Pâte feuillete: French name for puff pastry.

Patent flour: The fine meal of ground spring wheat, used mainly for making bread.

Pectin: A natural fruit substance that, when in the right balance with sugar and acid, forms fruit juice into a gel.

Peel: A flat wooden shovel used to place hearth breads in an oven and to remove them.

Petit four glacé: An iced or cream-filled petit four.

Petits fours: Small cakes of various shapes and flavors.

Phyllo: A paper-thin dough or pastry used to make strudels and various Middle Eastern and Greek desserts.

Piping jelly: A transparent, sweet jelly used for decorating cakes.

Polydextrose: A polymer made up primarily of dextrose (corn sugar, glucose) molecules, plus about 10% sorbitol and 1% citric acid. It has one-fourth the calories of sugar and is used as a replacement for sugar, starch, and fat, thereby reducing the number of calories in a food.

Polysorbate 60, 65, 80: Emulsifiers that make bread, rolls, and doughnuts more tender and help to prevent staling.

Polyunsaturated fats: Fats with fatty acids that contain two or more double bonds. Examples are canola, corn, and soybean oils.

Potassium bromate, calcium bromate: Used by millers and bakers to artificially age and improve the baking properties of flour.

Pour batter: A batter that is liquid enough to pour.

Preliminary proofing: A short period of fermentation after the dough has been scaled and rounded.

Press out: To divide a piece of dough into a specified number of pieces by means of a press machine.

Profiteroles: Small cream puffs filled with cream and covered with a sauce.

Proof: The last stage of fermentation before baking.

Proof box: Box or cabinet equipped with shelves that permits the introduction of heat and steam; it is used for fermenting dough.

Proofing period: The time during which dough rises.

Propylene glycol: Used to help maintain moisture content and texture in baked goods and icings.

Propylene glycol alginate: Extracted from seaweed and used as emulsifier, thickener, or stabilizer in baked goods as well as in puddings, ice milk, frostings, and cheeses.

Puff paste: Rich pastry with rolled butter and special shortening for added flakiness.

Puff pastry: Light, flaky pastry made with rolled-in dough and leavened by steam.

Pulled sugar: Sugar that is boiled to the hard crack stage, allowed to harden slightly, and then pulled or stretched until it develops a pearly sheen.

Pullman loaf: A long, rectangular loaf of bread.

Pumpernickel: Coarse, somewhat acid rye bread.

Pumpernickel flour: A course, flaky meal made from whole rye grains.

Pumpernickel meal: Coarse rye flour.

Punching: A method of expelling gases from fermented dough.

Quick bread: Biscuits, muffins, or popovers leavened quickly by chemicals and steam. No fermentation time is needed.

Retarding: Refrigerating a yeast dough to slow the fermented dough.

Rich dough: A dough high in fat, sugar, and/or eggs.

Rolled-in dough: Dough in which a fat has been incorporated in many layers by using a rolling and folding procedure.

Rolls: Soft breads sometimes called buns; hard-crusted pieces of lean dough.

Rope: A spoiling bacterial growth in bread formed during production and evidenced as an obnoxious odor from the center of the bread.

Rounding: A method of molding a piece of dough into a round ball with a smooth surface or skin. Rounding prevents the escape of fermentation gas.

Royal icing: Decorative frosting of cooked sugar and egg whites.

Rye blend: A mixture of rye flour and hard wheat flour.

Saturated fats: Fats with fatty acids that contain a large percentage of carbon-to-carbon single bonds; its energy connections (valences) are filled. Intake of saturated fats has been correlated with serum cholesterol and coronary heart disease. Animal fats are saturated. So are tropical oils, coconut, and palm kernel. Hydrogenation creates saturation.

Saturation: Absorption to the limit of capacity.

Scale: An instrument for weighing.

Scaling: Weighing, usually of ingredients or of doughs or batters to apportion them by unit.

Scone: Typical Scottish hot bread or cake baked on a griddle or in the oven. It contains shortening and often raisins or currants.

Scoring: Judging finished goods according to points of favor.

Scrape down: To clean the batter from the sides of the kettle so that it may blend in with the batter in the center.

Sesame seed: Seed imported from Asia. Creamy white, tiny, somewhat slippery to (the) touch, with faint nutty odor and nutlike flavor, it adds interest to breads, cookies, and other baked goods.

Short: Having a high fat content, which makes the product (such as a cookie or pastry) crumbly and tender.

Shortbread: Crisp cookie, rich in butter or other shortening, of Scottish origin.

Shortening: Fat or oil used to tenderize and add flavor to flour products.

Short pastry: A dough made with high fat content, such as pie crust.

Shrink: To roll out paste and allow it to rest before baking in order to prevent shrinkage.

Simple syrup: A syrup consisting of sucrose and water in varying proportions.

Slack dough: One that has more moisture than it should for the best handling.

Soft wheat: Wheat low in protein.

Solidifying point: Temperature at which a fluid changes to a solid.

Sorbic acid: Occurs naturally in some plants; one of several substances used to prevent growth of mold and fungi.

Sorbitan monostearate: Used as an emulsifier in cakes and cake icing.

Soufflé: Baked dish made basically of milk and eggs, to which the beaten egg whites, folded in last, give a high, puffed, airy lightness; may be a main dish or dessert.

Sourdough: 1. A yeast type of dough made with sponge or starter that has fermented so long that it has become very sour or acidic. 2. A bread made with such a dough.

Sponge: A batter or dough made of yeast, flour, and water that is allowed to ferment and is then mixed with more flour and other ingredients to make a bread dough.

Sponge cake: A type of cake made by whipping eggs and sugar to a foam and then folding in flour.

Sponge method: A cake-mixing method based on whipped eggs and sugar.

Spoon bread: Southern cornbread made in a casserole, so delicate it must be served with a spoon.

Spread: The flow of a cookie when placed in an oven. Adding granulated sugars increases the spread.

Staling: The change in texture and aroma of baked goods due to the loss of moisture by the starch granules and other changes.

Steaming: Injecting steam into the oven while baking.

Stollen: A type of sweet yeast bread, usually filled with raisins.

Straight dough: A dough in which all formula ingredients are mixed together at one time.

Straight flour: Flour made from the entire wheat kernel minus the bran and germ; termed 100% extraction flour.

Stippling or docking: Piercing with a straight piece of heavy wire to let gas escape during baking.

Strong flour: Flour with a high protein content.

Strudel: Rich pastry filled with apples, cherries, plums, or other fruit.

Succistearin: An emulsifier used in shortening to make baked goods more tender.

Sucrose: The chemical name for regular granulated sugar and confectioners' sugar; a crystalline disaccharide carbohydrate, $C_{12}H_{22}O_{11}$, found in many plants, mainly sugar cane and sugar beets.

Sucrose polyester (SPE): Looks, smells, and tastes like ordinary cooking oil but is not absorbed by the body.

Tart: A small, open-faced pie with a heavy fruit or cream filling.

Tea rolls: Small sweet buns.

Tempering: The process of melting and cooling chocolate to specific temperatures in order to prepare it for dipping, coating, or molding.

Testing: Checking a cake or bread at the oven for doneness; checking product or ingredients for quality, according to a set method.

Texture: Interior grain or structure of a baked product as shown by a cut surface; the feeling of substance under the fingers.

Torte: German word for various types of cakes, usually layer cakes. Large fancy cakes enriched with creams or marzipan.

Tragacanth gum: An exudate from *Astragalus* exhibits resistance to acids unexcelled among vegetable gums and is used as a thickener.

Trifle: Dessert of English origin made of layers of wine-sprinkled sponge cake slices, custard sauce or whipped cream, and preserves or jelly.

Triglycerides: Fatty acids composed of one molecule of glycerol and three molecules of fatty acids.

Troughs: Large, rather shallow containers, usually on wheels, used for holding large masses of rising dough.

Tunneling: A condition of muffin products characterized by large, elongated holes and caused by overmixing.

Turn: When puff paste is mixed, rolled out, folded over one-third, and then the other third is folded over this, the operation is called *giving one turn.*

Turntable: A pedestal with a flat, rotating top, used for holding cakes while they are being decorated.

Two-stage method: A cake-mixing method beginning with the blending of flour and high-ratio shortening, followed by the addition of liquids; also called the *high-ratio method.*

Unsaturated fats and oils: Also known as *polyunsaturated* fats and oils, those rich in double bonds between carbon atoms and able to form products by chemical addition such as hydrogen or oxygen; associated with high-density lipoproteins (HDL) in serum cholesterol.

Vacherin: A crisp meringue shell filled with cream, fruits, or other items.

Vienna bread: A hearth bread with a heavy, crisp crust, sometimes finished with a seed topping.

Vol-au-vent: A light puff paste, cut either round or oval, and usually filled with meat or fish.

Volume: The size a mixture obtains when baked.

Wash: A liquid brushed on the surface of an unbaked product (may be water, milk, starch solution, thin syrup, or egg).

Weak flour: Flour with a low protein content.

Wet peak: Usually a mixture of eggs and sugar whipped to the point at which it forms a peak that is wet and has a tendency to fold over.

Whip: 1. To beat to a froth. 2. An instrument consisting of strong wires held together by a handle and used for whipping.

Whole wheat: Unbolted wheat meal.

Yeast: A microscopic fungus (plant) that reproduces by budding and causes fermentation and the giving off of carbon dioxide.

Young dough: A dough that is underfermented.

Xanthan gum: An emulsifier and stabilizer in bakery fillings, syrups, and other processed foods that causes solutions to become very thick but still pourable. It was developed by scientists at the U.S. Department of Agriculture.

INDEX

A

Additives:
  calcium phosphate as, 37
  enzymes as, 35, 37
  flour, 33–38
Alginates, 123–24
All-purpose (family) flour, 12
Aluminum, conductivity of, 136
Amino acids, 7, 24
  essential, 215–16, 219
Ammonium-carbonate-type leaveners,
  43–45
Amylases, 129–30
Amylopectin, 4, 114, 115–16, 120
Amylose, 4, 114, 115–16, 120
Angel food cake, 180, 181, 182
  protein in, 219
Animal fats, 76
  cholesterol in, 216
Artifax dough-mixing machine, 235

B

Bagels, 164–65
Bagged cookies, 200, 201

Baked goods, vitamin content, 221–22,
  224–25
Baked puddings, 207
Bake-off operation, 1
Bakeries, types of, 1–2
Baking:
  cake, 184–86
  Danish dough, 171
  enzymes and, 126–32
  flavorings in, 107–12
  heat in, 133–39
  in microwave, 144–47
  pH and, 126–29
  pizza, 163
  spices, 108–10
  sweet yeast dough, 170
Baking powder, 41–43
  action of, 42–43, 44
  definition of, 42
  as "soul of the cake," 42
  storage of, 48–49
Baking Science and Technology (Pyler), *xi*
Baking soda, 43
Baking temperatures, 145
Baking time, heat and, 143–44
Barley flour, 37
Bars (cookie), 199, 201
Beaten eggs, leavening by, 48
Bleached flour, 13

Heat flow, 137
Heat of fusion, 142
Heat of vaporization, 142
High-ratio shortenings, *ix*
Homemade method, of filling fruit pies, 231
Honey, 58, 196
Hydrogenation, fat, 75–78, 81

I

Ice-box cookies, 200, 201
Ice creams, sauces for, 208
Icing, 191–98
  boiled, 193, 194, 195
  buttercream, 192, 194, 195
  categories of, 190–91, 194
  color of, 191
  creamed, 196
  flat, 193, 194, 195
  fondant, 192, 194
  fruit in, 191
  fudge, 193, 194
  functions of, 191
  marshmallow, 193, 194
  moisture-retaining ingredients, addition of, 195–96
  royal (decorative), 193, 194, 195
Instant starch, 118–19, 120, 239–41
Invert sugar, 56–58, 195
  amount/manner of use, 58
  commercial preparation, 57
  compared to sucrose, 196–97
  definition of, 56
  functions in cakemaking, 57

K

Karaya gum, 122
Kneading, 23

L

Lactose (milk sugar), 55
Lard, 75, 81–82, 234
  cholesterol in, 216
Lean dough, 150
  baking time, 143
Leavening agents:
  chemical leaveners, 41–45
  definition of, 41
  mechanically achieved leavening, 47–48
  purposes of, 41
  yeast, 45–47
    storage of, 48
Levulose, 55
Liquid eggs, 63
Liquid milk, 93
Locust bean gum, 122, 124
Low-density lipoprotein (LDL), 83
Low-fat, low-cholesterol products, 83–84, 216
Lysine, 215, 220

M

Make up:
  basic sweet dough, 169
  Danish dough, 170
  sweet yeast dough, 169
  yeast products, 162
Malted wheat flour, 37
Maltodextrin, 80
Malt sugar (maltose), 55, 113, 120
Malt syrup, 56, 195, 196
Margarine, 79, 234
Marshmallow icing, 193, 194
Mealy pie crust, 228, 234
Mechanically achieved leavening:
  leavening by beaten eggs, 48
  leavening by creaming, 47–48
Medium flour, 30
Microwave heating/baking, 144–47
  of cakes, 147
  definition of, 144
  defrosting, 144